SELLING OUT

SELLING OUT

A NOVEL BY

Dan Wakefield

LITTLE, BROWN AND COMPANY · BOSTON · TORONTO

FIRST EDITION

Library of Congress Cataloging in Publication Data
Wakefield, Dan.
  Selling out.

  I. Title.
PS3573.A413S44   1985   813'.54   85-4273
ISBN 0-316-91774-5

BP

Designed by Patricia Girvin Dunbar

Published simultaneously in Canada
by Little, Brown & Company (Canada) Limited

PRINTED IN THE UNITED STATES OF AMERICA

For Joe Hardy
and
for Agnes Nixon,
friends regardless of ratings

SELLING OUT

I

H<small>E WAS FLYING.</small>

He was thirty-five thousand feet above America, in the clouds, in first class, with the woman he loved, on his way to make more money than he'd ever dreamed of making, for doing something he had only dreamed of doing. The whole thing was so good that it seemed, if anything, *too* good. The idea of such abundant fortune stirred in Perry Moss a certain apprehension as well as elation, a nervous impulse to glance back over his shoulder and make sure nothing dangerous was bearing down on him.

Perry pressed his seat button back to upright, pulled off the earphones that were transmitting soothing tones from the Oldies but Goodies channel, tapped the shoulder of the lovely woman beside him, and cleared his throat in an official-sounding prelude to speech.

"Remember now. This whole thing's only a fantasy. You know? An adventure. We'll enjoy it, get the most out of it, but we won't be taken in by it. OK?"

Perry realized he was pointing a finger at her as he spoke, as if she were his student instead of his wife. His voice was pitched too loud, in the tone for giving a lecture to a hall full of raw freshmen. He suspected the audience he was trying so hard to educate was really himself.

"I know," she nodded solemnly, "we've got to keep our wits about us."

3

Then her sudden smile broke out, and she whispered with delicious conspiracy.

"But don't you love it?"

"Love *you*," he murmured happily.

He nuzzled a kiss on her neck and she tenderly stroked his head, then drew away to look at him. Her bright face glowed with a mischievous grin.

"You know what I love most about it?" she asked.

Perry pretended to muse on this, then snapped his fingers.

"You can take up surfing? I bet that's it. You've always wanted to hang ten."

She poked a finger in his side.

"What I love most," she went on, "is that nobody else can picture it. *Us*. In *Holly*wood!"

Perry couldn't help smiling as he recalled the dour, disapproving faces of most of his colleagues on the faculty, and even some of his favorite students, when they heard he was going out to Hollywood to write a script for some kind of *television* program — not even for PBS, but a regular commercial network!

There were dire mutterings about "tinseltown," "wasteland," "glitter," and even "selling out," as if any kind of involvement with mass entertainment — especially TV — was a betrayal of intellectual principle, a kind of consorting with the cultural enemy. Haviland College, in southern Vermont, was neither as prestigious nor as pompous as Harvard, but it did take pride in its reputation as an outlying adjunct of the Ivy League, and harbored the ingrained academic distrust of the "popular" in arts and entertainment.

His colleagues' knee-jerk reaction of shocked sensibility was followed by a wave of what Perry considered their condescending concern for his own welfare. They harrumphed and glowered and trotted out the tired old cliches about what Hollywood "did" to people (as if the place itself were some malevolent force, a form of infectious disease), capped by the old chestnut about poor Scott Fitzgerald meeting his early demise because of "Hollywood."

Jane of course came up with the perfect response for faculty cocktail parties.

"We're not going Hollywood," she explained sweetly. "We're just going *to* Hollywood."

Besides, they were only going for a month. The January semester break. It would be like a paid vacation with a lottery-sized bonus thrown in.

A lark.

Perry pressed his seat back again to a reclining position and stoked up his pipe. He secretly enjoyed the hullabaloo this trip was causing within his little community. It was not just the professional aspect of it that had all the tongues wagging, it was also the personal surprise, the seeming contradiction of "us in Hollywood."

The juxtaposition of images clashed in an almost comic way, like Supreme Court justices wearing funny hats, or the Pittsburgh Steelers performing *Swan Lake*. Perry and Jane Moss were regarded as the temperamental opposites of tinsel.

They were tweed. They were corduroy and cotton, with red flannel nightshirts in winter. They grew their own vegetables, made their own hearty stews. They even, literally, paddled their own canoe. Perry confided in Jane that seeing reruns of "Centennial" on television had rekindled his boyhood dream of playing intrepid explorer in his own canoe, and damned if she didn't insist they buy one. They not only made overnight camping trips down the nearby Musquam River, but sometimes "went on Jane's trip" by dressing up for Victorian picnics. Jane would loll in the bow of the canoe in a long dress and trail a parasol in the water while Perry, with hair slicked back and parted in the middle, happily did the paddling. He had never before known a woman with whom he not only shared but enacted personal fantasies, and the resulting trust and intimacy enriched their love and their lovemaking. Slowly lifting that long skirt as she lay on the blanket near the picnic hamper was the start of a waking dream he would never forget . . .

A gentle nudge from Jane roused Perry from his happy reverie, calling attention to the lavish cart of desserts the flight attendant had wheeled conveniently to his side. There were different flavors of ice cream, exotic sauces, and fruit and nut toppings to choose from, any combination of which the passenger could pick for his own personally selected sundae. It was a kind of do-it-yourself dessert, except the flight attendant did it for you.

Talk about first class!

Perry was already full, and he had sworn off rich desserts for the New Year, but this was a special circumstance. His virgin first-class flight, at someone else's expense, on a trip that might make the whole course of his life more luxurious. What the hell. He rapped out the ashes from his pipe and turned his full attention to the array of luscious possibilities.

Before he finished eating his fantasy sundae Perry wished he had held out for fruit and cheese, or at least something sweet but simple, like vanilla ice cream with chocolate syrup. The exotic mixture he had chosen had not upset his stomach, but rather his mind — or was it his conscience? Right in the midst of a glorious taste of the mocha royale ice cream topped with crushed pecans and Kahlúa sauce, he thought of the dean. The one person who had really put a damper on this whole adventure.

Dean Gordon Rackley was one of those smug academic types whose literary admiration was reserved for the kind of writer who could get the most footnotes on the head of a pin. Years ago, when Perry first started selling his short stories to magazines like *Playboy* and *Redbook* as well as *Ploughshares* and *Partisan Review*, it was Rackley alone among the faculty who made the obligatory snide remark about getting slick on us. Later, when some of those same stories were selected for publication in prestigious collections like *The Best American Short Stories*, and the O. Henry Prize stories, Perry with relish presented the dean with copies, adorned with excruciatingly polite inscriptions.

Perry had braced himself when he saw the dean bearing down on him at one of those faculty sherries just after the news of Hollywood broke. Instead of the expected needle in the ribs, however, Rackley gave him an unaccustomed clasp on the shoulder.

6

"What a delightful opportunity for you!" the dean exclaimed with robust good cheer.

"Why, thank you," Perry said, relaxing under the warm assurance of Rackley's smile and comradely grip. He gave the dean a bashful grin.

"Evidently, the idea of me in Hollywood boggles most people's minds around here," Perry confided to his unexpected new ally.

"Odd," mused the dean, "it doesn't surprise me in the least."

Perry felt himself tense again.

"Oh?" he asked cautiously.

"Mmmm," the dean purred. "I always thought you had a streak of it in you."

" 'A streak?' Of what?"

A slight smile played at the dean's lips.

"Of Hollywood," he said, then took a delicate sip of his sherry, savoring.

Perry could feel his cheeks burning, remembering the dean's little dig. It was like an accusation, a recognition of hidden corruption. He spooned up the last of the sundae, wondering if his choice of mocha royale with Kahlúa sauce was an early warning sign of creeping decadence.

For God sake, sit back and enjoy, he told himself.

He licked the last of the sauce from his spoon just as a festive tinkling sound heralded the return of the flight attendant, pushing a cart that was crowded with brandy and liqueur bottles.

"Care for an after-dinner drink?" she asked with a smile.

Perry automatically turned to Jane, not precisely for permission or even approval but more for guidance, advice as to what would be not necessarily the most virtuous but ultimately the most satisfying choice, in this as in all things. They huddled, whispering. Perry confessed he was happily flying on champagne and wine as well as on the plane itself, and was so enjoying the vacationlike high that he hated to bring himself down from it with coffee, yet feared that the dark alcoholic potions being proffered might lead to heaviness and headache. Jane understood, agreed, and as usual came up with what seemed to Perry the perfect answer. He smiled, nodded, and looked up at the waiting attendant.

"Instead of any of that, may we just have some more champagne?" he asked.

"Of course!" the attendant assured him, adding a wink, as if giving her personal approval to the plan, and in a few moments was back with fresh, fluted glasses and a frosty new bottle whose cork she popped on the spot.

When Perry and Jane touched their glasses in a toast, they didn't even speak, but just exchanged a nod, a sign of their mutual appreciation and understanding. They were on a wavelength that Perry had never imagined possible, a shared communication that was not only apparent to others, but even seemed unsettling to those whose own marriages were neither so harmonious nor close.

"You seem to have a symbiotic relationship," the elegant Professor Evelyn Parkhurst, chairman of anthropology, told them once, making it sound like a textbook neurosis rather than the actual meaning of mutual dependence they were both proud to acknowledge.

"We clicked right away," was how Jane explained it.

In spite of the circumstance, Perry always added in his mind, experiencing a nervous tremor and an automatic outbreak of perspiration that recurred whenever he was reminded of their first, near-disastrous meeting. Jane had come up to Vermont to take his photograph for the Boston *Globe* five years before, to accompany a Living page article on Perry prompted by publication of his latest book of stories. He had forgotten the appointment, and gone to the door a little after ten in the morning unshaven, shaking still from a monumental hangover, wearing only undershorts and a soiled button-down shirt he had grabbed from a pile of dirty clothes in his closet when he couldn't find his bathrobe.

"Oh God," he said when he saw Jane, "I had no idea —"

"Didn't we agree on ten o'clock?" she asked.

He remembered the appointment to have his picture taken

then, but what he could not have known beforehand was that the very sight of the photographer would cut through the fog of his hangover, of the fuzzy condition not only of his head at the moment but of the whole frayed feeling of his life at that time. There was a glow about this woman who had suddenly materialized at his doorway, an aura of brightness and energy. She was tall and big-boned (not at all his type), and her high cheeks were flushed a ruddy pink, without makeup, her shock of thick blond shoulder-length hair pulled casually to a pony tail and tied with a piece of bright green yarn. He felt a deep and immediate impulse to throw his arms around her, but managed to restrain himself.

"Come in — I'm sorry," he said, motioning toward the living room of his bachelor apartment, which he realized with a wince of embarrassment looked like the scene of a rock group's reunion. His record albums from the sixties — the last ones he had bought — were spilled all around the stereo cabinet out of their jackets, lying on the dusty floor, which was bare except for splayed piles of magazines and newspapers, an empty bottle of Scotch and a couple of decomposing Chicken McNuggets from last night's "dinner." Perry reached down and grabbed an old sock from the detritus, then added to it by brushing off the remains of cheese and crackers from a corner of the couch so Jane could sit down while he went to shower and shave.

"Make yourself at home," he said plaintively, trying to be unobtrusive as he kicked a large black frilly bra beneath the couch, then realized the subterfuge was senseless since the garment's owner was still in his bed. He plucked the incriminating item from the floor and bunched it behind him as he backed out of the room, wondering if there was any way he could slip his overnight guest out the bedroom window; but he knew in his heart that was hopeless, especially since Lana Molloy, the hair stylist who had driven up from Brattleboro to party with him, had brought along her faithful dog, who would have to be dispensed with at the same time.

When Lana came wobbling out of the bedroom a little later

in her violet spandex pants and high heels, carrying her brace of mambo drums and followed by her dog, Jane stood up and said uneasily, "Maybe I've come at a bad time."

"Oh no!" Perry exclaimed in true panic, adding like a plea from someone drowning, *"Stay!"*

"As for us, we're on the road," said Lana with a wink, and Perry, pulling himself together as best he could, smiled gamely and said, "Jane, I'd like you to meet Lana Molloy — and Langley Wallingford."

Perry held his breath as he watched Jane's eyes widen at the introduction and her mouth start to open in disbelief (or was it disgust?), but then to his surprise and delight she bent down and took the dog's paw as she broke out laughing.

"Why, Langley," she said, "I know *you* — you're Phoebe's husband on 'All My Children'!"

"Oh, you're a fan!" Lana exclaimed happily. "Do you remember back when Phoebe was married to Dr. Charles Tyler?"

"I never thought he'd leave her for Mona Kane, did you?"

As Jane and Lana, like long-lost sisters, began rehashing events on the soap, Perry snuck back to the bathroom and popped another four aspirin.

He tried to look self-assured and authorially wise when a half hour later he leaned dizzily against a pine tree as Jane focused her Nikon on him.

"Lana's not one of my students," he explained, for he wanted to make clear that he didn't stoop to such unfair exploitation. As soon as he said it he realized what a pathetic claim it was to any pretense of nobility.

"That's none of my concern," Jane said, and Perry felt even worse. She told him "Smile," and the effort to do so in order to please her, combined with the nausea he still felt from the night before, as well as the sickening sense that his very existence was a sham, led to the quick, unexpected moment he later claimed was the worst one of his adult life to that point: he vomited on his shoes.

Jane stayed and nursed him, prevailing against his weak avowals of unworthiness that she was simply an intrepid photographer who would go to any lengths to get her assignment. By midafternoon she was teaching him how to make a healthy stew and they were exchanging not only their views about literature and photography but also their personal histories. By the time they sat down to eat and lit the candles she had bought at the superette, Perry reached across the table to take her hand — the first time he had touched her — and said he wanted her to move up there and marry him.

"We'll see," she said, and he knew from her eyes this dream would come true and that along with his writing it was the most important one of his life.

The whole thing seemed so natural and easy that Perry's friends at first were skeptical (especially in light of his track record) and then, as they saw the relationship working, they settled into a mixed attitude of acceptance — relieved and at the same time a little bit envious. That was how good it was.

Perry reached past the glass of champagne on his tray table and took Jane's hand in his own, wanting and getting the reassuring squeeze.

"I sure am glad you're going with me," he said.

Jane took a long sip of champagne.

"Are you sure you're sure?"

"What does that mean?"

Jane took her hand from his and playfully poked a finger in his gut.

"Isn't it every man's fantasy to be on the loose in Hollywood? Have your pick of the sexy young starlets?"

Perry slipped his earphones off.

"Did I really hear you say that? Are you actually laying that old chestnut on me? *Me?* Your devoted husband and demon lover?"

Jane leaned over and blew in his ear.

"Well," she whispered, "as a matter of fact, there are those who think Perry Moss may revert to his old bachelor ways when he hits Hollywood. The old kid-set-loose-in-the-candy-store theory."

Perry could feel his ears get hot. He thought about launching into a tirade against the petty gossip of the campus, then drank down the last of his champagne instead. When he finished off the glass he turned and nuzzled Jane's neck.

"How sharper than a serpent's tooth," he said, "are the tongues of jealous faculty wives."

Jane nestled up against Perry's shoulder.

"Those bitches," she said.

"Hey — you didn't really let them get to you, did you?"

"Well, it *is* a little bit scary," Jane admitted. "Hollywood."

Perry put his arm around her and pulled her closely against him.

"You know, this whole thing's for you, too. For *us*. Otherwise I wouldn't — *we* wouldn't be doing it."

"I know," she said, fitting right and full in his arm.

They had talked long into the night about it, sitting much like this, staring into the living room fireplace, sharing their dreams of what this unexpected financial bonanza could mean. Solarizing the house. Traveling. Taking time off from teaching, maybe someday being free of it altogether, Perry being able to devote full time and attention to his writing, as Jane would to her photography. They did not want "things" but freedom, the freedom to develop their talent and make an even greater contribution to the culture and beauty of the world. They did not want money for ostentation or for luxury, but for *good*.

As for fame, well, any of that would only empower Perry to use his name more effectively in causes he and Jane both believed in — the nuclear freeze, the human rights of fellow artists living in nations with oppressive political regimes. Perry would of course not object to his name carrying the added power of one who counted in the world.

Sinking back comfortably in his seat and closing his eyes, he imagined himself on some kind of crucial mission with other responsible people in the television industry, people like Norman Lear and Edward Asner, the sort of people who would welcome the participation of a delegate like himself from the world of serious literature. He saw himself with Lear, Asner, Phil Don-

12

ahue, and possibly Norman Mailer (after all, he had written the script for the powerful television dramatization of his own book *The Executioner's Song* and so must be considered part of the medium now), debarking from a special Air Force diplomatic plane at the Cairo airport, awaited anxiously by leading representatives of the Middle Eastern nations — but just then another voice broke his fantasy.

He looked up to see the flight attendant smiling down, gently tilting the frosty bottle of champagne toward him.

"More?" she asked.

Perry smiled.

"You took the word right out of my mouth," he said.

"Here's to 'more,' " said Jane, lifting her glass.

Bubbles grew like the buoyant feeling between the happy couple as they soared toward this exciting new phase of their lives. Perry touched his glass to the one his wife held toward him.

"*More*," he said.

"More?"

Perry's best friend, Al Cohen, was genuinely perplexed.

"I thought you had everything you wanted," he said. "Didn't you tell me that, not so long ago?"

"I did. I do. I know this sounds crazy, but lately I've had this feeling, like an itch or something. I don't even know what it is I want more of — I just want more."

It was early autumn, before any thoughts of TV or Hollywood had entered Perry's mind. He had gone to join Al, as he often did, for the end, or walking part, of his buddy's daily five-mile run. Though everyone still marveled at how much Perry had shaped up his life since his second marriage, and his physical as well as emotional condition was now acceptably healthy, he had not gone so far as those colleagues like Al, whose rigorous regimens of diet and exercise made them seem like prizefighters training for the final rounds of life.

Perry puffed vigorously on his well-chewed pipe as he ambled along on this stroll he considered his own day's virtuous exercise. Al, still breathing heavily from his run, stopped and put his hands on his hips, bending at the waist a few times to limber himself, then stared out at the blue-green hills as if seeking there an answer to Perry's dilemma.

"Is it women?" he asked, still gazing at the hills. "You want girlfriends again?"

"Oh for God sake, man."

Perry was disappointed, not only that his wise old friend had failed to come up with some blazing insight into his conundrum, but that this most trusted confidant could be so far off the mark. The very notion of "girlfriends again" suggested regression to the sloppy days of boozy, random beddings that preceded and followed his brief, blighted first marriage, that in fact made up most of his allegedly adult life before he met Jane and achieved some semblance of maturity and order.

"Sorry," Al said as soon as he saw Perry's face. "Maybe it was the word 'itch' that made me think that. As in *The Seven Year Itch*."

"You realize I've been almost five years with Jane now?" Perry asked.

He smiled, proud of his record.

"Hell, for me, that's a miracle," he said. "And I have every hope of making it twenty-five more. As many more as I've got."

"Right," said Al, nodding affirmation and starting to walk ahead again on the dusty path, as Perry, locking his hands behind his back, followed along, concentrating, trying to solve his riddle.

"No, it isn't women," he mused, as if eliminating categories in a quiz game.

"You're pleased with the book, aren't you?" Al asked.

"Like a proud papa," Perry said. "Maybe more than I should be."

He had spent the past few weeks reading galley proofs of the new collection of short stories his publisher was bringing out the following spring, and enjoyed the warming sense of satisfaction that comes with seeing one's words in print, and the larger fulfillment of completion of a work. This would be his third book of stories, and he felt justified and pleased in the expectation that it would bring, not fame and fortune, but a continued growth

in what Al had called — with his usual candor and accuracy —
the "small celebrity" Perry had earned.

"Maybe you need a change of scene," Al suggested, pulling
up a stalk of foxtail grass from the side of the road.

Perry stopped in his tracks.

"From here? From *Haviland*?"

The idea of living in some other place, or teaching at some
other college, seemed not only disorienting to Perry, but worse,
disloyal. This was the place that had taken him in when he needed
a home, had given him shelter and sustenance, professionally
and financially, at a time when other colleges and universities
had looked down their academic nose at his credentials, or lack
of them. Dropping out of the Ph.D. race at Harvard to support
his short-story writing by bartending, baby-sitting, selling encyclopedias and vitamins door to door, and teaching freshman composition at a pharmaceutical college in Boston had not made him
an attractive candidate in the eyes of most of the English department chairmen around New England. There was one, however, who saw something more in him, and valued it.

"You're a writer!" old Professor Bryant had said to him seventeen years ago, looking up from Perry's short story in the *Atlantic Monthly*, lifting his hands in a gesture of honor and welcome.
With Bryant's influential backing, Haviland had given Perry the
time to write as well as teach, and the college community came
to regard him proudly as *their writer*. They nested and nourished
him, protected and praised him, shared the honor of his books
and prizes, put up with his black moods and drinking bouts, stood
by him through the busted marriage that sent him into a tailspin
at thirty-two and the ragged personal life that followed till Jane
came along, like a real-live happy ending, beginning brighter
days.

"I only meant a temporary change," Al said. "I never thought
I'd be saying this to you, of all people, but maybe you're *too*
comfortable now."

"Too fat and happy, huh?" Perry grinned. "Maybe that's it.
Maybe I do need a change — a challenge."

Al suggested he apply for a grant or fellowship to go abroad

15

for a while, and Perry pounced on the notion. He sent off to foundations for applications, lined up distinguished sponsors, and with Al's help concocted high-sounding proposals for literary projects. Yet all the time, underneath all the activity, he knew that none of it would really happen because in his heart he really didn't care. The romantic images he had held in his youth of "Paris" and "Ireland" — not the real places but the literary dream about them — had faded, lost their power. Trying to revive his feeling about them was as useless as trying to re-create the passion once felt for an old lover.

Jane did her admirable best at playing the game of enthusiasm for going abroad. She even revived Perry's fantasy of the two of them doing a book together, one of those color-filled coffee-table numbers, a marriage of her pictures and his words: *The Irish Coast–A New View,* or· *Sidestreets of Paris Reconsidered.* Perry brought home maps that they spread on the living room floor, bending over to study as assiduously as explorers, but under the bright pretense Jane sensed his real unrest and lack of interest. She was worried about him.

"What is it? What's happening?"

She would ask, with gentle concern, when she woke in the dark hour before dawn to find him noiselessly pacing the room in bare feet, or simply sitting in the old easy chair in the corner, smoking his pipe and staring.

"Nothing," he answered quietly, or "I don't know."

He came and kissed her gently on the forehead, wondering himself what it was that distracted him during the day, acting like a subtle itch on his concentration. His senses had never seemed so acute, yet when classes began in September he found himself losing thoughts in midsentence, suddenly standing and staring at the students' familiar faces and wondering who they were and how they got there.

All the girls seemed to be named Michelle now. When he started teaching they were mostly Mary Lou and Cindy and now they were Michelle and Dawn. Of course they weren't girls any more, they were women. It was difficult for Perry to look at the latest crop of rosy-cheeked, milky-skinned, lithe young damsels, some of them teenagers fresh from pubescence, and call them women, just as it was incongruous for him to think of their giggling, pimply male counterparts as men. It was all right to slip now and then and refer to the male species as boys (the football coach called them his kids), but calling the females girls was a real cultural-political gaffe, practically reportable as an incident of sexual harassment.

There was a gorgeous Michelle who sat in the front row of Perry's "Art of the Novel" class who he privately felt was sexually harassing *him*, and certainly contributing to his already acute condition of mental disorientation, by every ten minutes or so tossing back her head in such a way that her long mane of glossy hair swung like a golden curtain across her face and spread itself on her other shoulder. The execution of the movement involved an arching of the neck and back that thrust forward her high, ample breasts, which of course were not confined by the unnatural constriction of a bra, so that, under the low-cut T-shirt-type garment she wore above her skintight jeans, the breasts seemed to be shoved toward Perry like a kind of erotic taunt as he paced in front of the class. He wondered if alleging that this Michelle's breasts were invading his space would be an acceptably current kind of complaint.

As the swing of Michelle's golden mane one morning totally swept from Perry's mind an intricate formulation he was about to present in regard to Henry James's style in *The Golden Bowl*, he stopped and asked, "Excuse me, but do you have some kind of itch that makes you have to throw back your head like that?"

"No," Michelle said with eye-blinking innocence, "I don't have any kind of itch at all."

There were giggles beginning now.

"Then why do you do it so often?"

"To develop my breasts," she explained brightly.

The room cracked up, as Perry felt his face become a beet.

"Class dismissed," he said.

It was one of those days. He happened to be wearing his treasured old faded Jefferson Airplane sweatshirt, which usually made him feel mellow, if not still youthful. He often wore to class instead of the standard tweed jacket with suede elbow patches one of his colorful collection of sweatshirts emblazoned with images and names of sixties music groups, or offbeat places or events he had been to, like the Fifth Annual Joy Street Block Party held on Beacon Hill, in Boston, and the World Blueberry Capital, which was Union, Maine. Wearing one of those with one of his colorful hats (the brief-billed Chinese worker's cap, the Parisian beret were among his favorites), plus a pair of bright red or green corduroys with hiking boots, made Perry feel happily more like a crazy creative sort than a stodgy professor. It was not only tolerated, he felt it was rather expected of him, part of the fulfillment of his role as the English department's "real writer."

It of course was on that day, the day of Michelle's coming out with the line about her breast development exercises, that one of Perry's freshman comp students noticed his Jefferson Airplane sweatshirt and asked, with a kind of remote, antiquarian interest, "Were they around the same time as Elvis?"

Perry went home and stared at himself in the mirror before lunch, trying to see himself objectively, the way others saw him. His light brown curly hair had begun to go gray, and the boyish freckles now seemed out of place. Would those marks of youth, those happy daubs of Huck Finn innocence, soon be mistaken for liver spots?

He was, to his amazement, forty-three years old.

He had a sense of time slipping past, faster than intended, like water spilling from a jug that no one notices has tipped on its side.

Now — that was the word that kept popping into his mind — and then *Now is the time*, almost like a voice speaking, and then he would ask aloud, "For what?" But there was no answer, only the rushing of the leaves, of the hours and days.

Stretched out in front of the fireplace at the Cohens' after the other guests had gone home from one of Rachel's fabulous chili and strudel bashes, Perry felt a welcome respite from the nagging, gnatlike doubts that lately were assailing him. This was his home away from home, was in fact the only place he had thought of as home before Jane came along and made one he felt was his own.

The evening had been especially gratifying, for the Cohens had brought together in the warmth of their hospitality the newest member of the department, a brightly idealistic young man named Ed Branscom and his pregnant wife, Eileen, who were still so new to the place they had not until now met old Professor Bryant, who lived alone in a room at the Faculty Club and was too often taken as a fixture of the place rather than as the honored colleague emeritus and friend he was treated as tonight. In bringing those guests together with Perry and Jane (who was now curled peacefully asleep on the couch) the Cohens had created a sense of a continuum as well as a circle, a feeling of everyone's being a part of an ordered progression within a harmonious community.

"This is the way it s'pose to be," said Perry, sipping his brandy.

"We're all very fortunate," Rachel said, lifting her feet up toward the fire.

"The most," Perry agreed. "So why can't I do my work and be grateful? Why can't I stop worrying I ought to be somewhere else, doing something different?"

Al loomed up to put another log on the fire, looking like a big friendly sheepdog in the shadowy light.

"Maybe you've 'had too much of apple-picking,' " he said.

"What's that supposed to mean?" Perry asked.

"It's Frost," Rachel explained. "Don't you know 'After Apple-Picking'?"

"What the hell has Robert Frost got to do with anything?" Perry shouted, suddenly feeling on the verge of tears and wanting to strike c·it at someone or something, anything, as he scrambled to his feet and yelled, "We're practically in the year two thousand and you people are quoting me *Frost*, on *apples*, for God sake?"

The next morning he called to apologize profusely to both Al and Rachel. He went to the room where he did his writing to try to think, to try to figure out what was happening to him. From his window he saw distant hills, tall pines, and a rutted dirt road. Sun and shadow, land and sky, were focused and held in the order of rectangular glass framed with wood. This quiet place was more than his study, in fact he sometimes thought of it as the closest thing he had to a soul, if such a thing existed, or had a tangible look. It was, at least, his chosen view of the world — or view of the world he had chosen.

Jane could be seen in it on her way to or from her expeditions to photograph the plants and trees, birds and insects, leaves and flowers of the nearby fields and hills. When she moved up from the city she became absorbed with the land and its everyday treasures, began to make it the subject of her work, not only in traditional pictures she sold to magazines but in the more original, close-up investigations of nature that she brought together in a highly praised exhibit in a Boston gallery that prompted one critic to call her "an upcoming Annie Dillard of photography." The good reviews and sales resulting from the exhibit not only made Jane feel her work was understood and appreciated, but gave her professional status as an artist in her own right as Perry was in his, which made them both happy, being in reasonable balance in that way as in so many others.

Jane was a crucial element in the composition Perry saw from his window, and in fact had made the whole picture possible, not only emotionally, but practically. When she came up to live she found the old farmhouse and pooled her own savings with his so together they were able to buy it. Perry had never owned a place he had lived in before, and after the initial fears and panic arising from such unexperienced responsibility, he came to love it with a pride he laughingly admitted bordered on patriotism. The sense of ownership added to the tranquility he felt in the house, especially in this room, with its view of the shifting colors of the seasons, its ordered presentation of the world. But now he began to wonder and worry if the whole thing, this house and love, this very life he led, was *too* tranquil, was leading to nothing more worthy or noble than the snoozing peace of pipe and slippers.

He made himself sit at his typewriter every morning, but felt no inspiration or urgency. The new book of stories consolidated a certain cycle of experience in his life and art, and he did not yet see his new direction in this particular form. Ten years ago he would have felt driven to make another stab at the obligatory novel that custom and commerce required of writers of this time and place, but he had come to finally accept the fact that it was simply not his métier, and the security Haviland gave him, both financially and professionally, spared him that artificial compulsion.

Sometimes he toyed with the idea of writing a play because he so enjoyed devising dialogue, but the realistic thought of the odds involved in getting anything professionally produced seemed overwhelming. Worse still, the notion of ending up as one of those fuddy-duddy professors whose dramas are staged by the college Thespian Society was too depressing to even contemplate.

He wrote letters to friends, drank coffee, smoked his pipe, and left his study to pace through the house, poking into corners and rearranging pillows like an absentminded detective in search of a clue. Daydreaming often, he was startled by the voice of his wife in their own house.

"Hey — this guy is looking for *you!*"

Jane had gone out one cold, windy night to make a magazine raid on the drugstore, and she was curled on the couch reading *Time* when she sprang up and pushed the article from the Entertainment section right under Perry's nose.

NEW TUBE BOSS NO˘ BOOB.

Skimming the story, Perry at first could not figure out why he should care that some hot young whiz had taken over the moribund television department of Paragon Films. Archer Mellis sounded much like any other depressingly young, outrageously successful show biz executive on the make and the way up, except for his fancy and far-ranging cultural credentials: Phi Bete from Princeton, Fulbright scholar, musical director of the Off-Broadway hit *Matchbox Revue*, special advisor on youth to the governor of New Jersey, producer of the low-budget film *Cranks*, which won honorable mention at Cannes, dēveloper of the first holistic medicine cable TV network, and former vice-president of the New York office of I.S.I. (Inter-Stellar Images), the powerful worldwide talent agency.

In the latter position, while packaging colossal deals for his famous clients, Mellis had found time to dash off a provocative piece attacking the new television season that was published on the Op Ed page of the *New York Times*, and so shook up the major networks that the president of one issued a counterattack charging Mellis with "links to Third World rabble-rousers." The other two networks offered him vice-presidencies. Mellis in fact was swamped with offers from nearly every segment of the industry he had so scathingly attacked, and chose the post at Paragon because it gave him what he called "freedom of quality."

Perry's interest grew as he read further that Mellis's aim was to produce "entertainment that holds the mind as well as the eye," and to achieve this, his first goal was to enlist "writers of quality." Mellis vowed to look beyond the tired old "Hollywood hacks" and bring to the airwaves America's treasury of living fictional talent, those writers "whose powerful work is known only to a handful of readers of little magazines and hardcover books because no one has ever tried to present their vision to a vast public that would appreciate and welcome it."

Perry put down the magazine and stood up.

"Well?" Jane asked.

"He talks a good game," Perry said.

Obviously, this Mellis character was full of himself and no doubt enjoyed the sound of his own fine rhetoric. Still, Perry couldn't help feeling a bit of a tingle, the hint of a deep-down thrill, at the possibility the brash young man had articulated. He walked to the window, then back to the chair.

"The funny thing is, I've been thinking that sort of thing myself for years," Perry admitted.

Like most of the writers he knew whose work was appreciated by a small, discerning audience, Perry believed that it would be equally enjoyed and esteemed by the millions if only the archaic, expensive system of book sales, promotion, and distribution in America were designed to meet the needs and realities of the twentieth century.

Like most everyone he knew, whether writers, teachers, politicians or plumbers, he believed that if given half a chance he could, while blindfolded and with one hand tied behind him, create better entertainment than the drek that was served up to fill the hours of prime-time television.

"Didn't I tell you?" Jane asked. "This Mellis character is looking for *you*."

Perry laughed, nervously.

"How the hell is he going to find me?"

"Easy," said Jane. "You're going to send him a copy of your last book."

That night Perry went to his study after dinner and wrote a brief, businesslike note to Archer Mellis at Paragon Films, attaching it with a paperclip to a copy of his last collection of stories — the one that included the O. Henry Prize winner, two others that had been selected for *The Best American Short Stories* of their particular year of publication, and another that won an award from the National Endowment for the Humanities. Just in case Mellis was not impressed enough with those honors, the jacket was resplendent with quotes from noted critics and fellow authors extolling the virtues of the author and his work, flattering tributes studded with the glittering names of great writers whose tradition he was said to be carrying on with distinction: Cheever, two O'Connors (Flannery, Frank), even the great Papa of all twentieth-century American writers, Hemingway himself!

Perry wore the brim of his hat pulled down and the collar of his coat pulled up when he went to the town post office to mail his package to Archer Mellis in Hollywood. He felt skittish, as if he were doing something unsavory, like sending off for tapes of pornographic movies, or dispatching semiclassified documents to a foreign government. He knew his embarrassment was silly; still, he did not plan to mention this matter to his colleagues, not even to Al Cohen. He had thought about consulting some old friends he knew out there in the movie business about the whole thing, but was afraid they would laugh and put a damper on it. He was keeping this strictly to himself and Jane.

After making his drop at the post office, Perry went to the town diner for coffee and a blueberry muffin. He felt a sense of calm, as if he had finally plugged in to a waiting connection.

From the moment he mailed the package, his life felt different. He was no longer bored. He went about his duties, his classes and committee meetings, with efficiency and courtesy; if anything, he was more polite and gracious to students and colleagues than he ever had been in the past. He felt kindly toward them, yet a bit removed, knowing he carried a wonderful secret they had no way of suspecting, a dream they couldn't possibly share. He no longer felt confined by their concerns or judgments. He was still among them, but not of them.

Perry started watching "Entertainment Tonight," the television program that reported from Hollywood on the latest doings in show business. The first time Jane came in the den and caught him watching it (he felt like a schoolboy masturbating in secret) he quickly said, "I just thought I might see that Archer Mellis character on here some night being interviewed about the future of television or some such bullshit." Jane smiled and said yes, she wouldn't be at all surprised.

After that neither Jane nor Perry said anything about his watching "Entertainment Tonight" but simply took it as a matter of course, as if he were watching "Monday Night Football," to which he was harmlessly habituated, or another rerun of "Brideshead Revisited," his all-time favorite TV drama, or simply the eleven o'clock news from Boston's Channel Five, with the anchor team he found most reassuring (perhaps because he knew they were married to each other and had a baby daughter), Chet Curtis and Natalie Jacobson.

On one of its programs, "E.T." (as Perry's new favorite TV show was popularly known) took its viewers on the set of a movie being filmed in the Andes. It was not the dramatic setting that Perry found thrilling, but rather the showing of some anonymous crew member slapping down the arm of one of those black-and-white slateboards used in filmmaking, while the voice of another person not even visible called out, "Scene forty-two, take seven!"

Like most everyone else, Perry had seen that little ritual portrayed in countless old movies (the kind with directors in jodhpurs barking commands through megaphones), and in numerous documentaries about the business, probably even on other TV shows

24

reporting on some film in production, yet this time it electrified him.

Perry woke a little after dawn with the words ringing in his mind: "Scene forty-two, take seven."

He got up and dressed and bolted down some orange juice and went outside, needing to swing his arms, to walk, to be in motion. He could hear the click of the slateboard through the still country air, and the magical words, the numbers of *scene* and *take*. He responded to the ritual words as he had since childhood to the language of endeavor and challenge, the stirring phrases that put men on their mettle, sent them into action: "Full speed ahead," "To arms," "On guard," "Ready, set, *hup*," "Gentlemen, start your engines . . ."

They all were lines from a child's dreams of glory, the standard repertoire of adolescent fantasies, American-style, enacted in games and daydreams later in life than most people cared to admit, mixed in with additions along the way that fit into more adult realms of sex and success: "Take me, I'm yours"; "Nominated for Best Supporting Actor . . ."; "I want to thank . . . without whose help . . ." And now, on this lonely road in rural Vermont, such words rang in Perry's mind from a world away, sounding like the bugle call of a more exciting life: "Scene forty-two, take seven."

Perry stood on a ridge, looking down at the quiet houses scattered through the town and campus. He breathed deeply and went back down, invigorated and ready for coffee.

He was not really shocked when Jane walked into his study one afternoon a few weeks later, her cheeks slightly flushed, her eyes especially bright, and said in a casual tone, as if it were an everyday occurrence:

"Los Angeles is calling."

II

Is IT REAL?" Jane asked.

Perry laughed, but he knew exactly what she meant. Stepping off the plane in Los Angeles was like arriving in some fictional foreign country. They had boarded in the icy reality of Boston, with wind whipping snow across the frozen harbor. Five hours later, filled and lulled with food and champagne, plugged into music and then a movie, the travelers woozily materialized into a bright new world of tropical temperature and color. Jane had been to San Francisco several times, but that was not as much of a culture shock — it might have been another version of Boston, but facing the opposite direction. Perry was in L.A. for a week eight years ago, but that was during summer-vacation break, so the weather was roughly the same when he landed as when he took off. The difference this time between departure and arrival was not only three thousand miles, but seventy-five degrees.

Warm air enveloped them, seeming to reach beneath layers of clothing and touch the skin all over, like a soft, lascivious kiss. Blinking, their eyes readjusted from the steely cold blues and slate grays of New England to the citrus glow of Southern California, the orange and lemony light of a constant sun. Bright-colored, lightweight clothing hung loose on the natives, and Perry had an immediate impulse to strip off his tie.

Jane nudged him and giggled.

"Look! That says how I feel," she said, pointing to a large sign. Its three block letters simply spelled LAX.

It was, appropriately, the symbol of the Los Angeles International Airport.

Welcome to LAX.

Loosen your tie, strip off your coat, tilt your face up to the sun.

"Hang it up early tonight, hit the sack — it's the only way to beat the lag, for sure."

Margo, the Paragon transportation person dispatched by Archer Mellis to meet Perry and Jane at the airport, piloted the beat-up studio station wagon through the freeways with such dramatic flair the newcomers felt they were in some TV adventure series.

"Check in, take a dip, go out for some Mex, maybe Thai — there's both in the neighborhood," Margo advised, craning her neck back as she poured forth her helpful information, while Perry and Jane squeezed hands and wished their driver would establish eye contact with the freeway traffic instead of with them.

"Or order out from Greenblatt's — pastrami's kind of heavy on the fat but the smoked salmon's something else, even the New York deli freaks say it's outasight."

"Thanks," Perry said. "We'll remember."

"And remember you gotta take a network meeting in the morning. Dawnish. Archer should swing by at seven. Probably hit the Polo Lounge for breakfast before the Valley. Whatever fresh berries they got you can't go wrong, but you don't want to do any omelettes, not before you take your first network meeting. Believe me, I know you writers and your stomachs. Queaseville."

Safe in their suite after a shower and swim, the smart thing seemed simply to take the beautiful basket of fruit Archer had sent, picnic from it in bed, and go to sleep. Except they were too keyed up.

The Château Marmont was a residence hotel that looked like a Moorish castle stuck in the side of a hill overlooking Sunset

Boulevard. From their living room window they could see the lights of the city flung out below. It was pulsing, bright, enormous, alive.

Who could sleep?

They went out for Mex, complete with Margaritas and the house sangria, topping it all off with Fundador because Perry said that's the brandy Hemingway mentioned in his famous book on bullfighting, *Death in the Afternoon*.

"They came back from somewhere 'washing the dust out with Fundador!' " Perry quoted. "Gave me a chill when I read it first, back in college. Still does."

"Hemingway," Jane said, smiling and taking a sip of the brandy. "We're a long way from Hemingway."

"What's that supposed to mean?" Perry asked.

"Nothing bad. Finish your brandy."

Perry smiled.

"I bet he'd like it."

"Fundador?"

"Television."

"Tell me."

Perry leaned across the table, trying to focus.

"Hemingway young man now might have written for it. Set new standard. Simple, understandable. His own prose. Show can be quality and popular, 'peal to all."

Jane hiccupped.

"*Sun Also Rises* a series?"

"Sure. Can see it. Loni Anderson as Lady Brett.

"Who's she?"

"English girl they all fall for."

"I know Lady Brett, dummy. Who's Lottie?"

"*Loni*. Beautiful blonde on sitcom. WKP-something-or-other. Saw on reruns. Clever."

"You too. My genius."

She blew him a kiss.

Perry grinned and raised his glass.

"Sun also riseth in West! The best!"

They clasped hands; somehow careened back to hotel home, to bed.

"The sun already rises, sweetheart."

Jane gently prodded him at six the next morning.

"Hemingway," he groaned.

He felt as if he'd been trampled by all the bulls of Pamplona.

"How in the name of God did we get on to Hemingway?"

"He was going to write for TV. Just like you. If you make it to your meeting this morning."

"Thank God this one's just a formality."

"Still, you have to appear."

"Mmmm."

With all the will he could muster, Perry made his legs move, feet touch floor. Wobbling, he took his first step toward making his mark on American television.

Even in his pained and disoriented condition, Perry had no fears about recognizing Archer Mellis when he appeared, though the two men had only met once, a month before. Waiting then at the bar of the Four Seasons in New York City, Perry had been on the lookout for some young Hollywood type, a flamingo-garbed sport with a beard and lots of gold chains. His preconception only proved how wrong the cliches about Hollywood were. Mellis had turned out to be an immaculate, clean-shaven fellow impeccably garbed in a three-piece suit of a hue so dark and a weave so heavy as to seem downright gloomy. He looked so reassuringly conservative and Eastern that his image went beyond even the establishment aura of New York and actually seemed more old-school English. His suit was reminiscent of the sort worn by the stuffy Brideshead himself.

There was no one resembling the elegant Mellis, however, among the few stray oddballs hanging out in the Marmont lobby at this excruciating hour. A stunning black woman wearing a silver cape was perched on the grand piano, while a bearded man in a velvet tux picked out a vaguely familiar show tune. A blond in a string bikini and an old felt fedora was draped on a couch reading *Variety*, and a fellow who was dressed like a Castro-trained insurgent guerrilla was pacing back and forth, evidently planning the next raid. Perry figured the whole group was left over from an all-night party, or perhaps was the cast of a small musical revue, gathered for an early morning rehearsal. He started to walk out the door and wait on the porch when he noticed the Castro guerrilla type was waving at him, and now striding purposefully toward him.

Mellis had no doubt sent another of his minions to pick up the visiting writer. Perry was a little peeved and was mentally searching for some sharp comment when he realized the man wearing the camouflage shirt and trousers and the combat boots, as well as a black beret and silver wraparound glasses, was not one of Mellis's subordinates after all. It was Archer Mellis himself.

"Welcome to L.A.," the young executive said, giving Perry a brisk cuff on the arm, then leading him toward the door.

"Thanks. I didn't recognize you. Without your suit."

"That's right, we've only met in New York. Out here I wear my working clothes."

"Ah," said Perry, wondering apprehensively if they were on their way to overthrow the network or just have a meeting there. He would not have been surprised if Mellis had led him to a waiting Russian tank, or at least a World War II armored half-track, but his host opened the door for him to a sleek, low-slung vehicle that reminded him of the Batmobile.

Perry squeezed himself into it as well as he could, feeling as relaxed and comfortable as if he were about to be shot out of a cannon. Mellis, though taller than Perry, seemed to have trained his long limbs to slip easily into the seemingly awkward if not impossible position, and his arms and legs moved effortlessly into the proper places, as if they were the appendages of a praying mantis. He shifted the car into gear, sped from the driveway with a screech of rubber, and slammed a tape into the deck.

"You into reggae?" he asked, as a stereophonic system that would have broken any champagne glass blasted out a sultry, tropical rhythm. In his overall pain, Perry was at least thankful that the sound negated any need or possibility for even small talk, much less extended conversation.

There was also little opportunity at the Polo Lounge, since Mellis was almost constantly on his feet, making the rounds of friends and acquaintances at the tables, keeping up a rapid-fire chatter with others who stopped by when he was back at his own table, gobbling hotcakes, eggs, and sausage with the gusto of a kid at summer camp. Perry kept his head low and managed to get down most of a bowl of cold cereal. He remembered Margo's advice and was hardly tempted by the omelettes, but also avoided the fresh fruit because it was papaya today and the name itself sounded entirely too exotic for his condition. The cereal seemed to settle all right in his stomach, and that gave him hope that he would live through the day, if he didn't have to undergo any great exertions of mind, body, or emotion.

"You ready to knock 'em dead?" Archer asked as they roared toward network headquarters in his sleek sports car. The sound of the powerful engine throbbed in Perry's head, but at least Mellis had removed the reggae tape from the deck, which was some relief.

"I just got a little jet lag, I guess," Perry said, managing a feeble smile. "Otherwise I think I'm OK."

"Terrific!" Archer exclaimed, shoving in a new tape. "We really want to blitz 'em!"

"Oh? I didn't think this meeting was so important," Perry said with a wince.

"This is the biggie! This is when we sell 'em on it!"

Suddenly Beethoven's Ninth Symphony was exploding in Perry's eardrums.

"You said you sold it to the guy in New York!" Perry shouted over the music.

"I did — now we have to sell it to his West Coast people."

Perry bolted upright, knocking his head against the bubble top of the sports car.

"For God sake, man — you told me this meeting was just a formality!"

"In an hour, it will be. They're going to love it."

Perry forgot the pain in his head. He wondered if he had enough strength to strangle this madman.

"What if they don't?" he bellowed. "What if they don't like it at all, and you've dragged me and Jane all the way out here for nothing, and I've told everyone I'm getting paid to write a television script?"

"Speaking of the script," Mellis said calmly, "have you worked out any more of a plot?"

"No! I thought that's what you and I were going to do — together! I was waiting till we both sat down to work it out!"

"Terrific! Let's go at it right now."

"Can't we wait till after this meeting?"

"*Amigo*, that's what the meeting's *about*."

"Holy Mother of God."

There *was* no story. Oh, there was the short story of Perry's that Archer had bought the rights to make into the classiest, and at the same time, most popular series in the annals of television history, but it wasn't a story with a plot, it was simply a slice of life–type sketch, a brief scene from a youthful marriage. The story, "Burden of Innocence," had been selected from the O. Henry Prize collection two years previously, but its merits were more literary than dramatic, its success resulting from an evocation of mood and atmosphere, an incisive rendering of character, rather than any development of plot. Mellis had frankly explained to Perry that the story and its two appealing young characters in conflict would simply serve as a launching pad for the series, that the hour pilot script would have to be a fully developed dramatization with beginning, middle, and end.

"You mean these network people expect us to tell them the story for the pilot and we don't even have one?" Perry demanded. "Is that what you're telling me?"

"We don't have one *now*, this *moment*," Mellis said imperturbably, "but we aren't even there yet."

Perry stared at the dashboard, trying to focus, to pull his frag-

32

mented mind together. Yet all he could think of was James Bond. Maybe one of the dashboard buttons activated a device that would propel the car's cockpit back to real life, or at least to the right time zone.

"How can we have a meeting about a story if we don't have a story?" Perry asked, vaguely wondering if he was repeating himself. "They'll have to kick us out. I won't blame them."

Archer yawned.

"No way," he said. "They're going to be very impressed, meeting a prize-winning author from the East."

"The *East*? My God. You make it sound like I'm from Baghdad."

"Tell me, have you had any thoughts about the title?"

Perry blinked, fighting off a sense that the horizon was tilting. He pressed the thumb and fingers of his right hand to his forehead as hard as he could.

"The title?" he asked. "The title is the one thing we *do* have. 'Burden of Innocence.' *That's* the title."

"That's the title of the *short story*. I'm talking about the title for *television*."

"I thought you liked the title."

"I love it! 'Burden of Innocence' has a classic ring to it. A real reverberation. Brings to mind the masters — Chekhov, Turgenev. But it doesn't work for television."

Perry cringed.

"Wait," he said. "Didn't you *want* something literary? Bring a little class to prime time? Wasn't that the point, sort of?"

"That's not at issue. The point is the title's a downer, in terms of audience gut reaction. 'Burden' is heavy, weighs you down. It's something to be avoided. People don't want to turn on a show that's going to be a burden."

Perry forced himself to take a deep breath, instead of screaming. He leaned back in his seat and closed his eyes. It was almost lunchtime at home. In Haviland. He could be sitting at the kitchen table sipping some good hot coffee while Jane warmed up some stew for them, perhaps pulled some fresh-baked bread from the oven. Maybe they'd have a nice glass of red with it, and watch the snow fall outside the window. The wood stove would make things warm and cozy. Instead he was hurtling through some mountains with a jive-ass hustler on the way to try to shuck some unscrupulous television hucksters. This whole thing was a stupid farce, a waste of life's precious moments.

"So what about a title?" Archer asked. "Something sharp, pithy. But true to the story."

Perry sighed, and opened his eyes. As long as he was trapped in this silly game he might as well be a sport and try to play.

"How about just plain 'Innocence'? That has some mystery, some romance. Don't you think?"

Mellis lifted his right hand from the wheel and pointed his thumb straight down as they hurtled around a curve.

"Too soft. A real yawn. You'd have to juxtapose it with something opposite, a shocker — like 'Rape of Innocence.' "

Perry bolted upright in his seat.

"Damn you, Mellis! I'm not having anything to do with some cheap exploitation title!"

His voice boomed over Beethoven's Ninth. The righteous indignation surging through him was making him feel better, giving him strength.

Mellis patted him on the knee, then shifted into low as the car screeched down a new twist in the road.

"Relax, *amigo*. I wasn't suggesting we use that title, I was only trying to illustrate how far you'd have to go to counteract the softness of 'innocence.' "

"Damn. We not only don't have a plot, we don't even have a title. It's hopeless."

"Refresh me on the names of the young couple in the story."

"Jack and Laurie?"

"Jack and Laurie. Mmm. Let's see. Laurie and Jack. No. Doesn't work. Tell me, how would you describe the subtext of your story?"

"The what?"

"The subtext. What's going on underneath. What's really causing that argument Jack and Laurie are having."

"Oh, well, it's still the first year of their marriage. Like they say, 'the first year's the hardest.' "

"I love it," said Mellis.

"What?"

"That's our title. 'The First Year's the Hardest.' "

"For God sake, that's a cliche! As old as the hills."

"As a title, it's new. It's fresh. It kind of winks at you, lets you in on a little secret. Dramatic irony, really — the audience knowing more than the characters. *Amigo*, it has everything."

" 'The First Year's the Hardest,' " Perry said slowly, rolling it a bit in his mouth. It felt awkward. Still, it wasn't gross. It could be worse. After all, this was television.

"I guess I don't mind it that much," he sighed.

"It's a winner," said Archer Mellis as they came down out of the hills. "Trust me."

The awful moment was upon them.

Archer had prolonged it as long as possible by building up Perry's credentials as a "quality" writer, and praising his intrepid character as proved by his coming out for this meeting all the way from Vermont, making it seem as if the journey had been made by dogsled and wagon train.

Finally, the network people had politely posed the inevitable question.

They knew of course all about Perry's prize-winning story and its wonderful, warm qualities, the appealing young characters, the compelling atmosphere, the whole ball of wax.

Now they wanted to know the plot.

Perry pretended he wasn't in the room.

He looked out the window and waited to hear whatever spur-of-the-moment cock-and-bull story Mellis came up with. To ease his own sense of acute embarrassment, Perry reminded himself as he gazed into the blank blue morning that this whole thing would later make a marvelous story for some faculty cocktail party back at Haviland. He must remember every word and nuance, not only of Mellis's improvised phony sales pitch, but of the acid

35

response from the network people whose time had been so uselessly wasted. The whole thing would probably make Mellis *persona non grata* at the network, and perhaps even bring a quick end to his meteoric career.

But there was only silence.

Perry could sense the anticipation from the network people, who had been more than courteous through this whole sham, but who could surely not be expected to carry on the pretense without even a response to their specific and perfectly reasonable question.

Was Mellis trying to purposely insult them?

Had the young executive cracked under the strain and fallen into a coma or trance? Perry could stand it no longer, and cautiously shifted his glance to Archer Mellis.

The youthful hope of Paragon TV was intently scraping something from the bottom of one of his combat boots with an elaborate Swiss Army knife. With a final twist, he seemed to pry loose the offending substance, then he held it up and squinted at it, and shook his head with a wry smile.

"Bubble gum," he said. "Double Bubble, unless I miss my guess."

He stood up, took a few steps toward a wastebasket, and casually tossed in the congealed bit of gum, as the three network people looked on with evident sympathy and fascination. Mellis sat back down and held the Swiss Army knife in front of his eyes, closing and then opening again various of its myriad blades and hooks and screwlike appendages.

Then he spoke.

His voice was pitched low, almost a whisper, so that Perry as well as the network people had to lean toward him to hear his words. If anyone had been watching him without being able to hear, they would have assumed he was giving instructions in the use and care of the marvelous knife. This effect seemed to make his statement about the TV pilot all the more dramatic.

"We are not going to bore you by laying out the bare bones of a plot. The ideal young married couple squabbles over in-laws. Jack flips out when Laurie wants to postpone pregnancy till

36

she finishes law school. Any one of a thousand hacks could pitch you those standard story lines and then grind them out like sausages. We are offering something unique. Character. Style. The shock of recognition. We are offering the texture and quality that have made Perry Moss a proven, prize-winning writer of American fiction, translated into the medium of television. We are not offering pap. We are offering you a challenge, daring you to be different by being the best. All I am going to tell you about our project is the title. Either you will get it or you won't."

Mellis snapped shut all the projections of the Swiss Army knife except one. It was the nail file.

"We call it — 'The First Year's the Hardest,' " he said.

Then he began to file his nails.

There was a split second of silence, a hairsbreadth portion of time suspended when Perry could feel himself cringe, awaiting well-deserved hoots and jeers.

What he heard, however, was an audible intake of breath, something like a sudden gasp that sounded like a response to a thrill — most likely one of an erotic nature.

"I like it," Amanda LeMay said huskily.

She stood up, smoothing her hands over her hips, licking her tongue lightly over her lips, as she began to slowly walk back and forth, smiling and nodding as if bringing all aspects of the title into balance and reaffirming its rightness. From the time he saw her as he first walked into the room, Perry had trouble keeping his eyes off this beautifully proportioned woman in the tight leather skirt and loose, puffy-sleeved sweater. She reminded him of Faye Dunaway in the movie *Network*, yet seemed, if such were possible, even sexier, perhaps a bit younger, and far more gracious and less aggressively grating than the character Dunaway created.

"For sure," said Todd Robbie with a big grin, "it really does sing."

Robbie was a friendly guy in his mid-thirties who wore faded jeans with suspenders and a long-sleeved checkered shirt, as if he'd just come in from a hayride. He seemed to agree with Amanda on everything, yet Perry hadn't figured out whether his deference to her came from a feeling of chivalry to a beautiful woman, or the toadying of a subordinate.

It was hard to psych out the power hierarchy among the network people, except for the fact — or so Perry automatically assumed — that Harry Flanders, even though he didn't say anything, was the real head honcho. Perry assumed that because he was the only *man* wearing a *suit*. Also, he was the oldest.

Smiling warmly, Flanders suddenly spoke.

"Well, maybe the first year *is* the hardest, come to think of it. Why, I often say to Marge — 'Marge, if we lived through that honeymoon, we can live through most anything!' "

No one seemed to hear him.

" 'The First Year's the Hardest,' " Amanda repeated, almost in a trance.

Todd chimed in to say, "You're right, it really works, Amanda."

"This young married couple," Amanda went on, seemingly oblivious to everyone else, caught up in her own fascination for the subject, "they're going to continue to grow. We'll see their real-life story evolve. That evolution will in a sense be what the series is *about*, am I right?"

"I wish I had said that myself," Archer Mellis assured her.

"Then we have a problem," Amanda sighed.

Perry was feeling dizzy. Trying to follow the sense of the meeting was like riding a roller coaster. The dramatic ups and downs, at least to a newcomer, were not only emotionally exhausting, but mentally disorienting.

Mellis, of course, betrayed no confusion at all, but squinted at Amanda, as if trying to get her in focus.

"Suppose 'The First Year's the Hardest' goes right through the roof in the ratings?" she asked accusingly.

Mellis stretched his arms, and nodded.

"Shares in the high thirties, top ten every week," he said, stifling a yawn.

"So we want to renew it," Amanda continued, turning her back on Mellis and walking a few paces away, like a trial lawyer toying with a witness. She suddenly turned, bending toward the young executive, pointing a finger at him, and asked, "What if

'The First Year's the Hardest' runs for a *second* year? What do we call it *then*?"

Mellis put away his Swiss Army knife and looked at his watch, with an air of impatience.

"We call it 'The Second Year,' " he said casually.

"Look here, son," Harry Flanders blustered amiably, "you can't say 'The Second Year's the Hardest' if you've just said 'The First Year's the Hardest.' You can't fool the people like that, no sir. They'll remember. They'll hold you accountable."

"I couldn't agree with you more, sir," Mellis said with almost military respect. He even smiled, and looked around the room with a benign air of explanation, like a patient guru. "We won't be saying 'The Second Year's the Hardest,' we'll simply be saying 'The Second Year,' which by then will mean to the public the second year of this particular marriage between Jack and Laurie, and by extension the second year of every young contemporary marriage."

Amanda LeMay stood immobile, her eyes enlarged, her mouth slightly parted.

" 'The Second Year,' " she whispered huskily.

"Don't you love it?" Todd Robbie asked, clapping his hands together gleefully.

"I get it," Harry Flanders said amiably. "We'll just move right along from there — 'The Third Year,' 'The Fourth Year,' and so on."

Archer Mellis stood now, glancing at his watch again, then grinning his most charming boyish smile as he looked around the room.

"By 'The Seventh Year,' everyone will be dying to know if Jack gets the old Seven Year Itch, and if this very human marriage can survive its next test."

Amanda tossed her head back, laughing, her blond hair swinging over her shoulders.

"If they split," she said, "we can have two spinoffs — 'Jack' back to back with 'Laurie.' "

Archer gave her a wink, and started for the door, looking back over his shoulder to summon Perry with a quick nod.

"We've already taken too much of these good people's valuable time," he said.

"*Thank* you, Archer," Amanda said, grabbing Mellis's hand, "we'll get back to you *soon*."

"Whenever," Archer shrugged.

"I mean, like this after*noon*," she said.

"*Ciao*," said Archer, practically breaking into a run now as Perry, waving his good-byes, scurried along behind him.

"Cars!" Harry Flanders called after the departing visitors. "Don't forget lots of cars — the people love 'em."

"Pack," Perry said, kicking off his loafers and flinging himself on the bed. "We're getting out of here."

"Was it that bad?"

Jane came and sat beside him, instinctively putting her hands on his neck and beginning to knead.

"You wouldn't believe it," he groaned. "I wish I had it on tape."

"Didn't they like your short story? Hadn't they read it?"

"I doubt it, but that has nothing to do with it. The whole thing is bullshit. Archer spooned it out to them, and they ate it up."

"But if they liked what he said, don't they want you to go ahead with it?"

Perry sat upright and placed his hands on Jane's shoulders, as if at the time trying to steady himself and convey to his wife the bizarre quality of what he had just experienced.

"You don't understand," he said. "They probably *do* want me to go ahead."

"So what's the problem?"

"I'll regret it. I'll wish I'd never got involved with it. I already do. It's impossible. We've got to go home."

Jane kissed him on the forehead, and got up and went to the little kitchenette.

"How about some orange juice?" she asked. "I picked some up next door at that liquor place. It's like a little market."

"I'm serious! I can't deal with these people. They aren't like people we know."

"Who?"

"The network people. And Archer. He's like them too, at least when he's with them. They talk the same game. I think they're all on some kind of dope. Uppers and downers, mixed together."

Jane brought him the glass of orange juice, with a couple of ice cubes in it.

"Darling, you've got an awful hangover, and jet lag thrown in. No wonder everything seems weird."

"It *is* weird! Dammit, you've got to believe me!"

Perry slugged down the orange juice and got up and started yanking the drawers of the dresser open and tossing clothes on the bed.

"Call American Airlines," he said. "Find out what's the next flight to Boston."

"Darling. Slow down."

Jane put her arms around him and guided him back down to the bed, where she started massaging his neck again.

"You don't believe me," he said.

"I do believe you. I always believe you. I just want you to think this thing out.

"I already have. And you know what I think? I think all the faculty jerks back at Haviland were right about television and Hollywood. I'm the one who's misguided, imagining I could waltz out here and do something classy and 'literary.' Oh, what a chump!"

Perry clutched his forehead, and fell back on the bed.

"You're not a chump," Jane assured him, "you're a wonderful man and a sensitive writer."

"All the more reason I should get the hell out of here."

"All the more reason you should stay."

Jane took Perry's chin and tilted his face toward her so he was looking at her.

"Darling, these people sound like wonderful *material*," she told him. "This meeting you went to this morning, I bet you remember a lot of good dialogue from it, even though you didn't have a tape recorder."

Perry lifted himself up on his elbows, smiling slightly.

"You mean like —" he said, then squinted his face into the hip attitude of Todd Robbie and went on with a nasal inflection, " 'For sure — it really does sing.' "

"You see?" Jane said brightly. "You're going to get some terrific stories out of this."

Perry dropped back onto the bed with a sigh.

"It's a nice rationalization, anyway."

"It's the truth. Look at it as material — almost like anthropology. And you're in the field, observing the weird rites of the Dippy-dos at work and play."

"What if I turn into a Dippy-do myself?"

"No way. The first time anything or anyone violates your own sense of taste, or ethics, or whatever, that's when you pack it in. And if you don't know when it happens, I'll know, just from looking at you."

Perry sat up again.

"It would be a shame to turn right around and slink back home, I guess. Before we even got the vacation out of it."

"And before I had a chance to do some of the California coast with my camera. Like you promised me."

"I forgot. Honest."

"You also forgot this whole thing was supposed to be a lark."

Perry smiled.

"Thanks for reminding me."

He pulled Jane against him, hugging hard, happy again to have her good sense keep him on the right course.

More champagne!

Why not?

The network had commissioned the hour pilot script of Perry's show, which was surely a foregone conclusion after Archer's brilliant hype at the meeting, but anyway the official word provided an excuse to celebrate. Archer seized the opportunity to take Perry and Jane, along with a charming date of his own (an elegant UCLA grad student out of Westport, Connecticut, and Wellesley named Phyllis Clare), to dinner at Spoleto, the hot new celebrity restaurant in Beverly Hills.

Mel Brooks was across the room, simply having dinner. Digesting it, no doubt, much like everyone else. There was a woman — what was her name? — who used to play a detective's girlfriend on one of those nighttime series a couple of years ago. Every face was teasingly familiar. The sense that you either knew or ought to know who everyone was from having seen them in movies or TV or the pages of magazines or newspapers gave an interesting edge to the occasion, a sense of inherent drama, the illusion of being on the other side — the *in* side — of the screen or page or camera.

Perry was acutely aware of all this and was able to appreciate and enjoy it without being snowed by it. He had that light, buoyant feeling of being on top of things, of seeing and hearing everything around him with the special clarity that is the gift of an author. He was taking mental notes of his own reactions to what other people were doing and saying, and the realization of what a different scene this was from his usual academic and small-town Vermont milieus made it especially absorbing. What a ripe new setting for what Jane called his field anthropology! Yet part of the trick of being a good observer was not sticking out from the scene, not letting the natives know you had your eye on them, but rather, trying to relax and blend in. That was what Perry was doing as he listened in genuine fascination to the evening's host regaling his guests.

"Don't forget the cars, the people always love cars!" Archer said, doing his imitation of the old executive who had called out that exhortation to him and Perry as they left the network meeting. The women were delightedly amused at the comic rendition Archer was giving of the now historic meeting at which "The First Year's the Hardest" was pitched and sold.

"And then what?" Archer's date asked eagerly.

"And then," Perry said, adding his bit to the entertaining account, "I held my breath, terrified that Archer was going to tell me in the elevator that I had to write a couple of car chases into my script."

Everyone laughed at Perry's self-confessed naivete, and the misconception that Archer might be so gross.

43

"Perry didn't realize the car-chase man is simply one of those characters who's been around the business forever and has no power," Archer explained.

"That's right — I thought because he was the oldest *man* present, and was wearing a suit, he must be the head honcho," Perry admitted, to everyone's amusement.

"So who is he, really?" Jane asked with interest.

"Harry someone?" Perry asked.

"Harry Flanders," Archer affirmed with a nod. "Worked on the old 'Highway Patrol,' got a rep as a programming genius, and kept getting kicked upstairs at the network. He's part of the furniture now."

"And I guess he keeps suggesting putting cars into every program, no matter what it is," Perry said, displaying his new insider's knowledge.

" 'The people love 'em,' " Archer intoned, imitating the powerless old exec.

"That's him to a T," Perry laughed.

"I wish I could have been a fly on the wall at that meeting!" said Phyllis Clare.

"You should have seen Archer's performance," he told her. "The man is a true artist."

"That's what he keeps saying all the time about *you*," Phyllis purred.

"Hey, I'm going to expose you now," Archer told his beautiful date, then pouring more champagne into all the glasses he spoke confidingly to Jane with the same sort of wink he had given Amanda LeMay at the network meeting. "It just so happens that Phyllis here is Perry's biggest fan."

"Next to me, you mean," Jane said. "And I have seniority — and tenure!"

Perry nudged her under the table. The adulation was getting a bit thick, he felt, even for a literary man from the boonies who privately believed he wasn't appreciated as much as he might be by the world at large.

"It's you who deserve the kudos tonight," Perry said, raising his glass to Archer, and telling the women with a wink of his own, "His performance at the network meeting should have won him an Oscar — or should it be an Emmy, for television?"

"Better get that right, *amigo*," Archer said. "That's the one you'll be collecting for your trophy case a year from now. The Emmy, for best original screenplay."

"I'll drink to that," said Phyllis Clare, beaming as she lifted her glass.

Perry shifted uneasily in his seat.

"I think we're getting ahead of the game," he said. "I haven't put a word on paper yet."

"Not to worry," Archer assured him. "We'll get you under way first thing in the morning."

"With that in mind, I think we better order now," Perry said.

"What do you recommend here, Archer?" Jane asked.

"Let's find out what Dom is up to with the veal tonight," the suave young host said, raising a finger that immediately drew a waiter, captain, and sommelier at the same time. The sommelier poured the last of the champagne from the bottle at the table and Archer gave him a brisk nod and snapped out a single-syllable directive:

"*More.*"

"So what did you think of the amazing Archer Mellis, boy wonder?" Perry asked, as he stumbled out of his pants later that evening and aimed for bed.

"Amazing," said Jane.

"That's my adjective. Be original."

Jane stopped rolling down her panty hose and pondered for a moment.

"Smooth," she said.

"Smooth? I'd have bet you'd say 'slick.' "

"I don't know," Jane said, tossing her panty hose away, "I'm trying to convey his 'operator' quality. I kind of like 'smooth.' As in 'a real smoothie.' "

Perry started to laugh, but a hiccup interrupted.

" 'Smoothie?' That's an oldie but goodie, all right. I like it."

"It's closer to the mark than 'slick,' " Jane said, snuggling into bed next to Perry. "That sounds a little too 'oily,' too conniving."

"Well, I'll find out for sure tomorrow. When we really get down to the script. The nitty-gritty. That's when we find out just how much of a con artist this character really is."

"The only thing that matters is he can't con *you*."

"Nope. I come equipped with what good ole Papa Hemingway said all real writers got — my built-in shit detector."

"Mmm," Jane said. "Lucky you. That way you're able to tell the difference between a sincere fan like me and a snippy little fake like Phyllis Clare."

Perry smiled, turning out the light and pulling Jane close against him.

"Mmmm. I love you."

"Mmmm. You too . . ."

The earthenware mugs of black coffee in Archer's office were so hot that steam came off of them. The strands of gray steam curled upward in the lemon-tinted light of the cool morning, making Perry think of Indian smoke signals, secret communications among conspirators. Archer told his secretary to hold all calls. There was a sense of purpose and subdued excitement like that feeling in college when a couple of like-minded friends get together and decide to start a magazine.

Was it all planned, a deluding illusion?

Archer was quiet, concentrating. He had taken off his combat boots and was pacing the room in stockinged feet, wearing a one-piece orange jumpsuit that seemed to be made of parachute silk. Occasionally he blew on his mug of coffee or took a quick sip of it, speaking in low serious tones of "essences," of "values," nodding approval of the few suggestions Perry made.

Still, there was not exactly a story.

Yet.

Archer suddenly pointed at Perry.

"*What if* —" he said.

"Yes?"

"*What if* — Jack and Laurie are, like many newly married couples, broke."

"Yes? They would be. Sure."

"And what if — to solve some of their financial problems, they decided to move in with their in-laws."

"Which ones? His or hers?"

"Which would be more interesting? Create more problems?"

"Hers — because her father's a professor. He and Jack are kind of in competition."

"Perfect."

"Yeah — I mean, all kinds of things would happen. Funny. Sad. Real."

"You got it."

"Hey — this is not bad."

There was a buzz, and Archer grunted into the phone and said, "All right, if it's urgent — I'll get back to him in two minutes."

Archer turned and stared at Perry, seeming to look straight into him.

"This is your show," he said. "I have total confidence."

Perry stood up, feeling dizzy with panic.

"Listen, thanks, but — well, isn't there something more I should know? Some basic rules or something? About writing for television?"

Archer walked slowly up to Perry, coming so close their noses were almost touching. He uttered one word, like a command.

"*Don't,*" he said.

"What?" Perry asked, confused. "Don't what?"

"Don't try to 'write for television.' Write the best damn thing you can. Don't think about ratings or networks or any other bullshit. Just write the finest script that's in you."

Perry looked directly into Archer's eyes, trying to detect any sign of falseness, but the young executive gazed relentlessly back at him, back *into him,* it felt like.

"I hope you mean that," Perry said.

"Try me."

"I will."

Archer stepped back and gave Perry a quick squeeze on the shoulder.

47

"Go for it," he said, then turned away.

Perry walked out of the room, a slight smile playing on his lips as he savored the situation. All right, he'd been given free rein and he was going to take it. He was going to give Archer Mellis the classiest, most intelligent script that was in him. Then he'd find out just how much this character actually meant what he said about raising the quality of prime-time television.

III

E/VERYTHING WAS NEW.

It was really the same old stuff, of course, the tools and totems Perry Moss had used on thousands of days over years and years. There was the beat-up old manual Royal portable typewriter with the beige body and green keys (including the "k" that always stuck), the solid ream-size package of plain white typing paper, the yellow pencils arrayed with sharpened points sticking up from the chipped souvenir Red Sox mug, the tiny steel toy locomotive whose smokestack was actually a pencil sharpener, the plug-in electric percolator brewing the black coffee that was strong enough to "corrode nails," according to Jane, and, of most recent vintage, the color photo of Perry and Jane in the autumn flare of the mountains of Vermont that was taken by Al Cohen and given to Perry for a birthday gift in a plastic frame-stand. Perry had only planned to bring out the faithful Royal portable for this month-long stint but Jane had also prudently packed what she called "the essential toys" to insure his psychic ease and comfort.

The rituals were the same, also: the lighting of the pipe, sharpening of pencils, folding paper into halves to make notes and scribbles on, pacing back and forth across the room, moving in closer, then taking a deep breath and planting himself in the chair, down to business.

The words were the same, too. They were the ones he had always used, the ones that had served him so well. He had not had to learn some new vocabulary. Archer had even brushed aside his concern over mastering technical terms to put in the kind of stuff he had seen in some scripts like "pan to" and "dolly" and "angle on." Directors liked to put those things in themselves, Archer explained, and writers didn't really have to worry about it.

Just write.

Perry wrote, using the old familiar words, *but* — and this was an exciting difference that made the whole process he was undertaking seem more exotic — he was putting the words on paper in a new and different way.

They looked like this:

INTERIOR — JACK AND LAURIE'S BEDROOM — DAY

LAURIE stirs, wakes, and yawns. She looks around the room, looks next to her in the bed, sees JACK, her husband. She smiles, and rubs her hand soothingly along his back.

LAURIE
Jack?

JACK groans, and moves away from LAURIE.

JACK
Huh?

Perry looked at the page and felt an odd tingle of excitement. These were his first words — at least the first words he had written that would actually be spoken, by real actors, in front of a camera, for an audience of millions. Suddenly he started to laugh, at himself, at the foolishness of pride in getting a couple of gruntlike sounds on paper, yet he sensed that something important had occurred.

He was doing it. He was writing a script. Stoking his pipe, he returned to the work with a feeling of heightened energy and elation.

Several hours later he stood up and stretched and walked around the room, humming to himself. He had written three pages. Of a *script*. He was doing something he had never done before, something completely new.

At age forty-three.

Who said you couldn't teach an old dog new tricks?

He not only felt he was *doing* something new, but that *he* was new. Or *re*newed, anyway. He felt refreshed, revitalized, by a feeling of command, of creation. Maybe that's why the writer's credit for a TV series didn't just say "written by" but "created by."

Created.

Yes.

This was different from writing a story. Maybe it was the knowledge that live actors would be performing it that made the whole thing seem more palpable, real. He had the sense that instead of just writing, he was creating a world and putting people in it, making them move where he wanted and say what he wished. He could see Jack and Laurie in their bed, waking and moving; he could hear the tone of their voices.

He cared for them, of course, they were his own creatures, from the time when he imagined and named them back in the creation of the original short story, and now, in this new incarnation, he cared for them even more, felt even more protective of them. It was his duty to maintain their integrity, and of course in so doing he would maintain his own.

Smiling, he went to find Jane to tell her how happy he was she had made him stay.

Perry had wanted to see his old friends the Vardemans ever since he first arrived on the Coast, but he hadn't yet been able to reach them. All he got was their answering service. Of course he understood they were snowed under now, socially as well as professionally, what with their amazing success in the movie industry as, respectively, top directors' agent and producer.

Still, his friendship went back to grad-school days, when he and Vaughan had been restless, rebellious students at Harvard, shared a grungy one-bedroom apartment, and dropped out together after the first year — Perry to devote himself to dishwashing and short-story writing, Vaughan to marry the brilliant Radcliffe student editor Pru Pinchel and move with her to New York when she landed her first job as a literary agent. He pursued his own literary dreams on her salary, writing book reviews that were published and novels that were not.

When they shifted to the Coast a decade ago to courageously crash the movie business, Perry enjoyed keeping track of their rise. Pru took on an unknown director and got him his first film job, and soon convinced Vaughan through her own experience that writing gave the lowest prestige and profit in Hollywood. She turned him to producing projects she packaged with her growing list of hot young directors. Perry kept in touch through late-night phone calls and postcards and funny letters, even the occasional drink or dinner when the Vardemans came back East.

"Look!" Perry exclaimed to Jane over a breakfast of Huevos Rancheros at the Hamburger Hamlet on Sunset. "Here they are!"

Well, not in the flesh, of course, but in the Society page of the L.A. *Times*. He passed it to Jane, folding the page to the picture.

There was Pru wearing one of her basic black Bonwit dresses with the simple string of pearls, and Vaughan in his tweed sport-coat from J. Press in Cambridge, the ultimate Harvard haber-dasher. They still flew back East to buy their clothes, for stubbornly maintaining their Ivy League style amid the glitzy gold-chain culture of Hollywood had become a kind of trademark with them, a sign of principle that they carried into all areas of life, up to and including the culinary. Pru's popular New England Boiled Dinners were considered *the* social event of what the local press respectfully referred to as the "A List" of the Industry. No wonder then that Vaughan and Pru looked a little uncomfortably sheepish in this photograph, wearing Hawaiian-style leis around their necks — but the incongruity was explained in the headline over the picture:

VARDEMANS TO HOST LUAU FOR LEUKEMIA

The story said top directors' agent Pru Vardeman and her producer husband, Vaughan, were generously offering their Bel Air estate for this charity event which was being backed by the top people in the industry.

Perry grinned and shook his head in affectionate amusement.

"I can't wait to put them on about this," he chuckled.

"You may have to wait," Jane said. "I doubt they'll have time for their poor country cousins."

"Now, now, let's be fair. They took us to Locke's the last time they were in Boston."

"That was before they made their millions on that vampire movie. Besides, what was the alternative? A stroll down the Freedom Trail? Hang out at Quincy Market?"

"Darling, love of my life, as a big favor to me, do you think while we're out here you could try to just accept the Vardemans the way they are, maybe even enjoy them a little bit?"

Jane pulled down her chin, squeezed her nose with her fingers, and did an imitation of Pru Pinchel Vardeman's Radcliffe accent.

"Oh, *Lord*sies, why don't we all get 'faced and go skinny-dipping?"

"Why don't you think of them as your very own field anthropology? Something like 'At home with the Dippy-dos.' "

"Okay, touché. But promise me you won't go fishing for an invitation to their cozy little mansion. I don't want to have to plead to be invited anywhere."

"Darling, we're inviting *them*."

"For a tuna melt at the Hamburger Hamlet?"

Perry grinned, pleased with his plan.

"I'm going to invite them to be our guests at Spoleto. We'll take *them* to the hottest new restaurant in town."

Jane pinched her nose.

"Oh Lordsies," she said.

Archer Mellis was impressed with the ten pages Perry brought him. He said it was just what he hoped it would be — natural, fresh, charming; sad and funny at the same time.

Archer was even more impressed that Perry was such good friends with the Vees (as the Vardemans were popularly known around town) that they had agreed to go to dinner with him and Jane at Spoleto.

Archer knew them himself, of course. "If I didn't know the Vees I might as well be living in Tulsa," he said. He had met them around town, at screenings and parties, but he didn't go way back with them, like Perry did. At any rate, he was more than happy to ring up Dom and make sure Perry was welcomed with honor at Spoleto and given a choice table when he hosted his important friends.

Archer said to give the Vees his best, and tell them they were welcome on his lot anytime if they wanted to see their old *amigo's* first pilot in production when it got under way.

"The Vees talking up your show won't hurt us a bit," Archer said with a wink.

Spoleto was all aglitter. It was, as Vaughan Vardeman observed, "ass-deep" in stars the evening he and Pru joined Perry and Jane there for dinner. All the stars stopped by their table to say hello and pay court to the Vees — and, as was only natural, meet their dear old friends Perry and Jane Moss.

It was a long way from Haviland, Vermont.

The satisfying part of it for Perry was that he was not just sitting there like an outsider, listening to the in stories of Hollywood from the Vees like some visiting hick from the sticks — hell, he was talking *shop* with them.

"Tell me frankly," Perry said, sipping his Napa Valley Chardonnay, "what would you think of Renna Greaves as a bright, fairly kooky, recently married graduate student?"

Earlier that very day, when Archer Mellis had posed the same question to Perry, he had never even heard of Renna Greaves. Now he could hardly imagine *not* knowing she was the hottest new overnight sensation in town by virtue of raves on the Industry grapevine for her knockout performance in the new remake of "Streetcar," which wasn't even released yet.

The Vardemans didn't at once respond, looking at each other with curious glances, and Perry's heart leaped, pulsing with the wild hope that by some miraculous lapse the Vees had not yet heard of Renna Greaves. That meant he would be one up on them about the hottest new sensation in their own backyard!

Jane, evidently sensing another reason for their lack of response, quickly said, "Perry means can you see her playing the part of Laurie, the young wife in "The First Year's the Hardest.' "

Pru finally spoke, in her heaviest, most nasal Radcliffe accent.

"You mean hypo*thetic*ally, I presume, since she surely wouldn't actually *do* it?"

Perry smiled.

"I think you guys know me well enough to realize I don't go around tooting my own horn. But I gotta tell you, this script is something special. I mean, I'm only a little more than halfway through, but I'm really excited about it. So, who knows? Maybe even Renna Greaves will go for it."

"Oh Lordsies, I didn't mean any reflection on your script. I'm sure it's charming. I only meant I couldn't imagine now that she's hot she'd want to do *television*."

Vaughan burped and shrugged.

"For big bucks, Renna Greaves would hump a horse," he said.

Pru turned quickly to Vaughan and spoke in such a sharp, sudden manner it seemed as if she were spitting the words at him, through the slit of her thin smile.

"Since when do you know about Renna Greaves's humping habits?"

"Oh, for shit on a stick," Vaughan groaned, tossing his napkin up in the air.

Perry had to stifle a laugh, not of enjoyment over the Vees' little controversy, but really from affection at how little they had changed. Vaughan was still the raunchy little cock of the walk, enjoying his farts and belches just as he did back at Cronin's bar in Cambridge, and Pru was the stiff, horsey type, the eternal image of the Eastern socialite snob. They were an unlikely pair, physically as well as in personality, but somehow if you knew them they *went* together, an odd but credible combination. Perry wondered, though, if Vaughan's being — as he no doubt would put it himself — "ass-deep" in sexy young actresses in the line of duty as a producer was really causing trouble for them.

"By the way, I think you both know Archer Mellis," Perry said quickly, hoping to shift to neutral terrain.

"Mellis?" asked Pru. "Isn't he the real estate lawyer who fronted for those Iranians — the ones who wanted to buy the Santa Monica Mall?"

"No, no," Vaughan corrected her, "you're thinking of Arnold Melman. Archer Mellis is the new boy at Paragon."

"You must be mistaken," Pru shot back. "Rick Stutz is the new boy at Paragon."

"He's *features*," Vaughan explained. "Mellis is Paragon Television.

"Oh, *tele*-vision," Pru said, as if chewing on a prune.

"Anyway, Archer Mellis is the guy I'm working with over there," Perry said. "He told me he knew you guys, met you at parties, I guess."

"I'm sure," Pru said, looking blank. "We must have."

"Yeah, yeah, Archer Mellis," Vaughan said. "Long drink of water with aviator glasses."

"Lots of gold chains?" Pru asked.

"No, no. Only chains he'd have would be for his dog tags," Vaughan said. "Dresses like Che *before* coming down from the Sierra Madre."

"Ah," Pru nodded. "Sort of a Rodeo Drive Sandinista look?"

"Bulls-eye," Vaughan nodded.

"Is that where you shop, Pru?" Jane asked. "I've heard about Rodeo Drive on Johnny Carson."

"I still buy at Bonwit's, in Boston. But Rodeo is fun to browse. I wish I had time to take you some afternoon. Can we see what Dom's doing with the veal this evening? I'm afraid I have to take a meeting in the Valley tomorrow morning at an absolutely un-*civilized* hour."

"Whatever Dom's doing with the goddam veal, I hope he can grill me a decent sirloin," Vaughan grumbled. "I'm starved."

Perry grinned as he leaned back in the booth, enjoying the moment, the whole scene. Vaughan's grumbling made it seem like old times, and Perry thought how far he and Vaughan had come, from a couple of disgruntled grad students with literary dreams, wolfing down sandwiches from Elsie's in Harvard Square, to men of substance in the world of entertainment, partaking of a gourmet meal in a fashionable Beverly Hills watering place, surrounded by stars. Vaughan and Pru were among those few who had proved that Ivy League intellect, taste, and style could not only survive in the tinsel of Hollywood, but actually succeed. Perry Moss seemed fated to be the next of those rare birds whose talent could bridge the gap between East and West. He picked up the menu, happily scanning the impressive array of choices. The wise thing seemed to be to put oneself in Dom's hands as far as the veal, and, in terms of appetizers, Perry found the *Canastrelli Trifolata al Spoleto* intriguing, perhaps because he hadn't the remotest idea what it was.

"I really do believe they meant it when they said they wanted to invite us out to their place before we go back," Perry said while getting undressed for bed that night. "They *do* have a heavy schedule."

"Frankly, I can live very well without another dinner with the Vardemans as long as I live, thank you."

"Oh, come off it," Perry said. "I know they have their pretensions, but can't you just relax and enjoy them? Enjoy the show they put on?"

"Not when part of the show is Vaughan Vardeman trying to feel me up during dinner."

Perry let his pants drop.

"Are you *serious?*"

"I was squirming so much to try to keep his hand off my leg I couldn't even enjoy whatever it was Dom did with the veal."

Perry shook his head.

"That lousy bastard. What a pal."

Jane came over and slipped her arms around him, soothing.

"Don't be mad. It's sad, really."

She kissed him on the neck and he relaxed, unclenching his fist.

"The poor guy is probably jealous, I guess," Perry said. "There he is with Pru, who's getting bitchier and more unbearable all the time, and I have *you*."

57

"Honey, it isn't me he's jealous of, it isn't me he really wants. It's what we *have*. The two of us. Together."

"I know."

He kissed her, lightly, thankfully, and her lips moved with his, that special response, so tender and intimate, that led them, together, as one, to bed.

It was magic.

You could tell that right away, just by glancing at it. There wasn't anything flashy or hokey about the presentation, just the standard Paragon Studio script covers, with the logo in the bottom right-hand corner. Archer had chosen a conservative pale blue, with the title in black italic print, a slight scroll effect giving just a touch of elegance, without ostentation: *The First Year's the Hardest*.

It was class.

It was more than that. It really was magic, not just to Perry, who of course would have been impressed by seeing his first script bound for reading, no matter what the thing looked like. Everyone else at Paragon sensed it, too, though none of them as yet had had time to read it. The scripts had just come back from the printer late the previous afternoon and Archer had immediately messengered a dozen copies to the network. This morning he proudly took not only a copy of the script but its author in to Zack Spackford, the president of Paragon, not just the TV division that Archer headed but, as he explained to Perry, this man they were going to meet was his own boss, everyone's boss, boss of the whole enchilada, feature films and all.

"I like it," said Spackford, feeling the script, running his hands over the covers, then holding it gingerly on the upraised fingertips of one hand, as if balancing a serving platter.

"It feels good," he said. "It has a nice weight to it."

"Thank you," Perry said.

It was the first time his writing had ever been judged by the texture and weight of what it was written on. This would be a good one to recount back at some faculty bash; it was a kind of one-upmanship for those who said, "You can't judge a book by its cover," or those critics who had praised the jacket design of one of his books in the course of a review. Still, he was actually pleased at the mogul's positive response, and even sensed it was genuine; this was after all a world of signs and portents, of omens and fortunes, and he really believed there was something magical about the script, something Spackford sensed as he held it.

Terry Carver, the studio's young head of sales, didn't even have to touch the script to know it was a winner.

He sniffed it.

Carver, who looked like a surfer with skin that was tanned and jeans that were bleached by the sun, was lifting a dumbbell in each hand when Archer came into his office with Perry and laid the script on the edge of his desk. Carver approached it, and without putting down the weights, simply leaned over and sniffed at the crisp new document.

"Yeah," he said. "It's got a good smell to it."

Magic.

Perry wasn't surprised because the whole process of writing the hour script had been magic, too.

Fifty pages in three weeks!

It sometimes took him six months to write *ten* pages. Of course these were different kinds of pages, pages with a lot more white space on them, pages where complex descriptions could be done in a kind of shorthand (EXTERIOR — SUBURBAN HOUSE DRIVEWAY — NIGHT), but nevertheless, a real *story* was here, a drama with beginning, middle, end, a living, breathing creation of believable characters, dealing with real-life, adult dilemmas. This was no schlock sitcom stuff, this was *quality*, the sort of thing TV critics dreamed of seeing on network television.

Now it was up to the network to decide if they had the guts, the foresight, the imagination to put it on the air.

"You know what the odds are?" Perry asked Jane as they lay at the Marmont pool, sipping from bottles of cool dark Mexican beer. "The odds of a pilot getting produced and going on the air are fifty to one."

"Where do I place my bet?" Jane asked.

Perry smiled. He shared her confidence. It was part of the

amazing change that had come over him. Ordinarily, in any situation like this involving the outcome of something he cared about deeply, Perry was beset by anxiety, sunk in primordial gloom, fearing the worst. Now, knowing that the crucial word from the network would probably come today, might even this moment be waiting in the form of a pink message slip in his box at the reception desk, he was perfectly at ease, enjoying the gentle sun, the cool taste of the beer. The temperature was in the low seventies, the pool was heated at about the same degree. He reached over and rubbed Jane's shoulder. She was relaxed, too, almost purring.

Instead of causing any friction between them, this whole experience had brought them closer together. While Perry was writing in the mornings Jane took the rented Subaru and drove around the sprawling, magical county of Los Angeles, out to the beach, up in the canyons, exploring and taking photographs. Back in the afternoon she'd lie around the pool and Perry would come down and discuss a scene with her, get her ideas for some perspective on the domestic drama he was creating. She was like a collaborator, in a way she had never been with his more serious literary work.

How much more fun this was!

They had exchanged stories of their own early marriages, their conflicts with in-laws, and out of this real experience Perry drew the anecdotes and dramatic dilemmas of his story.

Every few days he had driven in to the studio to hash out the new pages with Archer Mellis, getting ideas about making the action more visual, the dialogue more pointed. What fun it was to share in the process of creation instead of just being locked up by yourself in your own room, your own mind!

They took a dip before toweling off and going up to get dressed for lunch — and, incidentally, stopping by the desk to see if any message — if *the* message — had arrived.

The pink slip was there, of course, waiting.

To Perry's surprise, however, it was not from Archer Mellis.

To his even greater surprise, it was from Pru Vardeman.

Perry and Jane were invited to the Vees' for a poolside brunch on Sunday!

That was the last day of their stay, the day they were going back to Vermont, but their flight didn't leave till five in the afternoon, and they could stop off at the Vees' on their way to the airport. It would be a kick to meet some of the stars who would surely be present at any event Vaughan and Pru put on, and besides, Perry would hate to admit back at Haviland that he hadn't seen any more of his old buddy's fabulous home than what everyone else saw in *People* magazine.

It seemed kind of silly now to cut off the Vees just because Vaughan tried to feel up Jane during dinner at Spoleto. Besides, they could be powerful connections for the future if Perry wanted to take a fling at writing a movie.

Jane agreed.

"I don't think Vaughan will try to feel me up in broad daylight," she said. "Besides, brunch with the stars is the perfect end to our Hollywood adventure!"

Perry felt a sudden apprehension.

"Well, it'll be perfect if the network says yes. I don't exactly relish the thought of sitting around with the Vees and their celebrity friends, telling how my TV pilot didn't get made."

Jane laughed.

"Darling! Don't you know it's a sure thing now? Otherwise we'd have never been invited to the Vardemans'!"

"Come on, you don't mean to say you think *they* know the network decision before *we* do?"

Jane grinned and put her arms around Perry's neck.

"I think they can smell it," she whispered.

Perry kissed her and started stepping her backward toward the bedroom, running his tongue in her mouth as they went, but before they got there the room phone rang.

It was Archer Mellis.

His voice was full, vibrant.

"The network loves you," he said.

"They liked the script, huh?"

Perry drew Jane to him, squeezing her waist as he spoke into the phone.

"They like it so much," Archer said, "they want you to write a second hour."

"What?"

"They want 'The First Year' to be a two-hour TV movie that will kick off the series."

"*Two* hours? Archer, I'm going back to Vermont on Sunday."

"Can you be in my office in an hour?"

"Sure — but Archer. What does all this mean?"

"You're hot, *amigo*."

Archer hung up before Perry could inquire further.

Jane and Perry walked along the water's edge, barefoot, the sand refreshingly moist between their toes. She'd discovered this place in her morning explorations while Perry was working, and thought it might be an ideal spot to talk, to think, to try to reach the right decision, together.

The sweep of beach was spectacular, a wide tan swath of sand that stretched with spacious ease along the coast from Venice all the way up to Santa Monica. There were mountains in the lower distance where the land curved out again, and a limitless expanse of azure sky blending to an endless indigo sea, broken by white froth of surf and slice of sails. Spinnakers added bursts of bright colors, oranges and reds and diagonals of gold, giving an illusion of pirate ships or Arab barks, adding to the ambience of fairy-tale strangeness and mystery, heightened by the deep green flare of palms, the molten tropical colors blending along the horizon.

This was not just a continent away but a world of distance and difference from the coasts they knew in Maine and Massachusetts.

This was Xanadu as opposed to Plymouth Rock.

Perry shivered, feeling a thrill of awe and excitement.

"What planet are you on?" Jane asked.

"Southern California," he said.

Jane took his hand in hers.

"It *is* like another planet," she said. "Or like being in a dream that you can't explain to someone outside it."

"Do you like it, though?" he asked. "Being in the California dream?"

"As long as I know I can wake up and go back home again."

"Of course. We'd go back in June, Archer says the whole two-hour movie will be filmed, produced, edited, finished by the end of May."

"That's of course dependent on your writing the second hour in the next month."

"By the end of February, yes. Of course, it's *theoretically* possible to go back home and write it, in between teaching."

"Darling, you're a genius, but you're not Superman, too."

"I could take a shot at it."

"But even if by some miracle you did it, you'd miss being on the set and seeing it produced, being on the inside of things."

"And even getting paid a little extra for doing it. And getting a consultant credit to boot. It really is kind of a once-in-a-lifetime opportunity."

"Even Dean Rackley can surely understand that."

"I doubt it. But good old Al will, of course. Thank God he's department chairman."

"You could do a stint in summer school — and take a heavier load in the fall."

"Mmm. And if it does become a series I can really be strictly a consultant, watch it on the tube at home, talk to Archer on the phone, send in my notes and comments. Whatever."

"And we can fly out over Thanksgiving. Maybe come for the January break again."

Perry laughed.

"We'll be what they call 'bi-coastal.' If it all sounds good to you?"

She squeezed his arm.

"I've got a book idea — photographing the two coasts. I don't mean big sweeps of mountains and beach, the usual stuff, but my kind of things — small, intimate, particular. I've been reading Rachel Carson — you know there are whole different types of life on this coast, even different varieties of seashells?"

"It's a fabulous idea."

Everything seemed to fit, for both of them.

The money was hard to pass up, too. Perry would of course be giving up his teaching salary, but at $13,000 for a half year, or one semester, that was a pittance compared to what he'd be making from his television work. The pay for the original one-hour pilot was $26,000, and now with the increase to two hours, that had escalated to $40,000. Even more amazing, the $20,000 for rights to the short story for the one-hour pilot would now *double*, bringing that to another $40,000! Evidently that was small potatoes in Hollywood terms, but for a guy who made $26,000 a year teaching, and was lucky to get a $5,000 advance for a book, it was a small fortune. And that wasn't even counting series royalties of $2,000 per hour-episode if the show went forward as planned.

Of course Paragon couldn't continue footing the bill for his living expenses all through the spring, but paying that himself would provide a tax write-off for him, Archer explained. He'd be actually making money by spending it out here!

"How can we lose?" Perry asked.

"We can't," said Jane, "if we keep on loving each other."

They kissed and nestled into one another as they walked up the wet, voluptuous sand, in step. They began to sing together, softly, in harmony.

The Vardemans' pool looked too perfect to actually swim in. Breaking the smooth surface of the water would have seemed like an act of vandalism, or, at the very least, a gauche violation of etiquette. It did not really seem like a swimming pool but rather a gigantic gem, a rectangular topaz, stunningly set in elegant tile, surrounded by tall, stately trees within a larger framework of manicured hedges and lawns as smooth and shimmering as glass.

It was like being on a movie set.

Except there weren't any stars.

At least not today, not for the Sunday brunch to which Pru and Vaughan had finally invited their old buddy Perry and his wife. Though the Vees were famous for hosting the Hollywood "A List," they must have reached back deep in the social alphabet for this occasion. Instead of Meryl, Glenn, Warren, or Joanne and Paul, the only other guests besides Perry and Jane were an expatriate English novelist and two lesbian librarians from Pacific Palisades.

Perry thought perhaps the Vees had thoughtfully rounded up the Hollywood literary set in his honor, but then, if this were really the cream of that crowd, where the hell was Gore?

"Of course we're familiar with your books, Mr. Moss," the librarian with the leather bracelets assured Perry politely, and her more demure companion said in fact she had read and admired a story of his in a recent O. Henry collection — something to do, she thought, with a rather *naif* young married couple?

"I'm frightfully afraid I'm not familiar with your *oeuvre*," said Cyril Heathrow, "but then I don't keep up with you Yanks and your fiction."

"Are you only here on a visit?" asked Jane.

"A rather extended one," Heathrow said sardonically, as he crossed one jodhpurred leg over the other and lightly rubbed the leather of his riding boot. "Twenty some years now."

"I'm afraid I don't know *your* work," Perry said, beaming. "Are you published here?"

Heathrow sighed.

"I'm afraid most serious fiction doesn't travel well across the Atlantic," he said.

"Cyril has been known to turn out a few sharp scripts between the heavy-duty stuff," Vaughan said. "But I don't think he's done any television — that so, Cyril?"

The Englishman winced.

"One would have to purposely write down, wouldn't one?"

"I guess I'm fortunate," Perry said. "The first thing the guy I'm working with told me was to forget about any preconceptions of television and do my best work. Fact is, Archer Mellis *demands* quality."

"He's no wetback, huh?" said Vaughan.

"I've never had the pleasure of working with a more creative mind," Perry declared.

"As long as it's fun!" Pru said brightly.

"Of course my academic friends are convinced I'm selling out," Perry said.

"Lordsies!" Pru exclaimed. "I haven't heard that expression in *eons*."

" 'Selling out'?" Heathrow asked, furrowing his brows with interest. "Isn't that peculiarly an Americanism?"

"It's pretty much a nineteen-fifties term," Vaughan explained. "The sort of thing the Man in the Gray Flannel Suit got his migraines about."

"Some people still take it seriously," Jane said. "At least out in the sticks, where we come from."

"Why not?" Pru said. "I think it's charming. Freshen your Chardonnay?"

She tilted up her straw garden-party hat and summoned the man of the live-in Mexican couple who had served the brunch and now hovered in attendance.

Jane finished off her glass of wine in a single gulp.

"Why, we're so deep in the boonies," she said with bright ferocity, "grown-ups even discuss things like *values* and *morals*."

Perry kicked her under the table. The cracked crab and avocado was elegant but not very filling, and he feared the mimosas followed by the Chardonnay might lead his wife to say some things she — or he, anyway — might regret.

"Speaking of the boonies," Perry said quickly, taking Jane's hand, "we better get you to the airport or you'll never get to Boston tonight, much less on to Vermont."

"She's not leaving you out here alone, surely?" Pru asked with sudden concern.

"She's just going back to rent the house, pack up our lightweight clothes."

"Well," Vaughan said with a leer, "don't leave him too long out here with his casting couch."

"Oh, I trust him," Jane said with a withering smile. "It's another sort of quaint old fifties thing we share — being faithful."

"Hell, Pru and I have the same deal," Vaughan said, "except we figure it's null and void when we're in different cities."

"It really was great to meet you all," Perry said, guiding Jane

66

firmly toward the house, and their departure. "We'll be in touch!"

"Don't be strangers," Pru called, "now that you know where we are!"

Thank God by the time they got to the airport Perry and Jane were giggling instead of fighting. They had a whiskey sour before the flight and then embraced, kissed, holding each other so tight that when Perry let her go he really felt part of him was being torn away. By the time the plane taxied down the runway for takeoff he was already missing her, wondering how the hell he was going to make it by himself for a whole week.

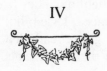

IV

Perry scanned both *Variety* and the *Hollywood Reporter* over a late, leisurely breakfast Monday morning at the Hamburger Hamlet, and at first was disappointed not to find any screaming headlines announcing that his hour pilot was so terrific the network was doubling its length and launching the series with a two-hour TV movie! He figured, however, the network probably wanted to keep the plans for its hottest new property under wraps, so the rival webs (as the networks were called in the trades) wouldn't frantically rush to start planning competitive shows about young married couples to try to compete with "The First Year's the Hardest."

Perry smiled, enjoying the secret of his own success, which was too hot to even be reported yet and was unknown by all the other aspiring show business moguls who were poring over the trades that morning at the Hamburger Hamlet. Leaving a big tip and whistling as he walked out onto Sunset Boulevard, Perry decided to reward himself, and at the same time put his mentor on notice that he wasn't any longer the square academic who was fresh off the plane from the East. He sauntered into one of the hip men's clothing stores on Sunset Boulevard.

Perry casually strolled into Archer's office at noon wearing a magenta T-shirt emblazoned with a silver palm tree, and a pair of tight bright yellow beltless slacks, whose cuffless bottoms rode high over his shoetops, Michael Jackson–style, revealing quality argyles worn with old tennis sneakers.

Mellis himself was clad in the sort of three-piece London suit he had worn in New York when Perry first met him, though this one seemed, if anything, more somber, like something Brideshead himself would have found too grim, except perhaps for his own funeral.

Today, of all days, Archer was evidently taking him to some elegant Eastern-style restaurant to have lunch. Perhaps they were going to meet some top network executive, maybe even its president! Perry slunk down in a chair, crossing his arms over his silver palm tree.

Archer in his ponderous elegance paced regally while speaking on the phone about some other pilot, one evidently involving a group of terrorists posing as Parisian prostitutes. He acknowledged Perry with a wave as if from a long distance, or from the deck of a departing ship. Hanging up the phone, he flipped open the sleek attaché case on his desk and began slipping scripts and papers into it. He hardly seemed to notice Perry's presence in the room, much less his exotic new outfit.

"Are we going somewhere?" Perry asked.

"I'm off to Paris," Archer said, snapping the clips of his attaché case shut. "Be back by the end of the week."

Perry jumped up, trembling.

"I thought you wanted to get me started on the second hour immediately!"

"Exactly. Ned Gurney will be here to take you to lunch in a few minutes."

"Who the hell is he?"

"Ever hear of *Spoons*?"

"You mean the Broadway play?"

"Won a Tony, ran for four years. Ned produced it, and he's been out here trying to get the movie off the ground, but it's run into some snags."

"What's that got to do with me?"

"I heard he was willing to do some television if he found

anything of quality. Of course he produced the Willa Cather for PBS, but I mean network. I gave him your script and he read it last night and loved it."

Before Perry could ask what all this meant, Archer had swung around the desk, and was shaking his hand.

"Congratulations. Ned is coming aboard as executive producer. This adds real class to your project."

"Wait!" Perry called after Archer, who was striding to the door. "What if I can't stand this guy? How can I work with him?"

"The man's a genius. He's worked with the very best."

"What if I hate his guts?"

Archer stopped just before he went out the door, and leveled his gaze at Perry.

"Trust me," he said.

Then he was gone.

To Paris. Leaving Perry to wait for this stranger who was now evidently in charge of his fate, his precious project, his sacred words. He felt as if he'd just been handed over to a new, unknown psychiatrist. Perry sighed and sat down, adjusting his tight new slacks that were riding up on his ass. Well, at least he wouldn't look like some academic hick from the East, not in his bright yellow pants and purple T-shirt with the silver palm tree.

Ned Gurney was wearing a tweed sport coat with suede patches at the elbows, a button-down shirt, and rep tie. He gave Perry a quick once-over, with a look of slight curiosity, and then the two men shook hands, politely, formally.

The initial meeting of producer and writer was like the first encounter of a couple of dogs of different breeds, cautiously circling, sniffing each other out.

Gurney was a handsome man in his early fifties with longish gray hair that curled up at his neck, and studious, horn-rimmed glasses that matched his ivyish style. He had an air of thoughtfulness about him even as he walked, with hands behind him, head slightly bent, as if studying the atmosphere, so when he commented on the weather it did not seem merely obligatory conversation-filler, but a matter he had actually pondered. The day was brisk, he mentioned, but not like autumn or winter in the East, rather like cool, high mountain air.

When they got to the studio commissary and opened the door, they were struck by the usual clash and clang of silver, as well as the heavy odor of institutional gravy.

Gurney winced, and said, "God, it always reminds me of a hospital."

Perry smiled.

"Or a high school," he said.

"Come on," said Gurney, "let's get out of here. You game?"

"Delighted. Lead the way."

Gurney drove them out of the Valley, smoothly and efficiently, without the idiosyncratic flair or urgency of Archer Mellis. Perry relaxed, enjoying Gurney's driving style, as well as the comfortable dark-blue Cadillac Seville, not a chic car in this world of Mercedes and sleek foreign sports jobs. They went to a restaurant in Westwood that reminded Perry of Boston.

"It's kind of like the Copley Plaza," Perry said.

"The food's all right, nothing gourmet, but what the hell, it's civilized."

Whatever Gurney really liked he conferred on it the judgment of "civilized."

He loved Perry's script, he thought it was really a rarity for television because it was not only funny and warm and real, it was "civilized."

"You can't believe the drek they send me to read," he told Perry over the glass of white wine each had. "What's already on the tube is bad enough, but this stuff is poor imitations of it. Nothing original. Hell, I'm tired of sitting on my can waiting for this feature to get put together, but I'd rather be bored than do drek. When Archer Mellis called me and said he had just the thing for me, I'd heard it all before, but when he mentioned your name I perked up."

Perry perked up himself.

It turned out Gurney had read one of his stories — in the *Hudson Review*, of all places!

71

"You really read the *Hudson Review?*" Perry asked.

"What the hell," said Gurney. "I'm a civilized man."

Perry agreed. He also agreed with the producer's few suggestions for changes in the first hour of the script.

"It's the second hour that's got me stymied," Perry confessed. "I hadn't even thought about expanding the story that way till a couple days ago, and I was kind of waiting to talk it over with Archer today, hoping he could help me come up with something."

"*What if* —" Ned said.

Aha. He too was a "what if" man. Perry leaned forward, intently.

"What if," Ned continued, "instead of Laurie and Jack resolving that little squabble and falling into each other's arms as you have it now, the argument escalates and Laurie splits."

"She leaves him? Then there's no show."

"Only for a while. Only till she realizes how much she loves him and comes back. In the meantime, Jack is stuck with living with his in-laws, and he and they are blaming each other for Laurie's leaving."

"That's marvelous! My God, I can't wait to start writing it."

"The sooner the better. I hope to get the director I want approved tomorrow, and begin casting right away for Jack and Laurie."

"*Casting?* My God, man, I can't get the second hour written overnight!"

"We don't need that for casting. It's still Jack and Laurie's story in the second hour, isn't it?"

"Well, sure, but —"

"And you're not going to change their looks or personalities, are you?"

"Of course not."

"So, we can start casting them."

"You sure don't waste any time," Perry said admiringly.

"I'm learning that in television we don't have any to waste," Ned said. "Decisions on new pilots are made by the networks in May. This is February. We're already running late."

Perry slugged down the rest of his coffee as Ned waved for the check.

"You're going to love this guy we got for executive producer," Perry proudly told Jane when he called her that night in Vermont.

"What's he like?" she asked.

Perry thought a moment.

"He's civilized," he said. "He's truly a civilized man."

"I can't wait to meet him."

"I can't wait for you to get back. Can you make it any sooner, you think?"

"I don't see how I can do everything in a week as it is. Especially with this god-awful weather."

It was ten above zero in Haviland. A big snow had fallen just the day before she arrived, and the roads had been cleared just in time for her to get through. If it hadn't been for Al Cohen's tramping over to the house in snowshoes to get the furnace going again, the pipes would have surely frozen.

From the half-open window above the bed where Perry lay with the phone a soft evening breeze wafted in, scented with sea air and oleander. Jane's voice sounded so immediate and close it seemed as if she might be calling from the corner, or from a booth at the Hamburger Hamlet, yet the words she was saying, the talk of roads blocked by snow, gave Perry the weird sensation she was speaking not just from across the country but from some other world, one of those sci-fi creations of Isaac Asimov or Ursula K. LeGuin.

Nor was it only the weather she described that seemed so oddly unreal and otherworldly. The people who only a month ago were familiar figures in Perry's daily life, the students and faculty, now seemed almost as remote, as Jane spoke their names and concerns — the books and classes, Al Cohen filling in for old Bozeman, who had suffered a mild heart attack, a basketball game canceled with Bowdoin, in Maine, because of the weather.

"I love you," Perry said. "Are you sure you're all right?"

Being in such different climates made him feel farther from her than he really was, gave him a bit of a panic.

"I'm fine, and I love you, too," she assured him. "I'll come back as soon as I can."

That night he dreamed of searching for her over ice floes.

It wasn't just the weather that was different in Southern California. Time was different, too.

It was faster.

Perry had imagined that, if anything, time out here at the edge of the vast Pacific, under the palm trees and constant sun, would probably be slower, lazier, than back in the brisk climate of the East. Like everyone else, Perry had read about the famous laid-back atmosphere of L.A., the mellow attitude of the natives of the region, whose casual clothes and morals were suited to the slow, sensual rhythm of surf and sun. Maybe that was true for some beach bums and bunnies, but it bore no relation to the full-throttle freeway race of show business. If Rome were the set for a TV movie, it surely would have been built in a day.

Overnight, literally, Perry's script had been transformed from the ethereal realm of imagination to the real world of production, even before he'd finished writing the second hour.

"The First Year's the Hardest" was not just a story any more, it was a company, with its own office. Of course the office was just another of the old, anonymous-looking motel-like buildings on the sprawling Paragon lot that happened to be vacant at the moment because the last production it sheltered was finished, either by completion or failure, leaving no trace of its character, leaving only the building, the shell, the office, ready to receive and be filled by the energy and spirit, the furniture and flesh of a new enterprise.

"The First Year's the Hardest."

That's what the secretary said when she answered the phone in Ned Gurney's office.

She said the name of Perry's story, Perry's show, as if it were General Motors or Lord & Taylor or Standard Oil.

As if it were *real*.

As if it were a regular business with typewriters and desks, secretaries and executives — and it was, it was all that.

Perry felt a little like a combination of Henry Ford and Rudyard Kipling — a literary man of action, an empire builder.

"You can pick your own office here in the building," Ned Gurney told him, "but don't feel you have to be here if you prefer to write back at your hotel. Whatever suits you best."

"Oh, I think I'd prefer to be right here now," Perry said.

Prefer, hell; you couldn't have kept him away from the place with armed guards.

This was where it was happening, the center of the action.

He selected an office on the second floor, right above Ned's; it was only a dingy cubicle, really, with some Salvation Army–vintage furniture, and a small window looking out on another identical building, but it seemed to Perry quite splendid. It was near a watercooler in the hall, and he could quickly run down to Ned's office and show him the latest pages that had just come out of his typewriter. Likewise, with an interoffice buzz on his phone, Ned could summon Perry down for important consultations, as he did later that very first afternoon.

"If you have a moment, Perry, there's someone here I'm anxious for you to meet."

He was a round, cherubic-looking young fellow. Perry realized at once he must be Ned's choice to play the part of Jack. He was even dressed for the part, sloppy collegiate, with baggy old jeans and a faded sweatshirt, tousled blond hair that he had to brush up from his eyes. He wasn't precisely the person Perry had imagined for the role, but the important thing was he didn't look like some slick Hollywood star. If anything, he looked a bit young for the part.

"Perry Moss, I'd like you to meet Kenton Spires, our director."

The pleasant, pudgy fellow blushed and shook hands, and Perry tried to hide his shock and disappointment.

How could he be a director? He was only a kid.

"Your script is the first really brilliant piece I've been shown for television," Spires said quietly.

Well, at least he was a *smart* kid.

Kenton had won an Obie and directed several prize-winning dramas for PBS, yet he'd been languishing out here for almost a year without getting a break because he didn't have what Ned called "schlock time," or commercial TV experience. But Ned made it a condition of his own involvement in "First Year" that Kenton direct the pilot, so Archer had gone out on a limb and raised hell to get the network's reluctant approval for him. Perry was soon delighted.

As the three new colleagues continued their discussion of the project over sandwiches and beer, the young director seemed not only as civilized as Ned, but also a fellow artist, a kindred spirit; hell, a buddy. It was as if time in L.A. moved faster in professional friendships, too, like an old-fashioned film run fast forward, so that what in the ordinary pace of life and relationships would require whole years was accelerated and experienced in a matter of hours.

By the time Ned and Kenton dropped Perry off at the Marmont late that evening it seemed as if the three of them had been best friends in high school and had just got together again to produce this show.

There was a couch in the room where Perry sat in on his first casting session, an old lump of Salvation Army furniture covered with faded brown slipcovers of some tired, nubby material. He figured this must be the infamous casting couch of Hollywood legend, but the actresses reading for the part of Laurie didn't even sit on it. Ned and Kenton sat there, while the young women stationed themselves in chairs by the window.

The faculty wives back at Haviland would have no doubt been relieved — or perhaps secretly disappointed — to find the symbolic casting couch was nonerotic and businesslike, as were the sessions themselves. After three or four readings, and the quick exchange of glances and comments afterward between Ned and Kenton, it was obvious that any other consideration than the actress's talent and suitability as Laurie was not only irrelevant, but annoying. Had some aspiring bombshell swiveled in and performed the most erotic disrobing since Salome, the reaction would have been that it was not the sort of thing Laurie would do.

At the end of two hours and eleven readings, Ned suggested they all get on with their other work for the rest of the day and "look at more Lauries" tomorrow.

"My God," Perry said, with a sudden sense of the neophyte's panic, "what if we don't find her — the right Laurie?"

"We'll find her," Ned told him.

Alton Saxby, the casting director, whose job was to send in a steady stream of potential Lauries until the right one was chosen, placed a reassuring hand on Perry's shoulder.

"We'll find her even if we have to make a search of graduate schools all over America."

Driving back from the studio that evening, Perry imagined a nationwide search to find the right Laurie, the 1980s version of the legendary quest to discover Scarlett O'Hara. Perry, of course, as creator of the character, was asked to lead the talent hunt, conducting interviews in grad schools all over America, where bevies of eager, gorgeous young women finagled their way into his hotel suite in imaginative attempts to seduce him into selecting them for the role.

At a stoplight on Cahuenga Boulevard, Perry was mentally in Madison, Wisconsin, where a voluptuous anthropology major who had just been elected Miss Dairyland tricked her way into his suite by identifying herself as Room Service. After pushing him onto the bed and ravishing him mercilessly, the aspiring star whispered in Perry's ear: "I'm Laurie," to which he replied, "I'm sorry, Laurie would never have done it that way."

Perry laughed at himself, and decided to stop off for something to eat at the Hamburger Hamlet, a mile or so down from the Marmont on Sunset. Usually he hated to dine alone in public, especially after dark, when being by yourself meant you were not only alone but lonely. Out here he didn't feel that way. Out here he felt that although he might be by himself he was not really alone, for he was part of the mystical fraternity of show business, to which everyone else either belonged or aspired to.

77

to which everyone else either belonged or aspired to.

The dream was not impossible. Though the Schwab's drugstore on Sunset with the counter where Lana Turner was discovered no longer existed, there were real and hopeful actors, actresses, directors and producers, camera people and set designers, in every luncheonette and coffee shop and drugstore in Hollywood, and for the price of that day's *Variety* or *Hollywood Reporter*, you could talk the language of the trades. You could speak of the latest deal and in the next breath talk of your own deal that might be tomorrow's box office boffo smash and you the producer or writer or star. And like the Megabucks Lottery back in Massachusetts, somebody's number eventually did come up, and everyone had hopes of hitting the next jackpot.

Perry sat at the counter and ordered the bacon and avocado sandwich on toast (anything with avocado reminded him with a pleasant rush he was out here in exotic Southern California). Though he was by himself, Perry was elated by the knowledge that he was one of the blessed at this or any other counter in Hollywood for he had his own show, not only "in development," but soon to be "in production."

Those magical terms, along with other stock phrases of show business, spoken like ritual incantations, were floating now as always in the very atmosphere of the room. A couple of places down from Perry a bald man was telling a tall young woman with an orange streak in her hair that he had just optioned a surefire property he was going to develop for a feature.

An option!

It was one of the magic words, one of the magic deeds. Everyone had options. Anyone could have options. For a dollar, you could take an option on your neighbor's laundry list, if he didn't already have it in development for a feature or perhaps for a pilot for a series!

Perry noticed a young woman alone, reading a paperback novel instead of the trades over her custard pie and coffee. Could be she was some kind of misplaced intellectual? She was hardly beautiful, with close-set eyes behind thick glasses, a long, aquiline nose, and stringy hair. Yet there was something appealing about

her, a kind of wistful quality, an innocence. . . . She might be —
Laurie!

Perhaps Perry himself was destined to be the one to discover
her, the one who happened by chance onto just the right woman
when all the pros had failed to produce her. All he had to do
was go up and explain who he was, why he was interested in
talking with her. It sounded like the oldest cliche in the books —
"Excuse me, young lady, but I can get you into show biz!" He
felt himself flush red at the awful corniness of it, and yet it was
true. It *could* happen. It wasn't likely, but it was damn well
possible.

Perry began to feel dizzy, almost disoriented. He found it hard
to discern what was real and what fantasy. It was a little like being
on the edge of the "twilight zone" and not knowing what thought
or deed would make you cross over from daily life into some
other dimension of experience. He concentrated on his sandwich.
That was real. In rising anxiety he gobbled it down, slurped the
rest of his coffee, and paid the check.

He hurried to his room and called Jane in Vermont, holding
his breath as the rings came, hoping and muttering a prayer she
was home. It was not just that he missed her, as he always did
the few times they had been apart in the past five years, it was
not just his desire for her companionship and lovemaking and
talk and intuitive understanding. What he longed for now was
her *reality*, her tangible, solid, commonsensical flesh and blood
presence to remind him who and where he was, to keep him
from slipping off into the "twilight zone" of show biz fantasy.

The sound of Jane's voice restored his balance.

"I love you, I miss you *too*," she said.

Perry relaxed, lay down on the bed, stretching and feeling the
tension flow from his body.

He dreamed Jane had been lost in a blizzard, and, with the
help of Ned Gurney, Kenton Spires, and Alton Saxby, Perry
conducted a nationwide search to find someone to play her part
in his life. The leading role. But no one was right. They might
even nearly look the part, but they kept doing things that Jane

wouldn't do — laughing at the wrong time, speaking ostenta-
tiously, moving awkwardly across a room.

"We still haven't found her," Ned Gurney said the next day.
"Don't worry, we *will*," Kenton said with quiet assurance.
"We've just begun to look," Alton Saxby added.
For a moment, Perry thought they were speaking of Jane, that
his dream of the night before was continuing into the day.
But of course they were speaking of Laurie.
Perry took a deep breath and, with a sense of relief and responsibility, exiled himself to his office cubicle to work on the
second hour of the script. There were hurrying footsteps in the
hall outside his door, and through the thin walls he could hear
phones ringing — phones being answered by secretaries saying,
"The First Year's the Hardest!"
Concentrate. He had to remind himself that if he didn't finish
this script for the second hour, the whole thing would come
tumbling down around him, the walls collapse, the phones stop
ringing. In several hours, he managed to squeeze out a couple
of pages of sizzling dialogue and decided to take it down to Ned,
rewarding himself with a break.
"Still looking at Lauries," Kenton reported, and Ned sighed
and handed Perry the glossy 8 x 10 photo with credits on the
back that announced the next candidate. Perry sat down, deciding
he'd indulge in watching just one reading before pressing back
to work.
Bad luck. He could tell just by looking at the photo this one
was wasting their time. Melinda Margulies may have done Shakespeare in the Park and had a lot of fancy New York stage credits,
as well as a good secondary role in a TV miniseries, but she
simply wasn't Laurie.
Laurie was pert, perky, and preppy. The Margulies girl was
big at 5 feet 10 inches, 135, not fat but certainly hefty and
decidedly broad-shouldered. A female linebacker, at least from
her photo.
In person, even more so. She chewed gum with loud smacks,

shook hands with a crusher grip, and spoke in a flat, anonymous tone.

"Ya want me to do it now?" she asked, slumping in her chair before Ned even had time to ask the few polite questions whose purpose primarily was to put the actress at ease.

"Please," Ned said, nodding.

Melinda first reached in her mouth and pulled a wad of gum from the back recesses, examined it critically, then stuck it under the chair. She closed her eyes a moment, took a deep breath, and pulled herself up so straight her spine was like a rifle placed against the chair's back. When she opened her eyes they were suddenly alert, excited. She smiled, and looked delighted by life, as if she found every aspect of it fascinating. When she spoke, her voice was warm, winning, energetic, not quite breathless but spirited, the voice of someone who was not only interesting but interested, and it was edged with that unmistakable, slightly nasal, r-softened sound that signals "preppy."

Perry recognized this voice at once, though he had never heard it before, except in his imagination.

It was the voice of Laurie.

By the end of the reading, this magical person had somehow so transformed herself that she even *looked* like Laurie — not the way the character was described in the words of the story, but the way it now seemed she ought to look, in living flesh and gesture.

When the reading was finished and Ned and Kenton thanked the actress, she slumped back down in her seat, reached to pull the wad of gum from beneath it, popped it back in her mouth, and shambled out of the room.

"How about that?" Kenton asked with a grin.

"Well, author," Ned said to Perry, "you should know — was that Laurie?"

"How did she do that?" Perry asked in a stunned voice. "What happened?"

"You just saw an actress," Ned explained.

Melinda Margulies was Laurie.

*

The next day Ned invited Perry to come down to hear a second reading for the part of Jack by an actor named Ronnie Banks.

A bit offbeat and quirky, Banks possessed great quantities of natural boyish charm as well as a wicked, spontaneous wit. He was obviously perfect for Jack, except for one hitch. He was short.

His bio said he was 5 feet 7 inches, but even that was a slight exaggeration. That was all right when they first had him in to read, but that was before they knew Melinda Margulies, the 5 foot 10 inch linebacker, was going to be Laurie.

Ned thanked Ronnie for coming in again and said they'd be in touch. When the hopeful young actor left the room Kenton Spires said softly, ruefully, "Shit."

"When Melinda wears heels, he won't even come up to her chin," Ned sighed.

"We can put him in lifts," said Alton Saxby.

"And stand him on orange crates during love scenes," Kenton said. "We'll never be able to shoot their feet."

"We'd look like the goddam 'Muppet Show,' " Ned groaned.

"I think they have feet now, too," said Perry, wanting to make a contribution, adding as the others turned to stare at him, "the Muppets, I mean. Have feet?"

"We got the right people of the wrong heights," Ned lamented, evidently ignoring Perry's observation.

Alton stood up and began to pace in an opposite direction from Ned.

"If we put him in lifts," Alton said, "maybe even cowboy boots, and kept her in flats all the time . . ."

"Why would a woman wear flats all the time," Ned asked, "unless she's got a gimpy leg?"

Perry cleared his throat and, fearful he might make a fool of himself, spoke in a rush.

"A woman might fall in love with a man even though he's shorter than she is, and if that were the case, she might simply want to wear flats to make him feel more comfortable about their difference in height. I imagine it happens sometimes."

The others turned to Perry and this time looked at him as if he'd just invented the light bulb.

"That's it!" Ned said, snapping his fingers.

"Beautiful," Kenton said. "Gives a whole new dimension to the relationship."

"And it's true to the two of them," Ned said excitedly. "It's almost symbolic of their love — kind of awkward, offbeat, giving, considerate . . ."

"I'll get them both back in tomorrow morning," Alton said, "and we can see how they look together. How they play off each other."

"Perfect," Ned said. "We'll know right away if it works."

It was magic.

"The network didn't go for it," Archer said flat out. "They think a tall wife and short husband is strictly sitcom stuff."

Kenton moaned, putting his head in his hands.

Ned exploded, rising off the floor of Archer's office like a rocket.

"The frigging Neanderthals!" he screamed.

"Besides," Archer said, "they've got Hal Thaxter under contract and they want to see him in this part."

Hal Thaxter was a burly blond macho type with a toothpaste ad smile and a high "TVQ."

Perry had just learned that a TVQ was a significant computerized personal rating of how popular an actor was with the American television audience. By virtue of his appeal as a mindless lifeguard in "Beach Bonanza," the long-running series of a few years before, Thaxter had a high TVQ and was thus regarded as a valuable element for a new, untried show.

"You ought to be pleased that the network wants him in your pilot," Archer said. "It means they're behind it."

"It also means they don't get the point," Ned Gurney yelled. "And it further means you let us down when you said you were all for Ronnie Banks and you'd back us on him all the way!"

As Ned's face grew redder, Archer's grew whiter. Perry for a moment wondered if the younger man was going to shrink before the older man's fury, but Archer Mellis became almost frighteningly rigid and frigid, a major of military bearing and command whose voice came out in saber strokes.

"I put myself on the line for you with Kenton, and I won that battle. I did the same with Ronnie Banks, and I lost. This is not Broadway, this is network television. If you don't like the way it plays, I recommend you look for more congenial action elsewhere."

Perry held his breath. Kenton Spires closed his eyes. Ned Gurney, his face not only red but puffed to the point of explosion, exhaled, then nodded.

"I hear you," he said.

"And that's the bottom line, *amigo*."

"Of course. I understand."

Ned extended his hand to Archer, who gave it a quick grip.

The meeting was over.

Ned, Kenton — and Perry, too, of course — calmed down and came to the conclusion that Hal Thaxter would be just fine as Jack. There was no sense in being down on an actor because he was handsome and had a high TVQ.

In fact, Ned said that casting the leads so well was cause to celebrate, and anyway, everyone needed to relax a bit, so he was having a little dinner at his house Friday night. Perry was of course delighted at the prospect of seeing the executive producer's home, as well as meeting his girlfriend. The only disappointment was that Jane wouldn't get back till the next day. He hated to have her miss this first social occasion with his new colleagues, and, in fact, he felt a bit uncomfortable about going alone. He realized it would be the first time in five years that he'd gone to a real party without Jane. He almost felt guilty, as if it were a small betrayal. He tried to call her just before going to Ned's, but there wasn't any answer. It was seven o'clock, which meant ten in Vermont. Where the hell was she? Should he try to reach her at the Cohens'?

Hell, he told himself to relax and enjoy, which Jane would

want him to do anyway. He poured a small glass of wine and drank it before leaving, feeling better and thinking he'd remember every detail of the evening so he could tell Jane all about it.

As Perry approached Ned Gurney's beautiful Spanish-style house in the Hollywood Hills, he thought it was a shame that it pressed so close to another one. But as he entered the interior courtyard he realized that what he thought was a second house was in fact a wing of the main house. He wondered if such grandeur meant the place qualified to be officially called a villa. He sure as hell wasn't going to show his hick ignorance by asking Ned, but he looked forward to discussing it with Jane. He also wondered if she would agree with his theory that Ned didn't have a swimming pool because it would seem too Hollywood, and that the elegant interior courtyard was more Eastern, even more intellectual than a pool would have been.

Ned's girlfriend matched the house.

She wasn't Spanish, but she was elegant and intellectual and, as opposed to the Hollywood type of woman, she was very Eastern. In fact, she was Far Eastern. From Thailand. Kim was small, with delicate features, and certainly young, early thirties, yet she had such assurance, such presence, she gave an impression of stature. Perry feared at first she might be aloof and formal, but in moments she had him laughing with her, relaxed.

She not only conveyed an enthusiasm but an understanding of his script; she was in the same business herself, a film editor. It was hard to imagine a more appropriate mate for Ned Gurney — surely not the former wife, whoever she was, who common gossip said he split up with back in New York.

Archer Mellis made a brief appearance, just for a glass of wine, with a girlfriend; she looked like the one he'd taken to Spoleto with Perry and Jane, but instead was fresh out of Yale Law School and working as an attorney in one of the prestigious entertainment law firms out here.

Kenton Spires came with his chatterbox wife, Alicia, who kept interrupting people to complain of the lack of culture in L.A., and how hideously she missed Bloomingdale's. When Alton Saxby arrived Perry was immediately curious to see if the casting director had brought some young sexpot he had plucked from the ranks of aspiring actresses, but instead he came arm in arm with a distinguished-looking gentleman who was a successful set designer.

Perry had assumed that since the party was to celebrate casting the leads of the show, Melinda Margulies and Hal Thaxter would be there, but Ned explained that he didn't think it wise to socialize with actors when you were working in a show with them.

"You mean they're too — uh, emotional?" Perry asked.

"They're too human," Ned said with a smile. "Worse still, they're artists. They want to tell you how it should all be done. As a writer, you have to be specially on guard. They'll have you rewriting every line."

"Oh, thanks!" Perry said, storing up this new bit of show biz lore and wanting automatically to share it with Jane.

Evidently it was all right to socialize with actors and actresses when you weren't working on a show with them, since one was there as a guest.

Perry did a double take when he saw her, not only because she was a striking-looking woman, but she also seemed familiar. He might have seen her on commercials, or minor roles in TV movies. She had short blond hair that glistened like a helmet, and tan, well-muscled legs, like a dancer. Her name was Liz Caddigan, and Perry found himself sitting next to her on a step of the courtyard terrace.

He declared to her, almost compulsively, that his wife was in Vermont, she'd be back tomorrow, and he missed her very much. He could feel himself blushing when he finished, and wondered if he sounded like a rube. Liz smiled and said she understood; the man she lived with was doing a play in New York, and she had to be in California for the filming of a TV miniseries.

There was some kind of wonderful curry for dinner, served buffet-style, and a young man in a red vest poured a nice white wine for everyone. Perry and Liz had something in common —

absent lovers — so they struck up a friendly conversation. They enjoyed each other's company.

Later on, Alton Saxby said he and his companion were going to catch a nightclub act of a singer who was a friend of theirs, and asked if anyone would like to join them. Liz said she had to be home early, and Perry offered to drop her off. She had mentioned she was staying in an actress friend's furnished apartment in West Hollywood, not far from the Marmont.

When Perry stopped in front of her apartment building, Liz invited him in for coffee.

Why not?

There was cognac, too, if he wanted. He hesitated, then said no, thanks, just the coffee, black would be fine. He already had enough wine in him, and besides, the idea of a drink gave the casual occasion a little more intimacy, or the possibility of it. He wanted to be able to tell Jane all about it, and "she invited me in for coffee" seemed more accurately innocent than "a drink." He started to sit on the roomy couch, then realized Liz might sit there too, so he chose a chair across from it with a low coffee table in between. He knew he was being compulsively proper, laughably so, yet this was the first time in more than five years he had sat alone in a room with another woman than Jane, with the exception of Rachel Cohen or some student or faculty colleague.

His ears felt hot, and he wondered if that meant Jane was listening, through some psychic transcontinental transmission. If she was, he had nothing to feel guilty about. Liz came in with the coffee and sat on the couch, and Perry told her how wonderful his wife was, while she in turn sang the praises of her own man back in New York. She slipped off her high-heeled sandals and tucked her long legs up on the couch, simply getting comfortable. She smoothed her short skirt down as far as it would go, yet Perry couldn't help noticing what looked like a tendon in her muscular thigh. It seemed to be pulsing or throbbing, and for some reason fascinated him. He looked away, and spoke even more extravagantly of Jane.

A window was open, and there was a scent of impending rain. It seemed as if Perry's sense of smell had sharpened, as if there were odors, aromas, everywhere, that windows and doors were perpetually open — that everything was open, like the land itself, the vast spaces, connected by freeways. *Free*ways. Ways of freedom. Perry shifted in his chair.

"It must be hard," he said. "I mean, having to spend so much time on opposite coasts, you and Jeffrey. It must mean a lot of trust."

"Mmmm," Liz nodded. "Also, we don't ask questions."

She uncurled one leg, raising the foot, staring at the toes.

"That's the only way it can work," she explained, lowering her leg again, curling it back underneath her.

"Of course," Perry said.

He set down his coffee cup, trying not to let it make a rattling noise on the saucer and only partially succeeding. He realized now he could walk a few steps to that couch and spend the rest of the night with this lovely, appealing woman. It was something he had never even imagined since the day he met Jane.

Would it matter, if it happened? Would it "count" if a man and woman made love to each other on one side of the continent while the man and woman they really loved were clear across the map on the edge of that other ocean? Did the barrier of continental distance, the difference of miles and hours, serve as a shield against the shattering of vows? Could fidelity bend instead of break in an arc of such enormous separation? Maybe there were different natural laws in operation in such cases; like gravity being suspended in space, perhaps fidelity was suspended in the warp of bi-coastal separation.

That was a comforting, a light-headed thought, but maybe it was only like an optical illusion, maybe there was something that caught up with you later, some phenomenon like "sex lag," in which what you did seemed all right at the time but three hours later boomeranged back and wiped you out, leaving you drained, disoriented, unable to sleep, groggy and aching.

Perry drank down the last of his coffee and stood up.

Liz uncurled from the couch.

Perry could see the two of them in his mind, like actors on a stage. It reminded him of one of those improvisational theater evenings, where the drama could move to all kinds of different endings, depending on the next gesture or the next line.

"As soon as Jane gets back, we'll get together," Perry said.

"I can't wait to meet her," Liz said. "And when Jeffrey comes out, we'll all do the town."

Liz walked him to the door and opened it, the musky scent of her perfume mixing with the other aromas of the night. Perry turned and hurried out, like a man fleeing a burning building. He sped home, careening around corners, wanting to call Jane, hear her voice, assure himself everything was the same between them, that she hadn't intuitively picked up any small "blip" of his momentary temptation on the screen of her own radar.

It was not quite one o'clock when he got in, which was still not terribly late. He picked up the phone and then put it back down, realizing it was almost four in the morning in Vermont. Damn. If he called her now, it would frighten her. It would seem like an emergency. He felt in fact like there almost had been one, but he didn't want her to know that. He got into his bathrobe, poured himself the cognac he was glad he hadn't had with Liz Caddigan, and sat on the bed, clutching the glass with both hands.

Perry went to meet Jane at the airport with flowers. He felt light, buoyant, as if he were walking around about five or six inches off the ground, just naturally, without any effort. He got up early and knocked out a couple of crucial scenes, and he was not only feeling good about himself as a writer but as a man, a person.

Instead of feeling guilty about the drink with Liz at her apartment, he had awakened feeling relief as he realized he had met and overcome the great cliche, Hollywood temptation. He had passed up the chance to go to bed with a real-live, attractive actress in the tan, taut, living flesh. He had remained true to his wife, to his marriage, to his old-fashioned concept of fidelity —

despite distance of miles or life-style — and so had remained true to himself. The whole experience made him feel less panicky about facing other temptations and tests of this place, for he had already passed one of the basic ones, the kind that changed people, changed the way they lived and looked at life.

He couldn't wait to get his arms around his wonderful, loving wife.

She was one of the last passengers off the plane, dragging her winter coat behind her, looking pale and disoriented, like some kind of refugee. When she saw Perry she lurched toward him and he caught her as she threw her arms around him and kissed him sloppily, her mouth like a cask of stale brandy.

"For God sake," he said, pulling away.

"Love me, love me not?" she asked, blinking, trying to focus.

He took her arm and turned her, hoping to steady her as they went to the luggage.

"You smell like a Saint Bernard," he said.

She wrenched her arm away from his grip.

"Oh, phoo. Phoo you."

She stuck her tongue out at him and stumbled, and he grabbed her again, guiding, gritting his teeth.

He had never seen her drunk, or rather, the few times she'd been drunk, he'd been in the same state, and so hadn't minded. This was different. This was disgusting. She was drunk and he was not. He tried to concentrate just on getting her home.

Driving back she rolled down the window and Perry was on the alert to pull over if she started getting sick. The fresh air seemed to revive her, though, as she stuck her head out the window, singing off key as she slurred her improvised words.

"Cal-a-forn-ya here I am,
like a great big candied yam . . ."

He blamed it on first class. They didn't stop pouring the booze for you. That, and after all, she had had to do all the dirty work of making the big switch, packing up, saying good-byes. He wasn't going to make a big issue of this, just get her to bed and start fresh the next day.

"I'm sorry," Jane said. "It finally got to me."

She slept it off the next morning, spent the day unpacking and soaking herself in a warm bath, and greeted Perry that night when he came home from the studio with crackers and brie, a Bloody Mary for him, and a Virgin Mary for herself.

"Hey, it's no wonder," he said. "You must have worked your tail off getting everything wrapped up out there."

He had put an arm around her but now she moved away, walking slowly toward the window, so her back was toward him.

"It wasn't the work," she said.

"What, then?"

"The whole thing. What we're doing — the move. I realized how big it is. The change."

"Lovey, it's only temporary."

"It's also enormous."

She turned and looked at him. There was a faint trace of red on her upper lip from the drink, and it accentuated the paleness of her face.

"Being back there," she said, "trying to explain to people what we're doing, what it's like out here, I felt sort of crazy. There were moments I wondered if maybe I'd dreamed it."

She lifted her arm, indicating the room, the window behind her, the bright lemon light falling in.

"All this," she said. "California."

"Yes," he said.

He knew just what she meant, for now, trying to conjure up his life in Vermont, the one that was real to him only a little more than a month ago, all *that* seemed like a dream.

Jane had just moved back and forth between dreams, and it must have been frightening as well as exhausting. Perry was struck by the scary notion that one of the two of them might get caught up in the opposite dream, and that it might really separate them, take them away from each other. That was something he had never before thought possible, under any circumstance. He got up and went to her and put his arms around her and she grabbed him, digging her fingers into his back as they swayed back and forth, together, tightly, holding each other in the same dream.

V

YOU HAD TO HOLD ON.

You not only had to hold on to each other, you had to hold on to yourself, to your own perspective.

You had to hold on because everything started going so fast.

You had to hold on or you might fall off.

"We're flying," Archer Mellis said.

The project was really off the ground now that Perry had finished writing the second hour. The network loved it so much they were willing to spring for the extra expense of shooting exteriors on location instead of just on the lot and around L.A., in an effort to preserve the original New England ambience of the story. Of course they couldn't afford to go all the way to Vermont, as Archer had originally assured Perry was the only way to do the piece properly, but the ingenious young executive had discovered a campus in a small town outside San Jose that miraculously conveyed what Archer assured everyone was "a heavy New England *flavor*." He was taking up some of the "First Year" staff that day to scout it out.

"Do all of us get to go?" Perry asked eagerly.

"I can only take one," said Archer.

Ned jumped up and started pacing, the vein in his temple turning red as it began to throb.

"Surely we can dig up a few more plane tickets out of the budget," he said. "Is that the problem?"

Archer, who was pacing in a different direction, wheeled and fixed Ned with narrowed eyes, as if he had him in the cross hairs of his rifle site.

"I don't pinch pennies, *amigo*," he said icily. "The problem is I only have room in my plane for one passenger."

Archer had a pair of goggles cocked up on his forehead and a silk ascot tucked into his tunic. Though he bore a striking resemblance to the young Errol Flynn as the flying ace of *The Dawn Patrol*, Perry had simply assumed this was another of his dashing costumes, rather than real aviation apparel. Come to think of it, though, he knew that flying a plane was one of Archer's many daring avocations, along with skydiving, scuba diving, steer wrestling, and white-water kayak racing.

"Forgive me, Archer!" Ned exclaimed. "I simply assumed we'd be flying up on PSA."

"We'd have to go to San Jose on commercial flights," Archer explained, "but I can take us right into Saratoga, where the college is. There's a small airfield at the edge of town. Saves lots of time."

"What a guy!" Ned said, throwing up his hands in tribute.

Kenton shifted his great bulk uneasily in his chair.

"Somebody better stay here and mind the store," he said. "I'd like to keep an eye on that set they're building for Jack and Laurie's living room."

Archer nodded.

"Perry, you get to work on those last notes from the network," he said. "See if you can wrap up revisions by tomorrow."

Archer pulled a couple of automatic cameras out of a drawer and tossed one to Ned as he flung the other around his neck.

"We'll take plenty of shots for you people," he assured Kenton and Perry with a brisk nod. "Come on, Ned — my Cessna's at Santa Monica."

Perry jumped up to get to his own task, exhilarated. It was like being in on a great military campaign, with excitement mounting as the shooting drew near.

"Great news!" Perry called out to Jane when he burst in the door that night. "We get to shoot on location!"

94

"Oh my God," she said.

She looked stricken.

"What the hell's the matter?" Perry demanded.

Jane sat down on the couch, holding her arms over her stomach as if she were fighting the onset of appendicitis.

"I thought that was all off," she said.

"The network loved the script so much they're willing to pay for it! You ought to be thrilled — this is a triumph!"

"Darling, I'm happy for you. But I just can't turn around and go back to Vermont, especially after this last trip, after all the explanations, all the good-byes. I'm not a human Ping-Pong ball."

Perry smiled and sighed.

"Lovey," he said, sitting down and putting an arm around her, "this has nothing to do with Vermont. The cost of that would be prohibitive — I thought you understood that."

"But you just said they like it so much they're willing to pay to go on location."

"Not in Vermont. That's out of the question. Archer found a place up north that he said has real New England ambience. He and Ned flew there today to scout locations."

"Up north?" she asked. "You mean Canada? I guess that would have a similar look."

"Not Canada, lovey. It's a college in a little town called Saratoga, near San Jose. California."

"San Jose! What in the name of heaven is New Englandy about San Jose? It's not even as far north as San Francisco!"

"How do you know? You haven't even been there."

Jane shook her head, smiling ruefully.

"Remember when you told Archer it had to be filmed in Vermont or the story wouldn't make sense?"

"That was ages ago, before I understood the realities."

Jane started giggling.

"What the hell's so funny?"

"Maybe no one will notice the redwoods," she said. "Maybe they can be disguised as giant pine trees."

"You really are hilarious," Perry said.

95

It was like standing in the middle of a dream.

His own dream.

This was the living room of Jack and Laurie's apartment, just as he'd conceived it — a combination of Salvation Army funk and academic chic. There was a swayback couch strewn with bright-colored corduroy pillows, blond Scandinavian-design chairs around a matching breakfast table, brick-and-board bookcases that held not only well-worn volumes but also gleaming chrome stereo components. There was the dark-shellacked door resting on sawhorses that held Jack's old Smith Corona as well as a mess of his books and papers. There was even Laurie's cello propped in a corner of the room next to an ironing board. There were framed posters of colored photographs on the wall: the tall wineglass filled with big, ripe strawberries that represented to them the abundance of life, and the canoe, empty except for the paddles pointing out to sea, that they knew meant the wonderful "mystery" of life, that high afternoon they bought the posters.

It was eerie, standing and walking around in that imagined room that now was real.

Or was it?

Perry suddenly plopped down into a chair to make sure it was solid, and not the stuff of dreams, or the illusion of madness.

The chair held him. Relieved, he stood up, walked to the bookshelves and pulled out a book, at random.

He looked at it and frowned.

It was one of those old one-volume Reader's Digest condensations.

"What's the matter?" Ned Gurney asked.

Perry looked up and saw that the two men standing with Ned were leaning forward, hanging on every word, looking as anxious as if they were about to hear a guilty verdict that would send them both to death row.

"Oh, it's no big deal," Perry said quickly. "It's just that a couple of grad students like Jack and Laurie would never have a book like this — a condensed book."

Tom, the big man who looked like a stevedore, grabbed the book out of Perry's hand, turned to the open side of the room that had no wall and hurled the book off the set.

"I'm sorry," said Larry, the fragile-looking man who served as Tom's assistant. "I pick up books by the boxful to stock shelves like this, it usually doesn't matter which books they really are."

"It doesn't really matter here either," said Ned. "The camera would never even pick up the title out of a whole shelf."

"It matters," said Tom, "that Perry here knows it was the wrong book to be in this room. We want this room to *feel* right, to *be* right, down to the last thumbtack in Jack's bulletin board."

Ned grinned and turned to Perry.

"These guys are the best," he said. "They'll get anything you want, from stained glass windows to real lightning bugs in mason jars."

"We did that once," Tom said proudly. "Got lightning bugs. For a 'Waltons' spisode."

"Oh, we'll get you whatever you want," Larry said. "And don't you hesitate to tell us if it isn't just right, Mr. Moss. After all, you're the creator."

Larry spoke the term with real awe.

The creator liked that.

He liked being recognized and appreciated, not only as a literary talent but now, for the first time in his life, the creator not only of stories but of jobs for all the people whose work it was to bring his fiction to life on film — the prop men like Tom and Larry, the set designer who built the living room he stood in, the set decorator who selected the furnishings, the location man who scouted places for exterior shooting, the camera crew that would soon begin shooting the two-hour script, the makeup people and hairdressers, the gofers and drivers, the whole array of men and women and their spouses and children who were now being supported, provided with food and clothing and medical benefits, all by the mere exercise of Perry's talent.

This was a far cry, a whole different order of experience and responsibility, from publishing a short story in the *Hudson Review*.

The heady feeling of power and command increased when he and Ned stopped in Kenton's office and saw the young director poring over the storyboard. The storyboard was like the master plan of any production, a long, graphlike chart showing each day of the shooting schedule, color-coded according to scenes, locations, and cast members. It was intricate and awesome, like some elaborate plan for the invasion of an enemy country, with troops and equipment amassed for carefully coordinated split-second action, yet all the more inspiring because this was not a campaign of destruction, but of creation.

"After all, you're the creator."

Larry's awed reminder rang in Perry's ears as he drove home from the studio that evening. Shooting was to start in two days. He had done it. He felt like celebrating.

After all, even creators took breaks. Perry had rarely even rested on the seventh day, and he'd now been out here working steadily, with concentration, for more than two months. In his focus on the all-consuming project he had paid little attention to Jane, and he felt now it was time for the creator's wife, too, to get a break.

Jane was at the table going over some contact prints with her magnifying glass.

The ungracious thought came to the creator that she didn't look much like a creator's wife.

He wasn't sure what such a glorified creature should look like, but he thought something rather on the elegant side would seem appropriate. At least around cocktail time.

Jane was wrapped in the fuzzy old bathrobe she wore around the house in winter, along with the matching pink bunny slippers. Perry hadn't seen this outfit since Vermont, where it seemed warm and cuddly. Now, here in Southern California, it simply looked sad.

The creator sat down with a sigh.

"Lovey," he said, "I thought you were only bringing back our *summer* clothes."

Jane looked up at him, then down at the tattered robe, automatically drawing it closer around herself, as if for protection.

"This is comfy," she said.

"Mmmm."

He paused a moment, held back his comment and asked, "Like a drink?"

"Thanks."

Perry made them both vodka and tonics, and sat down at the table with her. She was bent over the contacts again. Perry stoked up his pipe, trying to invoke in himself a reflective mood, a philosophic attitude.

"I was thinking," he said.

"Uh-huh?"

"Maybe we should buy some summer clothes."

"I *brought* our summer clothes out. We *have* everything."

"I meant new ones. You know. 'California' clothes."

Jane put down her magnifying glass, took a sip of her drink, and looked suspiciously at Perry.

"What do you mean, 'California' clothes?"

Perry shrugged, taking a sip of his own drink and trying to sound completely casual.

"The kind they wear out here. More casual."

"Why?"

"Why not? We're in California, aren't we? Shouldn't we dress as the Romans dress?"

"What's wrong with the way we always dressed?"

"Nothing! I like the way I've always dressed. Obviously. Or I wouldn't have dressed that way all my life. But I never lived in California before."

"We're only going to be here a few more months. Till the end of May. Aren't we? Is that still the plan?"

"Of course it's the plan! You think I'd change any plans without telling you?"

"Just checking."

"We start shooting next week. Then we go on location. I'd like to have some things to wear — you know, just some appropriate, casual stuff. Something besides my old sport jackets. They're too damn formal for this kind of thing."

99

Jane took a slug of her drink.

"You know what Thoreau said?"

"What has Thoreau got to do with this?"

"He said, 'Beware of all enterprises that require new clothes.' "

Perry took a long, cool pull of his vodka and tonic.

"Thoreau never lived in Los Angeles," he said.

They went in to Beverly Hills and had lunch the next day, both to celebrate the fact that shooting began the following morning, and to have the little shopping spree Perry was so intent upon. He really wanted to enjoy his role in the production and felt he had to look the part, just as his colleagues did. He wasn't out to top the flamboyant Archer Mellis with any orange silk jumpsuits, but at least he wanted to seem in the sartorial spirit of the others.

Once Ned assumed the mantle of executive producer, he switched from his Ivy League garb to the more casual, semi-military look of the working West Coast show business mogul, and even Kenton had a well-stocked wardrobe of the right stuff, clothing-wise.

Perry bought himself a fatigue jacket at a fashionable men's store on Rodeo Drive that except for its silk lining and London label might have been purchased at any Army Navy store for around thirty bucks, but seemed a wise investment at $465. He also got three pairs of pants with a mind-boggling array of pockets and flaps and brass buttons, and a half dozen sport shirts with epaulets on the shoulders. He felt himself to be now one of the many important officers in the Army of Entertainment, a veritable George S. Patton of show business, and it was only appropriate that he look the part.

Jane could tell he was pleased, like a kid with a new baseball outfit, and she relaxed and seemed genuinely happy for him.

"They'll never be able to tell you apart from Steven Spielberg," she said when they went to the dark, cool bar of the Beverly Wilshire for a glass of chilled Chablis.

"Well, now what about you?" he asked.

"I'm not part of the team," she said. "I don't need a uniform."

"It's not fair for me to be the only one in the family with new clothes."

"I don't need anything."

"Aw, c'mon. It's for fun. Get into the spirit of it, huh? For me?"

She agreed to go look for something just to please him, but not on Rodeo Drive, where the prices were so outlandish. He took her to one of the nice department stores in Century City. She put on a couple of the dresses he liked that were as tight as the skirts Amanda LeMay wore, but she pulled and tugged at them uncomfortably as she looked at herself in the mirror, grimacing and frowning. She wouldn't even try on any dress that was clingier than a sack, and absolutely refused to consider slipping into a pair of high heels. She said all this stuff made her feel like a hooker.

"This is what the top women executives wear out here!" Perry argued.

"Then thank God I'm not a top woman executive out here!"

Just to please him and be a sport, she bought a new slinky silk dress. It wasn't really slinky by Southern California standards, but she acted like it was something wild.

They ordered ribs and cole slaw from Greenblatt's Delicatessen that night. The idea was to eat in and get up early so Perry would be fresh for the first day of shooting. He wanted to be on the set before seven, along with the cast and crew. He didn't mean to drink much, but found that both he and Jane seemed to be constantly refilling their wineglasses instead of talking. He was disappointed with her obstinate refusal to get in the spirit of the shopping spree, but knew the subject was best left alone.

"You always used to like what I wore," she said suddenly.

Perry took a gulp of his wine.

"I do like it. I just don't see why you can't wear something different in a different place."

"I'm not a different person."

"Are you trying to say that I am?"

"Well, are you?"

"For God sake, are you accusing me of going Hollywood?"

"I didn't accuse you of anything."

"It sure sounds like it."

"Well, I don't like you accusing me of being a prude, either."

"I never said any such thing!"

"You acted like it. Just because I don't want to buy all my clothes now at Frederick's of Hollywood."

"That's a lie! You've distorted this whole thing!"

He jumped up and went to the kitchen to pour himself a brandy.

Then they really went at each other.

The tension the next morning was so great it seemed tangible. It was obvious that neither of them had slept well the night before. He was still in the shorts he wore to bed, while she was wrapped in her old ratty bathrobe.

"Coffee?" she asked.

"Thanks," he said.

She started to pour from the electric pot, but her hands were shaking so badly she couldn't hold the cup steady. She put it down and turned away from him. Instinctively, he started to reach for her, then drew back, and poured himself the coffee. He took a sip and winced. It was bitter and hot. He put the cup back down on the table.

Then everything went black.

Perry could feel his heart pounding. There were tears welling up in his eyes. He was all at once extremely sad and happy. The situation was so poignant, the pain of both husband and wife so real that the viewer had to feel sad, yet there was something deeply human, universal, about it that was oddly uplifting, even ennobling. In the silence and darkness that followed, Perry felt a sense of awe.

"Scene twenty-three, take two!"

The crisp voice jerked him from reverie as the screen flashed to life again, showing the torso of a man with head and feet cut off by the camera, holding the traditional black-and-white slateboard of film production. The hinged upper arm with diagonal stripes was held aloft and then smartly clapped down to signal the new take of the scene.

Perry felt a sudden déjà vu, and he realized he was living now an experience he had fantasized way back in his other life, while he was waiting for the call from Hollywood and watching "Entertainment Tonight." They had showed some film in production on location, with a close-up of the slateboard announcing the new take of a scene, and Perry had been electrified with the thought, like a precursor of the act, that he would someday himself be involved in such a ritual with his own work. And here he was, not just fantasizing his dreams of glory on a cow path in Vermont, but sitting in a darkened studio on a movie lot in Los Angeles. The slateboard bore in chalk the name of his own show, his own creation.

And now it came to life.

Perry's story. His characters.

They moved. They walked. They talked.

"Coffee?" she asked.

"Thanks," he said.

Perry was entranced, captivated. He was amazed at how much more wonderful the words sounded when spoken by the actors, instead of when only read on a page. The only dialogue in this scene were the two words, one word apiece, per actor, the most commonplace words in the most commonplace setting and situation, words that not only were uninspired but almost obligatory under the circumstances.

"Coffee?"

"Thanks."

But oh, when you heard human beings say them, when you saw their faces, their expressions, those simple words took on another life, new dimensions. Watching and hearing the words being spoken, they seemed now to Perry as profound as *Hamlet*.

Coffee.

Thanks.

"I can't explain it," he told Jane later.

"You just did, love," she said. "It was eloquent."

She touched him tenderly.

"No. I said the words, I told you what I felt like, but I know

I didn't convey the actual experience, the amazing feeling of seeing those actors on the screen, bigger than life, saying my lines."

"I can't wait to see it myself."

"I'm afraid you'll have to wait. We just started shooting."

"Can't I see what you're seeing? The little bits and pieces? What do you call them officially — the 'rushes'?"

"The 'dailies.' But lovey, only the staff gets to see the dailies."

"My God, do you have to have a national security clearance? It sounds like you're watching nuclear strategy secrets."

"I'll ask Red Simmons if he minds your coming."

"Who the hell is Red Simmons? Did I miss him in *People* magazine this month?"

"He's the director of photography. The head cameraman."

"Pardon my abysmal ignorance, but how was poor little me supposed to know?"

"Because I've told you about six million times, that's how!"

"You've also told me about six million names of other people I've never met, along with all the wonderful things they do, complete with your new terrific show biz terminology, and I can't even come and look at the pictures — or whatever you show biz insiders call them."

Perry started for the brandy, then stopped.

He went to the couch and sat down next to Jane, taking her hand.

"I'm sorry," he said. "All this is new to me, and I'm nervous as hell about it."

"I know. I didn't mean to jump down your throat."

"I was just about to get a brandy, and then we'd both be starting in again like we did last night. We can't fall into that. I have to have my mind clear in the morning. All day."

"I don't get any work done either when we do that. Shall we stop?"

"You mean altogether? Go dry?"

"I will if you will."

Perry tensed; that seemed a little extreme.

"Maybe we should just cut down. Cut out the hard stuff. Nobody out here drinks anything but wine, anyway."

"I guess that's more realistic. OK. Just wine with dinner. And we ought to cut back on our eating, too."

"Great. We'll diet, then," Perry said. "And get more exercise."

He had begun to feel self-conscious about that extra ten or so pounds around his middle. Also, he'd begun to notice that although before he liked Jane a little fulsome and fleshy, out here, compared to these amazing women whose stomachs seemed as flat as ironing boards, she began to look by comparison a little frumpy. Some diet and exercise would do them both good.

"I'm willing," Jane said.

They shook hands, smiling, and then embraced.

Then Perry pulled away. The fact is he didn't feel like making love. It wasn't just the thought of Jane's frumpiness compared to the sleek California women. Being on the set all day, involved in the shooting, was really exhausting. He simply didn't have a lot of energy left over for sex.

Perry was high, and about to get higher.

The feeling had nothing to do with drugs, though in fact he'd felt a real rush when he saw the tall director's chair with his own name on it in big black letters.

PERRY MOSS.

Now all he had to do was climb up onto it, as if this were a commonplace occurrence, in front of all these people whose eyes were on him. They were shooting on location at the little college up north near San Jose, and a crowd of students and faculty had gathered, as people always did around cameras, drawn to the magic of filming.

Perry felt like a star, for all the people who were watching knew he was one, or might be about to become one, just like the actors who also had their own director's chairs with their own names — MELINDA MARGULIES, HAL THAXTER — along with the executives, NED GURNEY and KENTON SPIRES.

All eyes were on him as he went to mount the chair that had

his name on it, and suddenly it seemed a challenge. It looked storklike and flimsy on its crossed toothpick legs. Bravely, he seized the arms as if he were going to mount a wild bronco, hefted himself up and onto the canvas seat, teetering only slightly, silently saying a prayer of thanks as he opened the large notebook that held the script and pointed his nose down into it, pretending to focus on the swimming words.

When he looked up, Ned and Kenton were beside him on their own personal thrones, each looking as comfortable in his perch as if he were born to it. Perry still felt slightly dizzy, as if he might tip himself over if he leaned too far one way or other, or coughed suddenly. He got out his pipe and lit up, hoping that process would distract him from his newest phobia — fear of falling off a director's chair while shooting a TV film on location and being watched by the natives.

"This is a big scene we have coming up," said Ned.

"Mmm," Kenton nodded. "Our happy couple's first big fight."

Perry smiled, proud of his drama. This was a scene where Jack thinks Laurie is flirting at a party; he leaves, she rushes after him, and they "grapple" before he runs off and she chases him.

"Kenton?" Ned asked. "Do you see this as a tag-team wrestling match — or something more subdued?"

"Frankly, I was grappling with the word *grapple*."

"Luckily," Ned said, looking at Perry, "we have our author here to elucidate."

"Oh, well, I just meant the way people do — I mean, a young man and woman, recently married."

He realized he was picturing a scene from his own first marriage and added quickly, "A couple like Jack and Laurie, I mean."

"Naturally," Ned said reassuringly.

"You know how people like that kind of grab each other, in an argument?" Perry asked.

"Like grabbing by the arm?" asked Kenton.

"Sure, right," Perry said, not wanting to reveal how he and his first wife had rolled around someone's gravel driveway in such an argument.

"Good," Ned said. "That suits our couple, I think, better than a knock-down, drag-out, roll-around kind of thing."

"We'll get more frustration and fury by having them hold back a bit," said Kenton.

"Exactly," said Ned. "Keep it civilized."

"Perfect," echoed Perry.

When they saw the scene in dailies they agreed it was both civilized and dramatic.

It was not till the next day that they heard a dissenting opinion.

At the crucial moment of shooting the picnic love scene in an open field near the campus, a plane began circling overhead. The soundman took off his earphones and complained he was picking up the drone.

"Cut!" said Kenton.

All eyes of cast and crew turned upward. They not only saw a plane circling, they saw someone jump out. There was a gasp and several shrieks. Then a sigh of relief as a parachute opened. Perry followed Ned and Kenton as they ran toward the uninvited paratrooper, who landed at the far end of the field and was pulling in his chute.

It was Archer Mellis.

"What's going on?" Ned asked.

"That's what I want to know after looking at yesterday's dailies," said Archer. "Doesn't anyone here know how to stage a real fight between a young married couple?"

"It was supposed to be understated," Kenton said.

"*Civilized*," Ned added with emphasis.

"I call it bloodless and boring," said Archer.

Sweat popped out on Kenton's brow, and the big vein in Ned's temple began to throb as his face grew lobster red.

"What the hell do you really want, Archer?" Ned demanded. "Violence?"

Archer looked as if someone had just insulted his mother.

"I didn't hear that," he said. "I didn't hear anyone in good conscience accuse me of resorting to something I entered this industry to oppose."

"So what is it you want?" Kenton asked.

"I want that scene reshot."

"I'm the executive producer here," Ned said. "What are you trying to do, take over the picture?"

"I'm trying to save it," said Archer, and, pulling in the last cords of his chute and balling it up, he strode toward the camera and crew.

VI

As the lights went down in the small executive screening room at Paragon, Perry could feel his pulse rising. He was about to see his dream from beginning to end. This wasn't even the final form of the film, it was only the rough cut, but it was the first time anyone except Kenton as the director and Kim as the film editor (along with her assistant) would view the work as a whole, in sequence, instead of just the disconnected pieces of the dailies. Perry was as nervous as if he were about to see a documentary of his own life on a large screen.

No matter how it came out, it would in a sense be a victory over many odds. There were times when Perry wondered if it ever would be finished, if the production would get past the conflicts and emergencies, the artistic tantrums and budget crises, the unexpected breakdowns of nerves and equipment, the acts of God, like the drenching rain that fell the day of reshooting the picnic scene (they used it to show Laurie and Jack's true grit by having them kiss and fondle under umbrellas).

From the time Archer Mellis landed in the field up at Saratoga like a paratroop guerrilla, challenging Kenton and Ned (and Perry by association), he came to seem almost like their adversary rather than their leader, relentlessly prodding and pressing, yet goading them on. They were the production company while he was the studio, a higher force, a more powerful critic and judge. Yet despite its disadvantages and tensions this new situation, if anything, brought the "First Year" company even closer together, made them more determined, more dedicated to their cause, and devoted to their eventual triumph.

The staff of the "First Year" company sat bunched together in the center of the first few rows of the screening room, while Archer Mellis, who had not come in the door but materialized at the last minute from inside the projection booth, sat in lofty isolation in the top row at the back of the room, his mouth a thin straight line, his eyes unblinking and inscrutable.

As the overhead lights in the room went out, the tiny lights attached to the clipboards of the professional filmmakers came on like the scattered glow of some exotic breed of illuminated insects. Perry again wished he had thought to ask Ned where you buy these things; he had never seen one for sale in an ordinary stationery store and presumed they could only be purchased at an official insiders' supply house that sold such stuff as the black-and-white-striped slateboards, and the old-fashioned megaphones of the kind still used on the set by Roger, the crusty first assistant director on their production. Perry was far too nervous now to use a lighted clipboard for its purpose of making notes while the film was being shown; he would simply have liked to have had one as a security prop.

Better still, he had Jane beside him. He was glad now he'd overcome his apprehensions of breaking protocol by bringing his wife, and he gratefully reached over now and took her hand. He squeezed her fingers tightly as the first of the film began to flicker to life on the big screen in front of them.

A rough cut runs long by definition, but this one was longer than most, running thirty-eight minutes over. It was especially — almost scandalously — long for television, a medium which by necessity emphasizes economy of time as well as money. This two-hour movie for television would be cut to ninety-six minutes with commercials on a $2.1 million budget, with a nineteen-day shooting schedule, whereas a feature film of similar scope would probably run at least three times that in budget even without any stars, and three or four times in the length of the shooting schedule. A director of a feature might indulge himself in as many as fifty or sixty takes of one angle of one scene, while any more than five or six takes for television was considered excessive. Everyone was doing his best but there was no time for "art," no extra hours much less days to spend in trying to get the slant of light just so across the cheek of the heroine at the moment the hero's lips brushed ever so lightly across the top of her brow. The public was waiting, switching the dials; the television tubes were like millions of hungry mouths all over America, waiting to be constantly fed. Making television was like making bread, as opposed to the gourmet cakes and tarts of the features, and in Perry's opinion, in many cases, the bread turned out better anyway.

A rough cut for a feature might run three or four *hours* over its eventual desired length, but in television anything more than ten minutes over was thought of as indulgent. Well, Kenton had wanted the luxury of this kind of indulgence and Ned had fought for him on it, and though Archer had sometimes fought back, he had himself demanded reshooting not only to get something just right by his standard but also to have what was considered in TV almost profligate — a choice.

So here it was at last in the rough and it was long and repetitious and awkward and Perry loved every minute of it. It seemed to move as slowly as syrup, yet to its author it was just as sweet. It was like the unrolling of some endless novel, endemically American in sight and speech and yet in scope seemingly created by one of those ponderous nineteenth-century Russians whose tales seemed to grow from and mimic the vastness of their land.

The pace of the work was quite like that of the foreign art films Perry found so excruciatingly tedious and boring, the hushed Bergman epics and snail-like Japanese morality tales he had hated from the start, when he first had to endure them during his twenties in order to accommodate the cultural longings of sophisticated young women so they would hopefully later satisfy his own baser appetites.

Unlike his faculty colleagues, who almost all were film buffs, Perry was frankly a movie fan, one who preferred real plots and lots of sparkling dialogue to amorphous moods and sullen stares. His taste was epitomized scandalously to his peers (and even to most of his students) by his sincere and unashamed avowal that *The Young Philadelphians* starring Paul Newman was far superior entertainment and more revealing of the human condition than Bergman's *Wild Strawberries*, and was even better with lots of buttered popcorn thrown in. He preferred to be entertained, he argued, rather than mesmerized or lulled to unconsciousness.

Now as he experienced an almost sensuous thrill from simply watching one of his own beloved characters walk across a room in the course of the film, or open a window, or pour a cup of coffee, he understood why the famous European *auteur* directors subjected their fans to such endlessly drawn-out sequences. To the "creator" (*auteur*) they were pure fascination, as the squalls and dumps of a newborn baby are completely captivating to its own parents.

When the lights came on, Jane squeezed Perry's hand. He squeezed back, and held his breath. The room was deadly silent. Slowly, heads turned back, craned up, looking toward Archer to see if any reaction could be discerned. Would he tell them to take the whole thing back to the drawing board? Would he curse them all as he had before, threatening to fire the whole damn lot of them if they couldn't produce the quality he had hired them to create? Would he stand up and read from his clipboard a series of elaborate notes that would mean everyone would have to start from scratch?

Archer sat immobile, inscrutable, his feet propped on the seat in front of him, his elbows resting on his knees, hands held together with the fingertips lightly touching in the symbolic gesture of prayer. But there was no sound or movement from him. Finally Kenton stood up in the front, and, proud but perspiring from every pore of his considerable flesh, he faced up toward Archer, his shoulders thrown back, like a man presenting himself to a firing squad. Ned got up and stood beside him. Perry was about to squirm out of his seat and go join them in the noble presentation of themselves and their work for execution, but just at that moment Archer suddenly shot up to a standing position, aimed a finger down toward Kenton and Ned and said, simply, in a clear, commanding voice: "Go for it."

Then, wheeling and disappearing back into the projection booth, he was gone. There was first a general sigh, a sound of relief, like pent-up breath released at last, and then someone was clapping and applause spread throughout the little band of fellow workers and all at once everyone in the room was standing, whistling, and cheering, acclaiming Kenton, and Ned, and Perry, and themselves, saluting and praising the work, the thing they had made together, the story and the dream.

"Tell me, what did you *really* think of it, I mean, your honest gut reaction."

Perry pulled Jane's hand away from his crotch and looked her straight in the eye. They had come home and opened a new bottle of good chilled Chardonnay to celebrate, and after a few sips Jane had leaned against Perry on the couch and begun to caress him with her hands as well as her mouth, slowly stroking him along the inside of the thigh while at the same time she made little fluttery butterfly kisses around his mouth.

"Darling love," she cooed, "I told you already — it's absolutely wonderful."

"You really think so?"

"Yes, and I know when it's really finished it will be incredibly better. All those slow, draggy parts will be gone."

She started in stroking and kissing him again, but Perry pulled gently away.

"What do you mean, 'slow, draggy parts'?" he asked.

"You know. Where you just see someone walk across a room, without saying anything."

"I thought you understood this was the rough cut. That's the kind of thing you see in a rough cut."

Jane giggled, and tweaked Perry's ear.

"I know, darling, but I couldn't help thinking how ironic it was — I mean, some of those drawn-out numbers reminded me of the kind of stuff that drives *you* up the wall in foreign films, where you wonder *when* the heroine is ever going to get to the door."

She nuzzled up under Perry's chin for a kiss, but he dodged it.

"Maybe you'll be disappointed in the final cut, too," he said. "I mean, Kenton isn't one of those razzle-dazzle sitcom directors."

Jane reached over to the table and picked up her glass of wine.

"Well, I hope he doesn't think he's Fellini, for God sake."

"You don't like his direction?"

Jane took a long sip of her wine.

"Is this the only thing we can talk about?"

"No, but I'm interested in your opinion."

Jane stood up and unhooked her skirt, then shucked it off, and kicked off her shoes.

"My opinion is I might as well go for a swim. Or take a cold shower."

"Hey. I'm sorry."

"Don't be," she said, stripping off her blouse and dropping it on the floor. "It's not your fault if I don't turn you on any more."

"Don't do this. I said I was sorry."

"I am too. I'm sorry the only thing in the world you can think about night and day is your damn movie."

She turned and left the room. Perry started to get up, but instead refilled his glass of wine and closed his eyes as he gulped it down.

"Jane has a headache," Perry said by way of explaining her absence that night for dinner with Ned and Kim.

They of course were incredibly gracious about it, pretending the age-old excuse was real. Perry was embarrassed, and depressed. In fact he really was more absorbed in the movie than anything else in the world, including lovemaking, and he feared it really was coming between him and Jane. He knew she was right when she said he would only be talking business with Ned and Kim, that she would inevitably feel out of it, a mere outsider.

They did talk business of course, going over impressions and ideas about the rough cut as they consumed one of Kim's delicious and seemingly effortless curries. Perry was so absorbed in the fascination of it that he didn't even think about Jane again till Ned poured him a second brandy. He was sure as hell glad that the new "wine only" policy he and Jane had pledged to keep as part of their California health and fitness plan officially counted brandy *as* wine.

The brandy really loosened him up. It loosened up his tongue, too.

"I'm worried about Jane," he confessed to Ned and Kim. "There wasn't any headache, of course. If anything, it's an ache in the butt. I guess I'm giving it to her."

Ned shrugged.

"It happens," he said.

Perry took a hit of the brandy and shook his head.

"Not to us. At least not till now. I mean, the last couple weeks. I guess I'm too wrapped up in the show."

Kim placed her hand on Perry's, giving it a reassuring squeeze.

"This business," she said, "lays a heavy stress on people. On relationships."

"You ought to get away for a while," Ned told him. "Just the two of you. There's nothing you can be doing on the show now anyway. We've got to let Kenton do his thing. Let him and Kim come up with the next cut, and then we'll get back into it. I've got to go to New York, which I'm glad of, since I won't be tempted to keep looking over their shoulder all the time."

Kim tweaked Ned's ear.

"Good boy. Stay at least a week."

She turned to Perry.

"And you get out of here, too. *With* Jane. I know what she's feeling. She's a show biz widow. You've been married to this show. Now go off and concentrate on *her* for a while."

"Where?" Perry asked.

He didn't know where people went to get away when they already lived in a sort of permanent vacationland. Ned and Kim exchanged a glance, and then Ned turned to Perry.

"Have you ever been to the desert?"

"No, but I heard about it. Palm Springs, you mean? I don't think Jane would like it — nightclubs and all that.

Kim shook her head.

"We mean the *real* desert."

"Where's that?" Perry asked.

Ned gave him a nudge.

"Shall we tell him?"

"Do you think we can trust him?"

"If you swear a secret oath," said Ned, "we'll tell you about our favorite spot. Our hideaway."

"It's magic," said Kim.

Borrego Springs.

You went to Palm Springs first, but only to stop for lunch. It was like an extension of L.A., a satellite of it, flung out in the space of sand and empty distance. Hotels and neon, nightclubs and swimming pools. You might run into Bob Hope or Gerald Ford. Civilization — Southern California–style. Show Biz. Shopping Malls.

You kept going south.

Into mountains. Mystery. Narrow winding roads with hairpin curves and purple horizons of rock and sage. Clouds merged into mirages. Cars became sparse as trees. The air thinned and sharpened. Spiraling, slowly, you rose, then saw below, breathtaking, a valley, spread out like peace, quiet and calming as sleep.

No neon here. No noise.

La Casa del Zorro. "House of the Fox." The name made Perry smile. It sounded like the set for one of those old swashbuckler movies with swords and capes, closed carriages, and midnight escapes over moats.

Or the Hollywood name for a desert motel or resort. But it wasn't funky enough to be a motel, or fancy enough to be a resort. It was simply a cluster of cottages scattered over several acres beyond a main house with a dining room, and an unobtrusive swimming pool.

Each little house had a name, and Perry and Jane were in *Mesquite*. It was cozy and private. They went into town and bought eggs and sandwich stuff and beer for the kitchen, and at sundown, sat outside on a little veranda and listened to the silence. They felt little need to speak. It was as if all the tension and muck and debris were being drained away and they were being washed clean by the desert air.

That night they made love.

Like new.

As of old.

Jane led them on nature walks, trails laid out in the desert with botanical names for varieties of cacti and flowering plants. Perry didn't mind the beating sun, and the sweat soaking through his shirts felt good, like being purged. They hiked into rocky valleys and discovered dramatic waterfalls and deep gorges decorated with bright exotic blooms, tropical pinks and blues. Giant palm trees grew in profusion, whole wild forests of them hidden from highways. It was like an imagined Amazon landscape, a child's Crayola dream.

"I needed this," Perry said that night.

"I needed *you*," Jane told him.

"You have me."

"For a while I didn't. You were gone. It was scary."

"I'm sorry."

"Don't be sorry. Be with me."

"I am. Now. Always."

"Even when we get back? To the show?"

"I won't let it come between us."

"God. It sounds like a woman."

"It's just a show. *You're* the woman."

"You won't forget that?"

"I promise."

They touched and clung, making love like a vow.

"You broke your promise! You went back on your word!"

Ned Gurney was furious. The veins in his neck were red ropes. His fists opened and shut, as if they were itching to grab the neck of Archer Mellis and squeeze.

Mellis himself looked cool, nearly Zenlike in his composure. Perhaps that image was heightened (even purposely) by the fact that he was wearing a flowing saffron robe, with thong sandals.

He raised his right hand, palm up, in a gesture of peace and reconciliation.

"Relax, *amigo*. Amanda and her people understand."

"Dammit, I know they say they understand!" Ned screamed. "They won't even know themselves how it affects them, or doesn't affect them, but without the music, it's going to be a bore. Believe me. The music is crucial to this show, more so than if it were cops and robbers or tits and ass. It creates the mood, it — it —"

Ned was wringing his hands as he groped for words.

"It sustains the action," whispered Kenton, who looked as if he might cry.

Archer leaned back in his chair and jabbed his foot against his desk, hefted up his robe, and retied the sandal thongs that crisscrossed up his calf, tightening the whole system with determined concentration.

"When they see it again, with the music, they'll be all the more knocked out."

"But today is what counts!" Ned shouted. "Today they'll decide its fate! *Without any music.*"

"*Our* fate," moaned Kenton, mopping his brow with a big bandana.

Archer took his leg down, stood up straight, and winked at Perry.

"Sounds like your colleagues don't have much faith in your story *qua* story."

"That's not the point!" Ned shouted, moving perilously close to Archer with a raised and trembling fist. Archer looked with detached curiosity at the fist, as if Ned were holding up some kind of art object for him to examine. Then he looked into Ned's eyes, calmly.

"Amanda and her people will not be 'deciding the fate' of your project today, or any other day. The real decision will come from Max Bloorman and the East Coast network brass."

"But Amanda and her people will decide if they're going to get behind it today, if they're going to push it when they go to the meetings in New York next week."

"Precisely. And they'll be much more likely to do that if they've had a preview, if they feel like they're in on it. I've already kept them shut out of it for longer than maybe is even wise because of your 'specialness' and your collective sense of artistic precocity. They've bought that from me up to now, but we can't keep them away any longer."

"Not even for a week?" Ned pleaded.

"We'll have the music in five days," Kenton said hoarsely.

Archer suddenly turned and hopped onto the top of his desk, drawing his legs up into the lotus position.

"Amanda and her people will be here in half an hour for the screening," he said. "I suggest we take this opportunity to compose ourselves."

He closed his eyes, took a gulp of breath, and bent his head forward in an attitude of deep meditation.

Ned, Kenton, and Perry looked at Archer, then at one another. Their very presence in the room now seemed an invasion of their boss's privacy. Bowing their own heads, either in respect or resignation, they tiptoed out.

In the darkened room, there was no way to read the network people's reactions. Every so often Amanda LeMay would emit a little giggle that was always followed a split second later by a hearty horselaugh from Todd Robbie. At other times, when nothing on the screen was supposed to be funny, a sudden guffaw would break forth from Harry Flanders. There were also moments that Perry considered hilarious, the height of wit, scenes that had simply cracked him up and practically sent Ned and Kenton rolling in the aisles, but now were witnessed by the network people in deadly quiet. Sometimes, in those awful stretches where music should have been, Perry could hear heavy breathing, and wondered with itching anxiety if any or all of the network people had fallen asleep.

Though this version of the film was almost a half hour shorter than the rough cut, it seemed interminably longer, and instead of producing the aura of power and massive meaning of the

Russian novels, as it had before, at this viewing Perry felt his precious story must seem to the outsiders who were sentenced to watch it simply tedious and boring. He shifted in his seat, feeling as if battalions of tiny, invisible ants were skirmishing up and down his legs and under his rump. Suddenly, he realized he needed to take a pee. Why the hell hadn't he done that before the screening started? He couldn't go now, or it might seem like his movie couldn't even hold the attention of its own author, much less a national audience of millions of viewers!

At last, the lights went on.

Perry scrunched down in his seat, not even wanting to look at Amanda, not wanting to go through the agony of trying to read and decipher her expression. But any such apprehension was quickly ended, as Amanda's voice rang out loud and clear through the room.

"This," she declared, "is what television should be!"

"I wouldn't go out and buy a new cabin cruiser yet," Ned advised.

Jane laughed.

"Thank God there's a voice of reason around," she said. "I think Perry was thinking of a somewhat larger purchase — Cape Cod."

"Now, now," Perry said, "I only mentioned a *house* on Cape Cod. I had in mind something modest — like the Kennedy Compound."

He joined in the laughter, sinking back in the pillows with his goblet of wine, his mood matching the sultanlike surroundings of Akbar, the new "in" Moroccan restaurant where he had taken Ned and Kim to dinner with Jane to celebrate the glowingly enthusiastic reaction of Amanda and the West Coast network people to the screening of "The First Year's the Hardest."

"Just keep in mind," Ned said, continuing his friendly caution, "the East Coast network brass may not necessarily go for 'what television *should* be' — they may just like it the way it is."

"That's always safest, you know," Kim added.

Perry shifted a bit uneasily on his cushion.

"Seriously," he said, "are you guys telling me you think they won't buy the pilot?"

"I think they'll probably buy the two-hour film," Ned said. "It can always go on and stand by itself as a quality made-for-television movie — something that's bound to get good reviews, and they can brag about."

Perry sat up now, leaning forward.

"You don't think they'll commission the series?"

"I doubt Archer will get them to order thirteen hours, not in these times," Ned said. "I think six would be more like it. Or maybe they won't take the gamble at all. There's no way to know."

"For heaven sake, Perry," Jane said, "be glad you have a wonderful movie that's going to be on television — probably."

"Hey, I am glad," Perry said. "And I'm grateful too."

He raised his goblet toward Ned, and went on.

"I'm grateful I got an executive producer who is so 'civilized' —"

He paused as they all chortled at Ned's trademark word, and then continued his salute:

"— he has become not only a trusted colleague, but also, I hope, a friend for life."

"Thank you," said Ned, raising his own goblet to Perry. "Not only for your kind words, but for your terrific script!"

"Here, here!" Kim called out, and Jane, beaming, reached across her pillows to hug her talented and happy husband.

Ned took a sip of his wine and then leaned forward saying, "All right — 'amigo' — now that the love fest is over, let's get down to business. How about writing another script I can produce?"

"Don't you dare tempt him," said Jane. "He's promised we're going back home the end of this month."

She grabbed Perry's hand protectively.

"I know you're pretty far up in the wilds," Ned said with a wink, "but I thought you had phones and a mailbox. In fact, I thought Perry was going to serve as our story consultant *in absentia* when you went back — no?"

"Sure, that's the deal!" Perry enthused. He relished the

thought — sitting up in his remote command post, watching his show on the tube and jotting down notes, calling up Ned the next day and hashing it over, getting the latest gossip from the front lines.

"I had presumed you might even scribble in a few sparkling phrases of your own to add a little class to the scripts we ship you?"

"Absolutely," Perry grinned.

In his own study he would pore over scripts, strike out awkward bits of dialogue, roll a fresh sheet of paper in his typewriter, and knock out a brilliant scene that he would mail off from the post office in town, stopping off afterward at the very diner where he'd gone for coffee after the historic mailing of his book to Archer a million years ago, last fall.

Ned raised his hands, palms up, as if he had demonstrated some point of logic.

"Therefore, it follows," he said, "that you could also write a new script of your own, working with me on it by mail and phone, and — "

Ned turned to Jane.

"You wouldn't object to coming out here again for a little visit, would you, while Perry and I molded our latest masterpiece into shape?"

"As long as I can live in my own house, and have my own garden," Jane said, "I wouldn't object to anything at all."

Kim smiled and touched Jane's arm.

"I'd love to see New England," Kim said. "Let's make the men agree to have this be a 'home and home' working arrangement — for every time you two come out to L.A., we have to go to Vermont!"

"It so happens Vermont is one of my favorite places in the world," Ned said. "I'd rather ski Stowe than the Alps."

"This is perfect," Jane said, genuinely delighted now. "We'll have a marvelous time!"

Of course. Perry could picture the very scene he knew Jane had in mind. The four of them sharing a hearty stew. Hot buttered rum by the fire. Surely back East it would be all right to drink something other than wine again. Especially something traditional, not for getting smashed but for observing the rituals of the region. Was it really a fantasy, too picturesquely ideal to be true?

"Uh, Ned," Perry said, clearing his throat, "were you thinking about this in general, us working on a script when I go back? Or did you have some particular idea in mind?"

Ned smiled and eased back in the pashalike pillows.

"I'd love to see a film of a haunting little story I happen to know and admire called "The Springtime Women.""

It was one of Perry's, a story he had published in *Redbook* and used as the title piece of his last collection. It was one of his favorites — two women in their forties leave their families in the Midwest and come to try a new life in Greenwich Village. Like most of Perry's stories it worked more on atmosphere than plot; an evocation of the Village of the late sixties was its greatest charm.

"That's a compliment," Perry said, "but I can't really see something that soft for television."

"I wasn't thinking of television."

"You mean a play? You want to go back to Broadway?"

"I mean a feature film," Ned said.

Jane squeezed Perry's arm.

"What a lovely thought," she said.

It was quite a tribute to Perry, not just because of Ned's liking his story, but more importantly of his having confidence in Perry's ability to write a feature. He had quickly learned out here that writers who worked in television were categorized — and even stigmatized — as being of a lower order of ability than was required for the more lucrative and prestigious realm of features.

"I'm overwhelmed," he said.

"Well, I'm being a little premature," Ned admitted. "We ought to keep our minds on 'The First Year,' but just between us, I think I'm finally going to get *Spoons* out of the starting block this year. It's over at Hamlin Productions now, and they're hot about it. If it goes, I'll be able to seriously start thinking features."

Kim put her hand on his shoulder, giving it a loving squeeze.

"This civilized guy has had some rough sledding in this town, but believe me, he's going to own it before he's through."

"Hey, this is all a bit premature," Ned cautioned, "including Kim's predictions of my rise to power in this town — but as soon as we see where we are with our TV project, I'd like to have my lawyer draw up an option for 'Springtime Women.' "

"It's a deal!" said Perry.

"Hey, hold on. I'm not in a position to lay out big bucks — this would just be a minimal thing, but if it went, you'd end up doing all right, I'm sure."

"Listen, the important thing here is your confidence in me. And the chance to work with you again."

Perry extended his hand, and Ned shook it warmly.

"All right, it's a deal then," Ned said.

Waitresses dressed as harem girls were bowing before them with steaming platters of lamb kebab. Perry picked up the bottle of wine, now empty, and waved it toward a sommelier wearing a red fez.

"More!" he said.

"More?" she asked.

Her face hovered over his cock. It was still only partially erect. A "semi" they used to call the condition back in high school.

Ha. If they could see him now. The old gang would never believe it. Perry Moss, the shy type, getting sucked off by his lovely, talented photographer wife in a hip hotel suite high above Sunset Boulevard, while he waited for a phone call from the other coast that might make him even more rich and successful. Not rich by Hollywood standards, of course, but certainly by Haviland standards. The Haviland College crowd would probably be surprised, too, seeing their tweedy literary man in his present condition — holding a glass of chilled Chardonnay in one hand, fondling the nipple of his wife's ample breast with the other.

"Perry?"

"Yes?"

"Does that mean yes, you want more, or yes, you remember I'm still down here?"

"Yes. I mean more. Please."

Jane sighed, then returned to her labors.

Perry took his idle hand, the one that wasn't fiddling with the nipple, and ran it through Jane's hair, wanting to show he was with her in this enterprise, was appreciating her efforts. They were, as always, artistic, the quick little butterfly kisses of the cock, interspersed with light, quick licks that lovingly lolled and lengthened into a lush, wet suck. Yet now he could not keep his mind on it, could simply not focus full attention on what was happening between his own legs while he wondered when the phone call would come and what news it would bring.

Even now, at this moment, while his wife's thumb and forefinger made little nips at his partially swollen stalk and the tip of her tongue tickled its tendermost top, the network brass in New York might be making the final — fatal? — decision about his show. Was it to be or not to be a series? How many episodes would they go for? Twenty hours constituted a whole season in these perilous, do-or-die times. Would they get, as Archer hoped, an order for thirteen hours with a chance for a pickup of seven? Or eleven and nine? Or none? He felt little nibblings around the root, and tried to concentrate on rising fully to the occasion here and now, instead of some smoky hotel room in New York. It was said that Max Bloorman, who was rumored to be the real power at the network even though he wasn't the president, smoked big black cigars; even in this day and age of health and pure air, he held fast to his habit, blowing smoke right at anyone who got in his way. So, the crucial meeting was no doubt muggy with the ash and fume of his fulminations.

Jane was tickling his testicles now. Nice, but still no cigar. Sometimes when it was fully erect his cock reminded him of that. A sort of cigar. He wondered what kind Bloorman smoked. Smuggled-in expensive Havanas no doubt. Damn! He had to get his mind off the show, on to the sex. That was one of the whole points of starting this up in the first place, to try to get his mind off worrying over what he had no way to control. Hell, he couldn't even control his own cock.

Perry suddenly switched tactics and positions, pulling Jane up beside him, kissing her wet on the mouth, with thanks, like saying hello, then sliding down, making stops at the breasts to deliver a few quick licks so as not to let them feel neglect, then continuing on below to his true target, burrowing in between her legs to pay back respects for her own arduous efforts and also to lose himself in this dark and lovely lair, forget his fears about the fate of the show, which now he saw as his own fate too, flee from those worries, and in so doing, not only give his wife pleasure but raise his own sex to the occasion of coupling, that occasion that recently was all too rare.

Kissing these other lips as affectionately as the ones above, he tried to forget about his business in New York. This really turned him on, kissing her down here. He had never kissed any woman like this before. He had licked his share, yes, sloppily slurped away as he thought was his duty, neither hating it nor enjoying it, just carrying on like a trouper in hopes of being good in bed, of getting a good rating.

Were there sexual Nielsens?

Perry lifted his head slightly and drew his hand to gently part her legs a bit more, then gently bent down and sought the exact spot with his tongue, the little protuberance in the hot center, touching and tasting it at the same time, sweetly giving moisture back from his own mouth. He had never taken this care before with a woman, never loved this dark, luscious place between the loins, and it was all tied up with loving *her*, Jane, wanting to make love here because it was her, hers, and so it was special, sacred almost, and that was how he approached it, treated it, felt it within his own experience.

The trouble with rating something, whether it was lovemaking or television, was that you couldn't measure quality. The fact that Perry had given head to other women before he met Jane could no doubt be charted in the numbers of women and amount of time spent in the exercise, but there was no way to compare that with the feeling of intensity and arousal and near reverence for life itself that came from his doing it with Jane. In terms of television, though of course it was possible to measure, for instance, the share of the audience and the numbers of people watching "Brideshead Revisited," it was certainly not possible to measure the depth or quality of the experience of those watching it from, say, their viewing of "Dynasty" or "Good Morning, America" or the local six o'clock news. There was no way Max Bloorman and the network honchos could measure the quality of experience, then, of something unique and special like "The First Year's the Hardest" as they judged its potential against all the ordinary, run-of-the-mill contenders it was no doubt competing against.

"Oooooooooh — aaaaaaaaahhhhh"

Jane's gentle moan brought him back again to where he was trying to be. He raised his head, placed his fingertips on the protuberance, and ducked down to move his tongue in deep below it, searching and sucking, feeling at the same time his own sex stiffen beneath as it hadn't yet in this whole session, thinking maybe now he was getting it, forgetting what was going on in New York. He wished now he'd have gone, though nobody asked him; he'd have loved to just hang around the hotel lobbies during the crucial week that all the networks declared as the "selling season," when all the studios and production companies brought their pilot films before the councils of judgment, like medieval peddlers bringing their wares to the market, to see what would be purchased — in this case not *by* the multitudes but *for* them.

"Please, *now*–"

She was pulling him back from New York again, where he kept slipping off — the very act of trying not to think of it made him think of it — pulling the hair of his head, tugging him upward to be on her and in her —

"Inside, I want you inside me now — "

And he thrust himself there, stiff and throbbing, and pulled the upper part of his torso up on his elbows to gaze down at his beloved and begin the real rhythm of his love, when, from the living room of the suite, the phone rang.

"That's it!"

"Owww!"

He yanked himself up and out and was hurtling toward the living room with his right arm already reaching for the phone and his cock like a magic wand pointing the way to glory as Jane yelled from the bed, "Screw you and screw your goddam television show!"

"Hello? Archer? What happened?"

"Congrats, *amigo*," the young executive's voice snapped smartly back, "You're a *series*."

"Wa-hoo-hoo-hoo-yah!"

Ecstasy. At least for a whole second until, the triumph absorbed, the victor wondered at once the extent of the victory.

"How many?" he asked. "How many episodes did they order?"

"Three."

Jane walked into the living room, nude.

"What?" Perry asked.

"*Tres*. A trio."

Jane knelt down on the floor in front of Perry.

"That's *all*?"

"With script commitments for three more if the show catches on."

Jane took Perry's cock in her hands.

"What the hell do you mean 'catches on'? How can only three shows 'catch on'? It's crazy!"

Perry firmly but gently tried to push Jane away but she held on to his cock and began licking it.

"Be cool, *compadre*," Archer said. "From your point of view, this order is *ideal*."

"How the hell can only three episodes be 'ideal?' "

Jane now had his whole cock in her mouth and was sucking back and forth on it, making love to it. Perry was afraid he might shoot off right in the middle of a sentence with Archer Mellis and let out some kind of ungodly yell. He tried to concentrate now on television and forget about the sex. If it wasn't one thing it was another.

"We can produce those three hour episodes before the end of summer," Archer explained. "You can serve as the real story consultant — not just *in absentia*, like we planned — and still be back for your classes in the fall."

"I said I'd teach summer school. To make up for the spring semester."

He looked down in fear that Jane might be getting upset by his even considering not going back for summer, might suddenly give him an angry bite, but *she* seemed to be succeeding in concentrating fully on what she was doing.

"Summer school," Archer said, so you could almost hear the smile in his voice. "That's no big deal, is it?"

"That's not the point. It's a commitment."

"You'll get twenty-five hundred dollars a week as story consultant," Archer said. "Also, we'll want you to write a 'bible' for the whole series. That's probably twenty grand. And I assume you'll want to write one of the episodes. Probably the first one, to set things up like you want them. Guild scale for an hour episode now is fourteen thousand three hundred and eighteen."

Perry's mind was whirling with the numbers. Twenty grand for bible, fourteen for episode, twenty-five hundred a week as story consultant, that was about ten grand a month for two, or would it be three, months? He reached down and tried to wrest his cock away from Jane, managing to get it out of her mouth but not out of her hands. He tried turning away from her but she yanked him back. He screamed.

"Aggghhhh!"

"You don't like those numbers?" Archer asked. "Those are very good numbers, especially for a neophyte."

"The numbers are fine," Perry gasped. "It's just the change in plan; I wasn't intending to stay out here past the end of this month — "

"The other beauty of it is that you can choose the other writers, work with them yourself, train the ones you'd like to take over when you go back in the fall."

"I'll have to talk to Jane," Perry said.

He tapped her on the head, trying to get her attention, but she was absorbed with the cock, had got it back in her mouth.

"Of course you do!" Archer said. "And give her my congrats

and my best. We'll all go break a little bread when I get back, schmooze all this over."

"Great."

Jane was pulling him down, pulling him by the cock.

"I've got to go now, Archer. Thanks for calling."

"*Ciao, amigo.*"

Perry slung the phone receiver onto the cradle as he bent, slumping forward, onto Jane as she guided him by the cock, fitting it into her now as he cooperated, wanting to make her happy, wanting her to cooperate with *him* in agreeing to stay, they had to stay, there was no turning back, everything was coming together, love and money, it all was his, the moment was his, and he entered it fully, feeling the force that carried him now, the very thing Shakespeare meant when he said, "there is a tide in the affairs of men, which taken at the flood, leads on to fortune." Oh yes, this was the one, and he wondered, wincing with ecstasy as he crested, if Shakespeare had ever heard of what California surfers called the perfect wave.

VII

SHE ALREADY KNEW. Jane saw it coming before Perry did. She knew he wouldn't want to go back to Vermont before the end of summer, and despite her own deep desire to return home — to literally "tend her own garden" — she agreed to stay on in Los Angeles another three months because it obviously meant so much to him.

On one condition.

"I need a home," she said.

"We have one. Remember? Back in Vermont."

"We're not living in it. I'm not the kind of person who can live my life in a hotel room."

"It's not your whole life, it's just for the summer."

"You forgot the late winter and the spring. We've been living in a hotel room since January."

"It's not a room, it's a suite."

"All right, two rooms."

"Three, counting the kitchen, if you have to get technical."

"Kitchen-*ette*, if you have to get technical."

"And swimming pool. And maid service. Everything we need."

"It may be all *you* need, fella."

When she called him "fella" he knew she was really pissed. Maybe he was being an ass, after all. It was little enough she was asking, especially when he was rolling in dough. When he finally tallied up Archer's numbers, they came out to something over

131

sixty-four grand for the summer's work. Of course he didn't have it yet, but it was all coming in. Rolling in.

"All right," he said, "but I don't have time to go around looking at real estate."

"I'll do the looking," Jane said. "When I find it, all you have to do is come give it your blessing."

"It's a deal."

Perry could hardly be expected to take time out from the lofty work he was now absorbed in, which was nothing less than writing the bible for the series. Not even the original Creator got to write his own Bible, but Perry, as the author of a pilot and thus by definition creator of the series that developed from it, had the opportunity to do just that. Of course it wasn't a lengthy epic tome of spiritual and moral dimension, but rather a forty- or fifty-page handbook that served as background for writers who would be doing episodes of the show, explaining the original concept of it, history and brief biographies of the characters, so that such vital statistics as their dates of birth, high school and college graduation, marriage, and other important landmarks could be looked up if reference was needed to them, as well as their personality portraits, habits, strong and weak points, and anec-dotes illustrating those things. Writing it was for Perry pure pleas-ure (to think he was getting paid twenty grand to do it!) as he filled in the full histories of these individuals he had conceived and brought to life. It made him feel more like a real creator, and he loved the sensation.

Maybe, he thought, Jane should find us a place to rent in that section of Hollywood that was actually called Mount Olympus!

The place she found that she thought was absolutely perfect was not on Mount Olympus, but in Topanga Canyon. That seemed awfully far from the studio, about an hour's drive, but Perry was learning that distances didn't mean anything to people in Los Angeles anyway. An hour and back to work was thought of as perfectly natural, and to question its convenience simply branded you as an inexperienced newcomer.

The place was quite far up a rural-looking, winding road, and certainly seemed far removed from the studio, in atmosphere as well as distance.

The house itself was quaint, a basic A-frame with wings added on each side, giving the effect of a small chalet. A hideaway. It sat on the top of a grassy hillside. From the edge of the property you could look down into the valley below, a picturesque spot with a stream running through it. The landscape looked oddly familiar — rocky and scrublike, with groves of trees — not the exotic palms of Southern California, but evergreens and oaks.

"Don't you just love it?" Jane asked, linking her arm in Perry's.

"It almost looks like New Hampshire," he observed. "Maybe even Vermont."

"I know! Isn't it amazing?" she asked, squeezing his arm.

Perry nodded.

"Amazing," he said.

Eagerly, like a child who is showing her favorite playmate a newly discovered secret hideout, Jane led him back of the house, to show him what was to be one of its master attractions: the vegetable garden.

"I guess zucchini is everywhere," Perry mused. "No matter where you go."

"I can do our summer casseroles."

"I bet there's zucchini growing in the goddam arctic. Even under the glaciers. The dinosaurs died out, but nothing could kill the zucchini."

"The garden's not even the best thing of all," Jane said.

"I should hope not."

She took him by the hand toward a sort of woods that seemed to border the property on one side. Tucked away, almost out of sight in a clump of trees, was a tiny one-room shack. It was formerly a woodshed, converted to a kind of studio.

"I could use it as a darkroom!" Jane exulted. "There's running water, a sink, everything. Isn't it perfect?"

Perry shifted from foot to foot.

"Well, that is nice," he had to admit.

Jane kissed him and took him back to the main house.

"Look, there's even a fireplace," she said, leading him into the living room. "And it's all furnished. They'll even leave their linen behind. And silverware."

Perry got out his pipe and packed the bowl.

"So," Jane asked, "don't you think it's like home?"

"Exactly," he said.

"What's wrong?"

Perry began to pace, feeling like a trapped animal. He lit up his pipe, sucking and drawing and puffing till great clouds of smoke were spewing forth, surrounding his head.

"Let's think about it," he said.

In silence, they went back to the car. In silence, they started driving down the winding road.

"Negotiating this road at night," said Perry, "with a little wine in the system, could be a little dicey."

"What's really bugging you? Why don't you like it?"

"Look," Perry said, trying for his most reasonable tone, "as long as we're out here, in Southern California, don't you think we might as well live in a place that's typical of the region, instead of trying to find an imitation of New England?"

"What would be 'typical of the region'?"

"Well, I suppose a house with a pool."

"A pool! You have to have your own private swimming pool now?"

"What's so weird about that? Lots of people out here have pools. It's no big deal, it's just part of the life-style."

"The 'life-style'! Oh, brother. Shall we stop off and buy our gold chains? Shall we score some coke on the way home?"

"I happen to like to swim. It's my favorite exercise."

"Oh, come off it! You're really into the scene out here. You love the whole thing — admit it!"

"All right, for God sake, I'm guilty! *Mea culpa!* I even like what I'm doing!"

The house they finally rented for the summer was a compromise. Jane gave up her dream of the New Englandy chalet with the garden and land and countrified atmosphere — even the little studio she could have used as a darkroom. Perry did feel badly about that particular point, but he graciously offered to rent her darkroom space away from home. She said it wasn't that big a deal, she wasn't sure she was going to do that much photography work out here anyway. Somehow she couldn't get herself in the right mood. She planned to do a lot of reading.

Perry in turn surrendered his own fantasy of a house. He had fallen in love with a pink stucco Moorish job with a kidney-shaped purple tile swimming pool in the Hollywood Hills that Jane protested was outlandish in taste as well as in price at $5,000 a month. They settled on a little gray frame bungalow in the unfashionable flats of Hollywood, down from the hills, on a quiet little street below Santa Monica Boulevard, for only $2,700. The house was small but comfortable, and most importantly the little backyard not only had a genuine redwood hot tub for Perry, but also a small patch of scratch soil that Jane got permission to use as a garden. She put in tomato plants and the inevitable zucchini, and planted a border of nasturtiums along one side of the neck-high green picket fence that enclosed the yard.

Give a little, take a little. Fine. The compromise of living quarters was OK with Perry. What mattered was the work.

It was thrilling.
It was show biz.
It was the opposite kind of work Perry had done all his life, that he had grown so bored with, so stale and stultified. Instead of mere contemplation, this was action. Instead of telling others how things had been done in the past, it was doing things now, in the moment, for showing in the future; and the audience, instead of a classroom, was a whole nation!

Instead of the leisurely pace of the academy, the Monday-Wednesday-Fridays of classes at ten, two, and four, with office hours nestled in between and a couple of faculty and committee meetings salted in, this was every day all day into the evening, and every moment meaningful, dedicated, dramatic, devoted to getting every single detail right in order to produce the most magnificent show ever seen on American television!

Perry felt so exalted by it all that he couldn't even share his

135

deepest emotions with Ned and Kenton for fear of sounding like the star-struck schoolboy he knew in some delicious way he had become. Once, walking across the lot back to his office, passing other shows in production, a group of men dressed as Cherokees, a couple of beautiful women in the full regalia of Old Western dancehall girls, he smiled and waved and felt with a lump in his throat the inspirational lines from Wordsworth: "Bliss was it in that dawn to be alive, but to be young was very heaven!"

And he was young again. At forty-three, he had rediscovered his youth.

He woke every morning before the alarm and bounced out of bed and into the kitchen to make a pot of coffee, drinking it by the window of the living room with the first cool, moist air of morning wafting in, and took a fresh cup and a glass of orange juice to Jane, switching on the TV to "Good Morning, America" and humming along with the theme song.

Jane good-naturedly grumbled, marveling that this was the same husband who at home she had to wake every morning herself, coaxing him from sleep as she would a drugged derelict coming out of a coma. He told her once way back then in that other life that waking each morning he felt as if he were reenacting the whole history of the human race, rising not just from the sleep of the previous night but from the protozoic slime, pushing upwards through aeons into the dawn of civilization and finally emerging, exhausted from it all, into the bleary new day.

His exhaustion now came at night. Where at home he was just getting into his stride around the cocktail hour, and hitting the sack around midnight or one o'clock, now after dinner he was bushed, done in, limp as a rag. In all ways. He couldn't even think about sex, except on Saturday night. Even then, he had to, as it were, "get himself up for it," and even during the act he found his mind straying to thoughts of "The First Year."

Nor was it any wonder Perry was distracted from everything in life not relating to the show. His position as story consultant for the series gave him a great deal of responsibility. It also gave him a lot of influence.

For the first time in his life, he had influence over the lives of others — not just in giving a passing or a failing grade to a student, but in affecting the careers and incomes of other adult human beings. What made this even more awesome was that these people were similar to him in talent, ambition, and sensitivity — even in vulnerability. They were writers.

They flocked to special screenings set up for groups of them at the studio. The word went out all over town, through the trades and the grapevine and calls to agents, that a new show was in the works, an hour drama series rumored to be that rarest of all birds, a quality prime-time network series. Since the show had not yet been on the air, potential writers had to see the pilot in order to know what the series was about. They had to know who the characters were and what sort of situations they might be involved in before they could pitch an appropriate story line for consideration. To inform themselves of these matters they dutifully trooped to screenings of the pilot, armed with notebooks and pencils and hope.

Those who were not invited to attend, who did not have agents to submit their names and samples of their work for consideration, called and sent in work on their own. The inundation of writers grew in geographic scope as well as variety of applicants and ideas when one of the wire services carried a small item about Perry, the college teacher and short-story writer who had originated a new television show.

Aspiring writers not only sent in scripts they had written, but poems and verse plays, biographies and musicals, comedy sketches and magazine articles, inspirational essays from religious publications and feature stories on beloved pets that had been published in small-town weeklies. There were telephone calls from writers who claimed to be old buddies of Perry's from college or the army or summers in the south of France or winters in the Alps or other such places where in fact he had never been in his life. There were those who swore they were best friends or sweethearts of people Perry had known in those or other places throughout his apparently teeming past, or friends of mysterious relatives who had allegedly assumed other identities.

Of the scores of inquiries and applications and supplications, the culmination came with the appearance of a wild-eyed man with a flaming red beard who gained entry to Perry's office posing as a window washer and claiming to be a psychic messenger of the late seer Edgar Cayce, dispatched from the logging camp where he had worked for five years solely on the sacred mission of writing an episode of "The First Year's the Hardest."

Security guards and efficient secretaries accustomed to such entreaties disposed of most of the eager but uninvited applicants, but that still left nearly a hundred or so valid, working professional writers vying for what came down to three script assignments. Or two, if Perry chose to write the first episode of the series himself. As story consultant, it was his own choice. He was not used to all these choices.

Thankfully, the selection of the writers was not his alone; it was a decision made jointly with Kenton and Ned, and had to have Archer's approval, as well as the network's.

This eased a bit the gnawing sense of guilt Perry felt about sitting in judgment on other writers, and his uneasiness about the whole process of writers having to come and sell themselves.

In Perry's own career as a writer he had never been required to "take meetings," but simply to write his stories and put them in the mail. The first and only meeting he ever "took" was the one at the network with Archer, but he luckily did not at the time comprehend its import.

Had he known then he was supposed to be selling himself as well as his writing, he would have freaked out and stayed home. No matter how tough it was to gather rejection slips, opening envelopes from your own mailbox in the privacy of your own home was far less agonizing than actually having to talk a good game at a meeting or pitch your story in a way that would sell it. Then, how degrading to read the indifference of disappointment on the faces of those with whom you were taking the meeting.

Yet Perry could see how it was necessary; he did not want to find himself working with some writer who he might feel was a schnook, or a bore, or had bad breath, no matter how brilliantly he put words on paper. Still, it was awful, and he bled for those candidates who obviously would not get the call alluded to in the obligatory phrase "We'll get back to you."

Perry quickly learned that writers with any success in the rugged field of television would not deign to do an hour of anyone else's series, for the form known as episodic television was lowest in pay and prestige (and the two always went together out here) of all the network script possibilities. So the writers who came seeking assignments for the show were basically the young ones who were breaking in and the old ones who were hanging in.

Perry's heart went out to the old guys, the veterans who in their forties and fifties were trying to make a living by knocking out some episodes for other people's shows, a "Hart to Hart" or a "Dynasty" or maybe now a "First Year's the Hardest," while keeping the dream that one of their own original scripts would someday hit the jackpot.

This could be me, Perry realized with chilling recognition when he saw the older applicants pitching a story.

Perry knew from reading their work that some of them were men and women of true talent, with unproduced screenplays or theater pieces that seemed to Perry every bit as good as or better than most of what was making it big, but who simply had not had the right combination of elements to make it happen — the star or director or producer or packager who could get the right pieces all to fit at the right time. Still, they hung in; they toiled and smiled and came to these meetings with new ideas, pitched their wares with humor and intelligence and decency, and then, with thanks for the chance, went off, to wait hopefully to hear a yes to something, anything.

"There's a term for it," Perry explained to Jane after work one night, "when the writers have to come in and sell themselves. It's called 'tap dancing.' "

"Ugh," she said, making a face. "It's disgusting."

She got up and started toward the house.

"Don't blame me, I didn't invent this system," Perry said.

"I was just going to get a drink."

"Oh. Would you bring me a glass of that good Chardonnay?"

Jane saluted in silence and went inside as Perry sank deeper into the hot tub. When he got down all the way to his chin and closed his eyes, letting the bubbling jets massage him, he almost didn't mind the deprivation of being without his own swimming pool.

"Here you go," Jane said, coming back out and handing Perry a long-stemmed glass filled with an almost golden-colored wine.

"You're not joining me?" he asked.

"I still have to do it a little at a time," she said, tentatively sticking a toe in the cauldron of water.

"I mean with the wine," he said.

She was holding a can of Michelob.

"I'm thirsty and hot and I feel like a beer," she said. "Do you mind?"

"Of course not," he said, lying.

She had never been a big beer drinker until this summer, and he secretly suspected her sudden love of the suds was not as she claimed because the heat and smog gave her a thirst that wine didn't slake, but rather because she regarded his sudden connoisseurship of California wines as more affectation than appreciation, and refused to share his enthusiasm.

He also minded that she was wearing her old one-piece, flower-patterned swimsuit from home, instead of the brief Day-Glo spandex bikini he had bought her. If she felt her body couldn't bear comparison with the sleek beauties on the Southern California beaches, that was understandable, but her refusal to wear the sexy bikini even in the privacy of the backyard hot tub, he took as an act of defiance, a purposeful turndown of the simple turn-on he was asking for.

"Yiii — help!" she yelled, as she edged down into the boiling waters, squinting with pain and holding her beer can aloft.

Perry tried to ignore this childish to-do, closing his eyes and taking a sip of the golden Chardonnay. He swished it around in his mouth, ruminating on the flavor, then opened his eyes.

"Is this the David Bruce eighty-one?" he asked suspiciously.

"It's whatever you had in the fridge," Jane said, hunkering down in the bubbling waters like some kind of refugee on the lam.

"Darling, I think that was the Simi Valley Cellars Sauvignon," Perry said moodily.

"For all I know it was the Bob's Bargain Basement Burgundy," she said, belting back a swig of her Michelob.

"Never mind," Perry said, taking a gulp of whatever the hell he was drinking.

"I didn't mean to blame you about the 'tap dancing,' " Jane said. "I know it must be tough on you, really, having to decide people's fates like that, and knowing how hard they're trying."

"It's the worst with the older guys," Perry said. "I feel for them, but when push comes to shove, I find myself wanting to go with the bright young faces."

"Why?"

"The point is, you can't afford to be doing someone a favor out of some misguided notion of charity. Or sentiment. It's your own ass on the line."

"But I thought you said some of the old veterans were really good writers."

Perry took another sip of wine and shifted a bit in the tub, trying to get a jet of water in the itchy place in his back.

"Well, you begin to wonder, though, if they're really good, how come they're still doing episodes of somebody else's series?"

"You're not exactly a boy genius yourself, darling."

"That's what makes it so painful when I feel myself edging away from some of these older guys."

"Still, you find yourself doing it, huh? Going for youth?"

"Going for what's good for the show. That's the bottom line."

Suddenly Jane pulled herself up from the tub and shook herself as if she were a dog drying off.

"What's wrong?"

"Nothing. I just can't stand being boiled alive any longer. I'm going in and read for a while."

Perry made a grunting sound of acknowledgment and took another sip of his wine. He wondered if the mention of reading was a bit of a barb since Jane noted recently that Perry didn't seem to have time for it any more. She went every week religiously to some intellectual bookshop on Sunset Boulevard and in addition to new novels, came home with copies of the *New Republic*, the *Nation*, sometimes even *Hudson* or *Partisan Review*. Seeing those little intellectual publications lying around on the coffee table seemed odd to Perry, as if they were artifacts of his other life back East; these magazines that seemed familiar at home struck him as exotic out here, a cultural juxtaposition, like finding the latest *Good Housekeeping* lying around some bazaar in Tangiers.

Of course Perry hadn't stopped reading, he was reading just as much or maybe more than he ever had, it was just a different kind of material. In the search for writers he had read dozens, hundreds of scripts and books, and in addition to that, he was now reading everything he could get his hands on about young married couples and graduate students in order not only to get ideas for the show but to make sure that everything in "The First Year" would be authentic, *real*. He had even had Ned's secretary call Washington to get all the government statistics and studies on youthful marriage and couples in grad school. He wanted every scene of his show to be not only dramatically but sociologically valid. He felt he had a mission, not merely to entertain but to inform, to raise the educational as well as the entertainment level of prime-time television in America.

He finished off his wine, set the glass on the rim of the tub, and tilted his head back. The day was not only hot but the smog was heavy, making his eyes smart and his nose burn. Such small discomforts, however, were canceled out by the fine native wine and the action of the jet-streamed water massaging his flesh. He didn't even mind the smog, for it was like a trademark of the place; he imagined for a moment the brown film staining the sky above was like the smoke of action hanging over a battlefield and he was a general, calmly preparing for the fray, experiencing now a thrilling hint of the charred scent of triumph.

"Jack and Laurie would never go to a porno flick," Perry explained. "They're not prudes, they'd just find it boring, kind of beside the point."

"Right."

"Of course."

"Got it."

His writers agreed.

Of course they agreed. They were *his* writers. He hadn't "created" them exactly, they were writers before he met them, but now they were working to portray his characters on his show and so they naturally deferred to his judgment. How much more responsive they were, how much more eager to understand than a roomful of questioning, carping students, always trying to trip you up!

"Do you think Jack and Laurie might ever go *bowling?*" Hal Hagedorn asked, and the way he said it cracked everyone up.

Hal was clearly the prize of the group. Witty and wise, with a well-tanned, muscular body and curly blond hair, he seemed more like a California surfer-turned-actor than a writer, yet his credits included scripts for some of television's classiest series, like "Family" and "Fame," as well as action stuff like "Remington Steele," sitcoms such as "One Day at a Time" and "Three's Company," and the big hit melodramas "Dynasty" and "Dallas." He said he preferred to work on other people's shows and live the good life out on the beach in Venice rather than take the responsibility and undergo the grind of a show of his own. His laid-back life-style and philosophy kept him young, for in spite of his many credits and his actual age of thirty-nine, he could have passed for a young grad student like Jack, and his ideas and dialogue were right on the mark.

It was only his experience and string of credits, though, that made him seem a more ideal writer for the show than Estelle Blau, a bubbly twenty-six-year-old housewife who had written seventeen paperback romance novels and was now attacking TV with the same energy and enthusiasm. She had just sold an original after-school special about teenagers on dialysis, as well as an episode of "Falcon Crest."

"Bowling!" she exclaimed in response to Hal's idea, jumping up and clapping her hands. "Oh, for sure — I know some lanes over on Melrose we could go and research it, and get a few games ourselves!"

"What the hell," said R. V. Hensel, "let's have some fun with this thing."

R.V. (now known to all of them affectionately as Arvy) was an owlish fellow in his middle fifties whose potbelly bulged through the buttons of old-fashioned Hawaiian-style sports shirts of the kind once worn by Harry S Truman. When Archer Mellis wangled one additional script commitment out of the network even before the pilot went on, it meant they could hire an additional writer (Perry himself was of course doing the opening show), and Perry, Ned, and Kenton had all wanted to take a chance on Buddy Byler, a brilliant UCLA Film School dropout who had broken into TV with an after-school special on teenage break dancers. To Perry's shocked surprise, Archer had vetoed that vote for youth, saying they should keep Byler in the wings if the show took off, and insisted on going with quality, as proven by the aging Hensel's having won an Obie back East twenty years before! The poor guy must rub it every night for luck.

"Bowling might really work," Perry mused, about to expound on how a hip young couple might see this lower-class pastime as kind of campy fun and then really get into it, joining a local league, but his creative stream of thought was interrupted by a sudden knock at his door and the sweating head of Kenton popping in to say, "Archer wants us — *now*."

Perry leaped up.

"May Allah be with you," Hal Hagedorn said.

The others, with sincere concern, chimed in their prayers of support.

144

Their own fate, after all, was now tied in with the fate of the show and its creator.

"What could be wrong?" Perry asked, hurrying to keep in stride with Ned and Kenton as they grimly made their way to Archer's office.

Whenever they were summoned like this it meant trouble. It must have been especially serious for Kenton to be called off the set, while directing the first of the hour episodes. It was not the first one that would be aired — that was Perry's, but he had been so busy he hadn't even finished his own script before the first draft of Hal Hagedorn's episode about Laurie taking karate lessons came in. It was so beautifully polished and expertly done that it was practically ready to shoot, so Ned and Kenton decided to go with it right away instead of waiting for Perry. The creator suffered a twinge of envy that this newcomer to the show had taken to it so perfectly, but it meant they had found a real successor to assume the writing leadership when Perry returned to Vermont. That, too, stirred mixed feelings in Perry: a grudging sort of gratitude.

"It must be the barbarians at the network," Ned growled. "They probably find Kenton's dailies too subtle. Not crass enough."

"At least if they make us reshoot anything we're not under the gun with time pressure," the perspiring young director said. "Thank God we don't go on the air till the fall."

"That's right," Ned said. "Once we're on the air week to week there's no stopping the express train without a crash."

"Why don't we not think about it," Perry said, with rising anxiety, "till we hear what it is."

When they walked into Archer Mellis's office they found the young executive standing on his head. He was wearing a Los Angeles Lakers warm-up suit.

"You're going on the air in three weeks," he announced from his inverted position.

"That's crazy!" Ned Gurney shouted. "That's the first week in August."

"They don't start new shows till the fall, do they?" Perry inquired.

"They can't start this one," Kenton said. "We won't be finished shooting."

"They're just putting on the pilot," Archer said, remaining unperturbed and upside down.

"In the name of all reason, why?" demanded Ned.

"It tested well at Preview House."

Preview House was a theater on Hollywood Boulevard where random audiences of people with nothing better to do were rounded up and subjected to screenings of TV pilots and other assorted film material not yet seen or heard of by the public. The reaction was thus supposed to be pure. Viewers registered their like or dislike or indifference to particular scenes and actors by pressing buttons located at their seats, and by filling out a detailed questionnaire upon leaving the theater.

"Is that any reason to put it on the air before the season even begins?" Ned inquired, getting down on the floor and trying to look Archer in the eyes.

Archer let his legs fall behind him and sprang up to a standing position.

"Since it's not typical prime-time material they want to give it a chance to score well against soft opposition. They're putting it on against a National League game between two cellar dwellers, and an amateur magic show contest among senior citizens at Sun City, Arizona."

"Baseball and magic sound like pretty potent stuff to me, no matter how bad it is," Kenton moaned, "especially against an unknown pilot of a never-seen series."

Archer went to his closet, flung it open, and grabbed a metal bar that was installed above his head in the door frame. He began doing chin-ups.

"Think victory," he said. "If you beat the opposition you'll have proven yourself in combat. Your fans at the 'network will strengthen their hand."

"*Television!*" Ned Gurney roared, throwing up his hands in frustration.

"That's the business we're in," said Archer, chinning himself with precise rhythm. "Remember?"

It was D day.

The three weeks seemed to have passed in three seconds. It was the several hours before the show that seemed to drag like eons.

Perry and Jane, along with Kenton and his wife, had been invited to Ned's to have one of Kim's curry dinners and watch the show together. The triumvirate and their women. The ones who had made it happen.

If this were a Broadway production, they would know they had a hit on their hands. The major reviews were already in, since the network arranges advance screenings for TV critics whose judgments must appear the day of the show's airing to be of any use to the audience. Perry had run in excitedly that morning to show Ned the *New York Times*, whose critic had called "The First Year" an "unexpected pleasure . . . uncommonly intelligent." Ned pointed out that "uncommonly intelligent" might be a turn-off to the mass audience, and was happier with the Associated Press review that called the show "a real heartwarmer," and *Variety*'s label of it as "this season's socko sleeper," but, as he ruefully explained, you could take all those reviews and with a buck fifty buy yourself an enchilada.

What counted was not the critics but the public, not the words of praise but the numbers of sets in use and percentage of viewers as tabulated by the Nielsens. That's why Ned wanted his colleagues to view it on an ordinary TV set on a regular-sized screen right in his own living room, just the way all those other millions of Americans would tonight, for they were the ones whose reaction would determine the fate of the show.

When the first notes of the upbeat theme music sounded, Perry felt as if he might go through the roof. When his credit appeared in a scroll of gold letters on the screen — *Written by Perry Moss* — he felt what he could only describe as a rush, a sensation surely as powerful as the high produced by any drug in the world.

147

Though he'd seen the show dozens of times, watching it now as it was aired was an entirely different experience, for he knew at this very moment the picture on the screen before him was being seen on other such sets by millions of people all over the country.

Millions.

In New York and Dallas, Peoria and Pittsburgh, in mansions and hovels from Maine to Seattle, his scenes, his words, were being witnessed by people of all ages and sizes and sexes, people of all political and religious persuasions, people who had doctoral degrees and people who had never read a book in their lives, people who could not even read at all, but were now, all of them, separately but together, unified by the simultaneous showing of the image that Perry himself was watching. This massive national viewing audience was now being gathered and held, entranced, entertained, by his story. And his story was true to his own best perception, his own understanding of life; it was not just drivel or junk, but a tale of which the teller was proud.

He had never seen the film with commercials before, the screenings had simply gone to black at the ending of the acts, the breaks where commercials would be shown, and he had feared that the appearance of the usual hyped-up jingle-jangle pitches for cars and colas, pizza and pantyhose, would break the dramatic spell of the film, would seem like simpleminded mockery of the emotions being portrayed so poignantly.

To his total surprise, however, the commercial interruptions seemed to him to actually *enhance* the overall effect of the story. After the action had gone to a certain pitch of emotion or point of plot, the total break from it seemed a relief, a chance to catch your breath — yes, even go to the bathroom, what was so bad about that need? — refill your glass, stand up and stretch, or simply to watch the sales pitch for whatever it was and divert your mind from concentrating on what had just been absorbing it. Besides, if it weren't for the commercials, this miracle wouldn't be happening at all, this fabulous transmission of a wonderful drama into homes all over America wouldn't be possible.

To the amusement of the others, Perry actually *cheered* the commercials!

"Eat those vitamins!" he shouted, standing up and shaking his fist with frenetic fervor.

Perry had also fretted beforehand that seeing the show on the small screen would be a real downer after having viewed it so often in the luxurious large expanse of a movie-size screen in a projection room, and yet in fact the whole thing looked *better* to him. During one commercial break he stopped cheering long enough to ask the others if in fact he was crazy, or if the film didn't seem more effective on the smaller screen.

"That," explained Kenton with a smile, "is what it was made for, you see."

"It's amazing but true," Ned said. "In this case, smaller is better."

What a miracle.

The next morning the miracle grew.

Ned's secretary let out such a scream that office doors flew open all up and down the hall, and Perry joined everyone else in rushing to see what happened.

"We got great numbers!" she shouted, waving a single sheet of mimeographed paper that Ned Gurney grabbed from her hand and began to pore over as if it were some kind of code that foretold the future.

In a way, it was. These were the overnights, the Nielsen ratings computed on the spot in the three major markets of New York City, Chicago, and Los Angeles. The final computations of the previous evening's television viewing audience for the whole nation would not be ready and released till the following week, but this first quick bulletin from the entertainment battlefront conveyed to the contending forces the running of the tides that would carry them irrevocably on to victory or defeat.

Executives and secretaries, electricians and actresses, makeup artists and film editors, all rushed as breathlessly and eagerly to hear the news, for whatever their age or experience, their income or status, their immediate fate and future would be determined by these results; like the members of an army, from the top-ranked general to the most menial private, they shared a common stake in the outcome. Their survival — as part of this particular show, anyway — depended on it.

"We got a forty-two share in Chicago!" Ned shouted.

A cheer went up.

That meant that 42 percent of the people who had their television sets turned on the night before in the city of Chicago had chosen to watch "The First Year's the Hardest."

More people came running to hear the news, and the whoops and screeches increased as Ned continued, his own voice rising to a higher pitch of triumph as he called out the victorious statistics: "A forty-four in New York . . . forty-one in Los Angeles!"

There was pandemonium.

They had done it.

They had triumphed.

The show had not only "won its time" against the opposition in all three big cities, it had captured more than a forty-percent share of the audience in each of those major markets.

They had clobbered the opposition, not only beating the expectedly weak baseball game between two noncontending clubs, but also handily thrashing the magic show special on NBC.

In Ned's office, he and Kenton explained to Perry the full dimensions of their success, in the ratings.

A thirty share means you did OK, you held your own and showed your viability, proved your worth as a potential series. You can stay on the air and get renewed with a consistent thirty share.

A forty share is solid gold. A forty share in TV ratings is like a baseball pitcher's twenty-five-victory season, a rock singer's platinum record, a jockey's winning the Triple Crown.

Anything over that is gravy.

Golden gravy.

The forty share not only gave the "First Year" team credibility, it gave them prestige, and more importantly, it gave them power.

Power is a magnet. It even drew Archer Mellis to their office. Since the time he had assembled this team and hired them and got them signed to contracts, Archer had never come to visit them. It was understood that for any meeting, they went to Archer.

Now he came to them, not of course in humility, but in professional respect. It was rather like a state visit, when the commander in chief himself comes to shake the hands of the troops, the people whose hard work has made him look good, affirmed the wisdom of his own judgment.

Archer was muted, subdued, on this day of triumph. He was wearing a starched blue work shirt, crisp jeans, and those heavy orange boots with leather thong laces favored by construction men. The very simplicity of his garb, without adornment, seemed to identify him with the ordinary labors of those beneath him, conveying the kind of impression of solidarity that the young Mao Tse-tung must have shown his faithful followers in the early days of the revolution.

He spoke softly, warmly, expressing not only his own gratitude but that of the Paragon executive board, whose chairman he had heard from early that morning, and passing on also the heady enthusiasm of the network people. Amanda LeMay was absolutely bubbly, Archer reported with a smile, as, in comradely chat with Ned, Kenton, and Perry, he quietly sipped a diet cola, before going on down the halls and over to the stage to convey his personal congratulations to each and every member of the cast and crew, with the firm handshake, the confidential wink, the bolstering squeeze of the shoulder bent at the wheel of production.

The point of course now was not to sit around in idle celebration but to move ahead even more purposefully to the task of turning out the first shows of the series that would solidify, perhaps even build more strongly, on the popularity of the pilot. When lunchtime came no one suggested going off the lot to celebrate, but rather the triumvirate went as usual to the commissary, consuming their Cobb salads and iced teas as they consorted over problems and plans. Who needed booze when the spirits were lifted naturally, by the fruits of creative, collaborative labor, to a pure and clarified sense of nearly superhuman elation?

It was the work that counted, and Perry was determined to plunge back into his script revisions, just as he would have done on any other day; yet he couldn't escape the indications of his triumph. There was a stack of pink phone message slips as thick as an overstuffed wallet, and even several yellow envelopes from Western Union waiting for him on his desk.

Though friends back home had no way of knowing about the real triumph of the numbers, they had seen the show and many had seen the rave reviews in the papers from the wire service reports the day before. Perry smiled as he leafed through the messages of congratulation and requests for calls from publishers, newspaper and magazine interviewers, invitations to speak at seminars on the problems of young married couples and the future of television in the arts.

But above all else, one message told him of the true dimensions of his triumph as the creator of a hit show, and the new status it gave him in the great world of entertainment.

Vaughan Vardeman had called to invite him and Jane to dine at their home Saturday night.

It was not going to be just any old potluck supper.

This was an invitation to one of Pru Vardeman's New England Boiled Dinners.

Perry knew he now had really *arrived* in L.A.

VIII

P
OWER HAD NEVER been one of Perry's dreams.

He had fantasized about fame and glory, even riches — not the great wealth of oil barons or shipping tycoons, but enough to afford the ease of luxury travel and nice homes in several choice spots around the globe — but he had never, even in his secret self, hungered for power.

Perhaps because he had never tasted it.

When it came to him, in his middle years, in the modest portion allotted the creator of a hit TV show — he was totally unprepared for its effects. Having never experienced it, nor even been interested by it as a subject of study or passing fascination, he didn't even realize he had fallen under its influence. No one mentioned the phenomenon, since admission of it is the last true taboo, more so than any aspect of sexual preference or proclivity, no matter how bizarre. He was, then, completely uninformed about the nature of this crucial new force in his life, and only in retrospect did he come to understand its elements.

Power is addictive.

Power is a drug.

It is the only serious drug of the film and television industry. The rest of the stuff — cocaine, marijuana, acid, alcohol — is for lightweights, for kooks, for a few far-out actors whose talent is matched by their irresponsibility; for those on the way down; for fringe people. No person of any kind of power in the field would succumb to the frivolous lure of such indulgences, since addiction to them would threaten one's maintenance of the headiest, most soothing, satisfying opiate of all: power.

No matter when it comes in life, power feels natural, as if it should have been there all along.

How could a feeling so natural be anything but right? How could anything the body and mind respond to so beautifully be wrong? Unlike drugs that gave you temporary feelings of elation or relief at a damaging cost to your physical and mental well-being, power did not in any way seem to endanger your health, but if anything, enhanced it!

That was surely true in Perry's case in a very specific way. He had already cut down his habitual intake of alcohol from the sheer exhaustion and absorption of work, but now he felt even less of an urge to drink, beyond a few glasses of wine, since the very sensation he once frenziedly imbibed to achieve was no longer desirable. Why subdue what felt good? Alcohol is a depressant. Alcohol numbs.

Power exhilarates.

This is how it feels:

There is a rush, an exhilaration, a buoyancy, a feeling of command, a sense of being taller, stronger, wiser, of imperceptibly lifting off the ground and having the capacity to look down and see things from the advantageous perspective of pinnacle vision, as in viewing people and events from the top of a private mountain, or, more emotionally accurate, a Valhalla. You are not alone, but happily surrounded by your peers, the other gods.

Perry could feel the power swelling within him, transforming him.

His voice even changed.

"Hey, are you *on* something?" his old friend back in Vemont, Al Cohen, asked when Perry returned his call of congratulations about the show.

Perry laughed, with benevolent joviality.

"You been reading the *Enquirer?* Scare stories about drugs and TV?"

"I don't know what it is, but I swear your voice sounds different."

"How?" Perry asked, pleased and intrigued now, knowing he *was* different, delighted that other people could tell, even on the phone, a continent away. He leaned back in his chair, smiling, feeling the contented ease of a cat stretching in the sun.

"Different how?"

"Louder, for one thing."

"I'm not shouting, Al. You must mean *stronger* — my voice sounds stronger. Is that it?"

"Hell, you sound kind of *aggressive*, you know?"

Perry chuckled, pleased with himself. It meant he was fitting in out here, as was only appropriate to his role as molder of taste and opinion, mores and morals, of the mass American audience.

"Well, I guess that's what happens," Perry said, "when your show gets more than a forty share."

"Got what?"

Perry sighed, and looked at his watch.

"Never mind — I was talking Nielsen stuff. It just means more people watched us than any other show, the whole goddam night. We even beat NBC's magic show special. Beat 'em to a pulp, as a matter of fact."

"To a pulp? Well, I guess that's good," Al said, with some hesitancy, as if he didn't really understand. "Anyway, everyone watched your program out here, of course. Big gathering in the Student Union. Packed house."

"Mmmm," Perry said, realizing those viewers wouldn't even register in the ratings. The Nielsen boxes that calculated the audience were only attached to TV sets in homes.

". . . was really high-quality stuff, especially for television," Al was saying. "Of course some of the academic satire was a little *broad*, but I guess . . ."

Perry was drumming his fingers, impatient now. He hadn't really asked for a goddam literary critique.

"Listen, Al, give my love to Rachel. Everyone. I've got to run, but I'll keep you posted on what's going on here."

"Maybe I'll come and check things out in person."

"What's that?"

"Someone mentioned there's one of those charter deals from Boston to L.A. next week. I was thinking I might just drop in on you. See the Coast, as long as you're out there."

"Oh? Well, hey — terrific," Perry said, noticing his voice getting lighter. Damn. He didn't want to tell his best friend not to come, but the prospect seemed awkward, especially now. He wanted to end the conversation without saying yes or no, so he'd have time to think up a good excuse. Fortunately, a brand-new phrase came to mind, one he had only heard and learned to use out here in the last month or so.

"Listen," he said, "I'll get back to you."

It was a nice way of telling the other person not to hold his breath. He hoped Al would understand.

Perry took Jane to dinner that night at Spoleto. It was the first time they'd gone to the prestigious restaurant on their own, rather than just as guests of powerful people in the Industry like Archer Mellis or the Vardemans. A week before Perry would never have had the balls to call for a reservation there just for himself, for fear of being politely told they were all booked up for the evening — for all foreseeable evenings. A week before, hell, he wouldn't have called the *day* before.

Perry's seemingly reckless new confidence in his power, restaurant-wise, turned out to be more than justified.

Dom himself came out of the kitchen to tell the new TV hit creator and his lovely wife what special magic he was working with the veal that evening. It involved an unexpected shipment of truffles flown in that day direct from his home district of Umbria, something he was doing up only for his special guests.

Perry closed the menu and said he and his wife would put themselves entirely in Dom's hands.

"Trust me," said Dom with a wink, sounding like a culinary Archer Mellis.

Carlos, the captain, personally accompanied the sommelier, suggesting, to start, a California Schwamsberg Blanc de Blanc champagne ideal for "the celebration of a forty-four share."

"Sold," said Perry.

"My God," Jane whispered under her breath, "how did *he* know? How do they all know? It hasn't even been in the papers yet. The share."

Perry grinned.

"In this town," he said, "everyone knows."

He took Jane's hand beneath the table, giving it a powerful squeeze.

He wanted her to share and enjoy his newly won power, wanted the heady feeling it gave him to rub off on her as well. He felt full of love for his wonderful wife and wanted to make up to her for his recent neglect and indifference, even irritation, as his energies had flowed so fully into the show. He knew she was trying, too, to get in the spirit of things. She had worn the semi-slinky new silk dress she had bought on their abortive shopping spree, and the pair of medium heels that were as high as she would go toward the locally fashionable spikes. She had even put some gloss on her lips, and her hair was tied loosely with a pretty silk ribbon instead of the usual yarn.

"You're beautiful," he told her. "I mean, you're always beautiful, but tonight you're especially beautiful."

"I guess I better be," she said, "to keep up with a forty-four share."

She smiled, letting him know it wasn't a dig, and returned his powerful hand-squeeze under the table.

"You're my best share of all," he said. "Always."

The champagne soon was bubbling in their glasses and Perry sipped, rather than gulped, savoring the taste and sensation as he also savored the events of the day, recounting them to Jane, embroidering for her amusement Archer's "state visit," reporting the amazing pile of messages, the requests for interviews and articles, the calls from well-wishers, new hangers-on, and old friends. She perked up especially when he told her about talking to Al Cohen, and how back at Haviland the Student Union was packed for the show.

He stopped short of mentioning Al's idea about coming out to visit on some kind of charter flight. He didn't want to try to explain why he didn't really want to encourage it. She wouldn't understand. In fact, she'd probably want Al to bring Rachel and the kids out, too, charter a whole plane for friends and faculty of Haviland, pack a few pine trees to put in the backyard, and sock in a month's supply of Vermont maple sugar. Perry didn't want to get into explaining how he loved all those people but wanted to keep his California experience pure, to enjoy it unadulterated by intrusions from his other life, so he just didn't mention that part. He didn't want to argue with Jane tonight, he wanted to make love to her.

The forty-four share had made him horny. Not "horny" in the old sense of being desperate, of feeling an almost adolescent itch and fever for sex, but rather, a deep surge of sexual energy, a strong, confident fullness of desire. He imagined himself as being like some prize bull ready to bestow his favors on the luckiest of the herd, the one that in his prime wisdom and experience, in the swollen heat of his own power, he had personally chosen as mate.

He was glad that it was Jane because she was his wife and he loved her, and he wanted, among other things, to make up for his sexual neglect of her these past months; yet, on some other, deeper level, he knew it did not matter at all that she was the precious, singular, beloved woman with whom he had shared his deepest intimacies of mind and body and soul. He did not want or need to fantasize her as any other woman, imagine her a sex goddess or movie star or elegant, expensive, professional mistress. It mattered only that she was a woman, or even more simply and basically, *was woman*.

Man of power. Man in command. Man whose own prick seemed to have swelled beyond itself, royal purple pulsing and perfectly rigid, rock-hard, pumping up and down, in and around, in total control, no spillage or early unwanted eruption — this was a tool programmed for performance and Perry had only to guide it, go with it. He moved and molded Jane to his wish, above and below and alongside, over and under, feeling her let go and glide with his — or its — own rhythm, and her responding to it, peaking and pouring again and later again, more fully than he'd ever felt her before, and finally, in his own sweat and juice of lust and fission, entirely by his own removed decision (for somehow he felt distant from what was happening, as if he were looking on it from outside his own body), he let himself go with her too, exploding, the two of them together, dying in one another's arms, slumping and sliding off the bed and falling to the floor, bodies sprawled like battle victims.

Afterward, they usually touched and murmured soft made-up, spontaneous words of sweet pleasure and love, but now both were silent, staring at one another, almost like strangers. Perry went off and took a shower and returned to find Jane lying on her back in bed, her hands beneath her head, staring at the ceiling. There were tears in the corners of her eyes. Perry didn't ask about them, or anything else. He rolled over and fell at once into a dead, dreamless sleep.

The party at the Vardemans' Saturday night did not, after all, turn out to be one of Pru's New England Boiled Dinners, but it was, according to guests in the know, the next best thing in terms of invitational prestige. It was one of Vaughan's Five-Alarm Texas Chilis. Vaughan did not make the chili himself, of course, it was just from his own recipe, or rather, a recipe he had allegedly won in a high-stakes poker game with the scion of one of Texas's wealthiest old oil wildcatting families, while raising financial backing for one of his first productions. This was back in the days before any studio in town would have been glad to bankroll anything that he wanted to do.

Vaughan's Five-Alarm Chili was actually made by a staff of Mexican chefs schooled at Cordon Bleu in Paris, and served by a bevy of beautiful young women wearing high-heeled boots with jangling spurs, miniskirts, and halters made of red and white bandanas. One rumor was they were the actual Dallas Cowgirls, which might well have been true, since their service at such a power-packed party could have meant the discovery of any one of them for a role in a movie or television show; what aspiring young show business beauty would not have been more than happy to serve?

Perry pointed out to Jane just a few of the powerful directors he recognized — Steven, of course, Randy, and the brooding Francis. She was of course more interested in the stars, right there in the flesh, and Perry, though he tried to be cool and not betray his greenness to power, was awed himself. He tried to keep up a good front of casual, almost-about-to-yawn composure, on seeing the likes of such legendary older greats as Gregory, Jimmy, and the ageless George, as well as contemporary legends like Warren, Meryl, Harrison, and Teri.

There was another category of stars whom Perry knew not by their real names but the names of the characters they portrayed, characters who had become part of the national consciousness. They were known by anyone who had flipped the dials of the TV set on idle evenings at home or scanned the pages of *People* while waiting in a supermarket checkout line. Here in living color were such famous faces as J.R., Fonzie, Archie and Mindy. Perry realized they had become part of the background of the times, like reference points for personality traits, just as characters in novels had been a century ago when Simon Legree, Huck Finn, Mister Pickwick and Little Nell were familiar symbols. It was an eerie, exciting feeling to be rubbing shoulders with them, fictional characters come to life.

"Lapping it up, are we?"

The arrogant, almost sneering voice broke Perry's pleasurable sense of being part of this real-life fantasy, and he turned to see the snide countenance of the Vees' pet English novelist, Cyril Heathrow.

"Oh," Perry said, deflated, "it's you."

It was not only the Englishman's insolent remark that brought him down, but the very fact of his presence made the party seem less brilliant in Perry's mind, as if the guest list had to be padded at the last minute by such third-string hangers-on, which brought into question the value Perry might attach to his own presence on the scene.

Heathrow was not in his riding garb, but was decked out in white duck pants, white buck shoes, and a sports jacket of wide pastel stripes, topped by a straw skimmer tilted jauntily on his head. He touched a finger to its brim in a sort of salute to Jane.

"You should have brought your camera, shouldn't you?" he asked. "Snapshots of the stars, sent back to the hometown gazette? A sure sale, I should think."

"Sounds a bit old hat, Mr. Heathrow," Jane said with a wide smile. "I'm sure they'd rather see a genuine English literary figure in the midst of the Hollywood scene, looking so . . . *croquet?*"

The left corner of Heathrow's thin mouth made a slight downward twitch, expressing disdain.

"Possibly so," he said, then turned, his pastels melting into the crowd.

The Englishman's barbs were quickly forgotten when Pru Vardeman suddenly swept down on Perry and Jane, bestowing on the cheeks of each a quick, dry peck, making them feel as if they were being greeted on the Merv Griffin show.

"How too sweet of you to come," she said, then grasped one of Jane's hands in her own. "May I borrow your decorous wife, Perry? There's someone absolutely dying to meet her."

"*Me?*" Jane asked.

Perry felt himself reddening, wondering if one of the famously lascivious stars, known for his hobbylike conquest of women, had picked Jane out of the crowd as his new morsel. But before he could ask any questions Pru was already towing her off at almost a run, pulling Jane behind her like a kite she was trying to get airborne. Perry started to follow, when a sudden goose from behind made him jump. He turned to see his host.

"Friggin' chili," Vaughan said, emitting a spicy belch, and shaking his head, "stuff's hot enough to scorch a wetback."

He threw an arm around Perry's shoulder and started guiding him toward the house. Now Perry understood why Jane had been suddenly swept away; Vaughan wanted a little private time with his old pal who was now making a mark in this new scene. OK, fine. Let's see what's up. He was ready for anything.

Vaughan and Pru each had their own office at home, conveniently located on either side of the comfortable private screening room they shared. Pru's office featured authentic New England antiques, while Vaughan's was a clashing combination of Danishmodern desks and tables, along with scruffy leather club chairs and couch that seemed to have been rescued from some ancient college fraternity house. There were framed posters of the movies he had produced, as well as autographed photos of Vaughan with celebrities ranging from Tommy Lasorda to Don Ho.

Vaughan opened a desk drawer and pulled out a scruffy, slightly deflated football that he tossed to Perry.

"Was rereading some of your stuff the other day," Vaughan said casually.

Perry smiled. He bet he knew exactly what day. He bet it was the day the Nielsen overnights came in on "The First Day's the Hardest." Vaughan probably had some kind of hookup to the Nielsens like the Dow-Jones ticker tape that provided the latest numbers. Maybe they were fed right into his own home computer.

"That so," said Perry, noncommittally. He gripped the football along the laces and lofted it back to Vaughan in a graceful arc. He was enjoying the game they were playing. Not long ago he would have thought Vaughan's sudden interest in his old short stories after all these years was disgustingly phony and hypocritical. Now he realized it was just part of the business, part of the game. When you're hot, you're hot. Might as well enjoy it.

When Vaughan got the ball he tossed it up toward the ceiling and caught it himself.

"There's one in your latest collection that grabbed me," Vaughan said. " 'The Springtime Women.' I think it might make a feature."

"So does Ned Gurney," Perry shot back, as if hurling a bullet pass.

Vaughan caught the comment without so much as a wince.

"Did he take an option on it?" he asked, casually tossing up the football again.

"We agreed that when 'The First Year' is all set, he'd take an option. I think his lawyer is drawing up some papers."

"So you just have a verbal agreement, is that it?"

Vaughan sent the football in a hard spiral that stung Perry's hands as he caught it.

"Well, I guess so."

Vaughan made a long whistle and shook his head.

"You probably gave it to him for a song."

Perry felt himself flushing. He cradled the ball against himself, as if in protection.

"Ned and I are friends," he said.

"At least you don't have anything in writing," Vaughan said, giving out another five-alarm belch.

Perry squeezed the ball harder against his belly, feeling his gut heaving.

"Ned and I really work well together," he said. "He sparks ideas in me."

"Too bad he never got his feature off the ground."

Perry gave the ball a fling. It wobbled in the air toward Vaughan.

"Hamlin Productions has it now. Ned says they're really hot about it."

"*Hamlin?* I wish him all the luck."

Vaughan tossed the ball across the room, past Perry's head. It ricocheted into a corner, and Perry went scrambling after it, puffing as he trapped and held it and called back to Vaughan, out of breath.

"What were you going to do with 'The Springtime Women?' I mean, if it was free."

Vaughan yawned, and scratched at his crotch.

"I wanted to show it to Harrison."

"Harrison *Ford?*"

"Why not? You can't see him as the starving artist–type who lives in the pad below the two women?"

"Well, it's not a very big part in the story."

"If Harrison was interested, we'd build it up. Maybe the artist ends up getting it on with one of the chicks."

"I guess that's possible."

"With Harrison involved, we could take it to any studio in town."

Perry was squeezing the football.

"But he's all booked up, isn't he?"

Vaughan shrugged.

163

"No harm in showing it to him."

That wasn't just Hollywood talk. Harrison Ford was here, at this party, tonight. Perry had actually seen the guy with his own eyes.

Vaughan held out his hands for the ball, beckoning.

"I guess there's no harm," Perry said. "After all, Ned and I don't have anything in writing."

He tossed the ball to Vaughan.

Outside on the lawn, among the stars and cowgirls, Jane was enmeshed in some animated conversation with a middle-aged woman who looked, like so many other people present, hauntingly familiar. Her name was Mona Halsted, which didn't ring a bell, and when Jane introduced her Perry asked her if she used to be on that excellent show called "Family," one of the only classy prime-time series.

Mona laughed.

"No, but a lot of people mistake me for Sada Thompson," she said. "The actress who played the mother."

That was it! This woman looked like the ultimate mother, the warm, slightly hefty source of all-American comfort. She must have been the mother in a number of movies, if not a series.

"Mona's not an actress," Jane explained, "she's a *producer.*"

"Oh?" Perry asked with rising interest, "features?"

"No, we only do television. I'm with Allerton, a production company."

Perry felt his attention slightly sag.

"They're doing what sounds like a wonderful series for teenagers," Jane enthused, "and best of all — oh Perry, this is so amazing I can hardly believe it — Mona went to college at *Middlebury!* And she loves *Vermont!*"

"It's not only my favorite state of the union, it's my favorite state of mind," the motherly Mona said sweetly.

"Mmmm," Perry said with a nod of acknowledgment.

So that was it. Pru Vardeman had played the good hostess by getting Jane together with the one person in the whole glittery crowd who got her rocks off reminiscing about *Vermont*, for God sake. Well, he guessed it was harmless; better than introducing his wife to one of those well-tanned seduction artists among the sucessful-actor set.

"I loved 'The First Year's the Hardest,' " Mona said. "It's the sort of thing that makes all of us proud."

"Thanks," Perry said, beginning to look around the lawn, trying to spot more stars.

"Maybe you and Mona could even work together some day," Jane said. "She's read your stories!"

"I'm sure you have many fans out here, Perry," Mona said, "but I hope you'll remember me as a genuine one of them."

"Sure. It was nice to meet you," he said, and pulled Jane away to the bar.

"You could at least have been polite," Jane whispered at him harshly. "She's a wonderful person."

"I'll vote for her," Perry said, "for the Mother of the Year Look-Alike."

He had bigger fish to fry than Mona Halsted.

Perry was on a roll.

When the final compilation of national Nielsen ratings came in, "The First Year's the Hardest" not only won the night it was aired, it was number one for the whole week, barely — but still, amazingly — beating out the highly touted "Frills," a lascivious four-part miniseries about an orphaned transvestite who overcomes a crippling bone disease and ruthlessly rises to the top of a worldwide lingerie empire. Analysis showed that "Frills" was up against stiff competition, going head-to-head against "Dallas" one night and "Love Boat" the next, while "First Year" had only the hapless magic show special and the bottom-drawer baseball game to contend against, but still, number one was number one, no matter how you sliced it, and the creators of the new hit were enjoying their growing prestige and power in the Industry.

"We're number one for the whole damn week," Perry intoned with slow emphasis when he called Jane the morning of the latest momentous news.

"Perry? Is that you?" his wife asked.

"Who else, love? Is Archer himself calling to tell you the ratings news?"

"No. It was just — you sounded kind of like Orson Welles."

Perry roared. Like a lion.

Evidently his voice was getting even deeper. If his success continued at this accelerated pace, he would soon sound like James Earl Jones doing Darth Vader.

And why not? It seemed his work meant death to the opposition. In a few seasons, rival networks would tremble on hearing that a new Perry Moss show was going on the air.

"Do you feel like a traitor to the world you came from?"

Perry felt himself start to flush, then laughed expansively.

"You make it sound like I'm a visitor from another planet. Some kind of Isaac Asimov character."

The reporter, who was working on his second Dos Equis, and had hardly touched his enchiladas, was obviously trying to bait him. Perry took a delicate sip of his Virgin Margarita, feeling cool and in control. The reporter was obviously hostile, probably jealous, which made it all the more essential for Perry to stay calm, aloof. He didn't want to look a fool in the Entertainment section of the Los Angeles *Times*.

"Aren't the values of the academic world some light years away from those of network television?" the reporter pressed.

Perry dabbed a napkin at the salt around the corner of his mouth and settled back in his banquette.

"I can only go by my own experience," he said. "I'm lucky to be working with topflight people like Ned Gurney, Kenton Spires. And of course Archer Mellis, of Paragon, whose sole purpose in bringing us together was to try to do quality television. His faith has sustained us, and the network has loyally supported us."

"So you're giving up teaching for television?"

"Oh no! I'm going back to Vermont for the fall semester. We'll have finished our current order of shows by then, and if we get picked up, I'll of course be in constant touch on a consultancy basis. If not, I'll still come back here during our holidays and our midsemester break in January. There's lots of other offers

I've had, and lots of ideas of my own I'd like to develop. But I'll alternate that with teaching."

"Don't you think trying to do both will make you schizophrenic?"

Perry smiled.

"I hope it will only make me like what so many people are becoming who commute from East to West — bi-coastal."

The reporter flipped his notebook shut, and finished off his beer.

"I can't wait to talk to you a year from now," he said.

"It's a date," Perry said with a smile. "In the meantime, I really have to run back to the lot."

At the very end of the interview-lunch at Casa Tio, a fancy Mexican restaurant, Perry had begun to experience uncomfortable feelings of shortness of breath and a beginning of trembling in his fingers. The anxiety was like he used to feel before his life with Jane when he was always hung over and trying to go a few days without a drink, but this time it was not because of any such envy brought on by the reporter's swilling of the Mexican beers, while he sipped his pure citrus Margarita without the tequila. That in fact gave him a sense of calm, and control, of superiority. Nor was it the reporter's aggressive questions, for though they were annoying they weren't really upsetting. The fact was, Perry now found he simply didn't want to be away from the lot. He suffered what felt like withdrawal pains whenever he had to leave it during the working day.

The damn lunch made him miss dailies. The only comfort was that it meant publicity for the show.

"How was your interview?" Ned asked him.

"The usual. A bore. The guy was all right, I guess. He just didn't understand — I mean, I knew I couldn't really explain to him what it's like, what we're doing, why I love it."

"Of course not," Ned said. "You never can, to civilians. Reporters are civilians."

Yes.

Perry understood that now. He had heard guys on the lot speak of anyone outside the business as "civilians" and it was true. They might be smart, and sympathetic, and curious, but they didn't understand the world you were working in, any more than people at home understood about the life of soldiers in combat. It was simply a different experience, a different life — more intense, exciting, adventurous, meaningful.

Perry was not a civilian any more, he was part of the army of entertainment, part of the elite troops. Maybe that was why so many of them wore shirts with epaulets on them, and semimilitary jackets. They *were* an army, fighting the never-ending battle against boredom, against emptiness, against the threat of blank television screens or movie screens or stages all across America and the world. They were on a mission to make pictures, stories, images, symbols, to fill the gap, the maw, the waiting wandering attentions and hungry minds of a whole society.

He realized that was why he didn't want his best friend — or best friend from his other world — Al Cohen, to come and visit. Not because Perry was a snob and didn't care for Al any more, not that he thought less of him, but the fact was, Al was a civilian. When you were fighting on the front lines, for the life of your cause (the show), you simply didn't want to be distracted by having civilians around, no matter how bright they were, no matter how you might care for them. He wrote to Al as graciously as he could, explaining it just wasn't a good time for him to come out, there wouldn't be any chance to talk or show him around the way he'd like to do, but anyway, he and Jane would be back in Vermont in just a few weeks, he'd explain everything then.

He had to tell Jane about turning down Al's request to come visit, since he knew she'd find out sooner or later. Naturally, she didn't understand.

"I'm not turning my back on my best friend, I'm not doing anything like that," Perry tried to explain. "It's just that he wouldn't understand what I'm doing now, not because he's a jerk, for God sake, he's the most perceptive, brightest guy I know, but he's — well, dammit, he's a *civilian*."

"Like me," said Jane.

"I didn't say that."

"But it's true, isn't it?"

"Even if it is, it doesn't mean I love you any less."

"I know what it means," Jane said.

Perry figured anything else he might say would only get him in deeper. He went to the bedroom to study a script.

IX

WE'LL HOLD OUR FIRE till the end," Archer commanded his men. He was bent forward over the wheel in determination, driving at breakneck speed through the high hairpin curves that led up out of the Valley and on to network headquarters. Perry was bending forward, too, not only to catch Archer's instructions over the booming sound system, but also because of the sense of urgency about this unexpected meeting. Ned Gurney was crunched onto the shelf behind the two seats of the tiny sports car, seemingly resigned if not relaxed.

"Ignorant bastards," he murmured.

"Don't blow your cool, don't let them put you on the defensive," Archer warned. "We have a beautiful script, and we're proud of it."

"I thought they were too," Perry said in genuine confusion. "I thought they loved it."

Only a few days before, word had come down through channels from Archer to Ned to Perry (the writer being by tradition the last to hear any vital information, even about what he had written) that Amanda LeMay was simply gaga over Perry's first hour script to lead off the series, and even more amazing, though of course less verifiable, was the rumor from higher on high that Max Bloorman had scanned it himself in New York and was not displeased!

"This is purely an E. and A. problem," Archer said.

Over the blast of the music, Perry thought he heard T. and A. Like any other sophisticated citizen who followed the media's inside accounts of the entertainment world, he knew that T. and A. was television code for tits and ass, a gross shorthand for the kind of show that appealed to the most base instinct of viewers by the most flamboyant possible display of the female anatomy. He understood that although one network in particular was most renowned for its belief in the foolproof lure of the T. and A. factor, there were executives at each network who felt that the addition of that lure could strengthen a weak show, just as there were some like Harry Flanders who thought that cars were the answer for bolstering any drama.

"My God!" he shouted in genuine shock. "You mean they want us to put in more tits and ass?"

Both Archer and Ned looked at Perry with alarm, as if they feared he had taken leave of his senses.

"Well," he said defensively, "isn't that what T. and A. means?"

Archer dialed down the musical volume.

"Not T. and A.," he said patiently, "E. and A."

"What's that?" Perry asked, his mind reeling at the possible meaning of this new bit of TV esoterica. Elbows and Armpits? Elastic and Action?

"E. and A.," Archer said patiently, "is the network Department of Ethics and Attitudes."

"The censors," Ned explained.

Perry felt like a real rookie. Of course he knew about the network censors, but so far he had been shielded from them. There was really very little of a controversial nature in the pilot story of his innocent young married couple, and the few issues of censorship had to do with the language, which Archer gently explained to him had to be a bit toned down for television. Perry had been realistically agreeable about removing a few harsh bits of dialogue to satisfy the censors, a couple of "Screw yous" and "Up yourses" that would have been perfectly OK in the pages of a magazine but would not do for the ears of millions on national television.

He also knew that although every network had its own censors,

they were never officially called censors, which smacked of to-
talitarianism, of un-American practice. Rather, each network, as
part of its keeping of the public trust, maintained boards or de-
partments devoted to the protection of what it conceived to be
society's accepted standards of morality, taste, and behavior. Each
was called by a lofty title appropriate to this high function, such
as, at Perry's network, the Department of Ethics and Attitudes.

"But what could they possibly object to?" Perry asked. "We
don't even have any 'damns' or 'hells' in this script."

"Don't even try to outguess them," said Ned.

"And don't try to challenge them," Archer warned. "Our best
strategy is to see the problem from their point of view and try to
accommodate them without losing any story point we feel is
crucial."

Before Perry could inquire as to how such a feat might be
accomplished, Archer turned the music back up to an even higher
volume.

Stu Sturdivant, chairman of the network's Department of Ethics and Attitudes, was a warm, jovial man in his fifties, the sort
who in Perry's childhood would have been described in the terms
of his father's generation as a hail-fellow-well-met. He wore a
plaid sport coat, bow tie, bright slacks, cordovan shoes, and argyle
socks.

"How *about* those Dodgers?" Sturdivant asked the group with
a shake of the head and a wide grin, and though Gurney was
obviously at as much of a loss about the local team's baseball
fortunes as was Perry, Archer quickly responded with arcane talk
about RBI's and ERA's, matching Sturdivant cliche for cliche as
they batted back and forth observations on so-and-so's performance at "the hot corner" and the relative strengths of the "wings"
of various starting "hurlers" of skipper Lasorda's "mound staff."

Perry joined Ned in nodding and grinning and grunting through
this seemingly interminable "warm-up," till finally Sturdivant lit
up a Dutch Masters cigar, and, amid billowing clouds of smoke,
came to the point of his complaint about the script.

"We don't mind him jumping on her bones in that last scene," he said. "What the hell, the guy may be some kind of college teacher, but he's no pansy. Am I right?"

"You called it exactly, Stu," Archer said approvingly.

"Our hero's a regular guy," Ned said, nodding.

"When does he 'jump' anywhere?" Perry asked in genuine confusion.

Archer slapped him on the knee in a seemingly friendly manner, then added a sharp squeeze that meant, keep quiet.

"You know, after the argument, they make up, and he 'jumps on her bones.' "

"The lovemaking scene," Ned whispered.

"Oh! Sure, right, you mean *that*," Perry said heartily.

He tried not to grimace, pasting a manly smile on, trying to black out the mental image of a pervert pouncing on a skeleton.

"It's not what they do," Sturdivant continued, "it's *where* they do it."

The hour script was a low-key, familiar story of the married couple's arguments over money that led to a cooling of sexual ardor, that were finally resolved over a "budget meal" so funny that it broke the ice of the couple's hostility and led to a sudden, loving rekindling of passion right there on the kitchen floor. Of course the scene only suggested it would end in lovemaking, there wasn't even any nudity, but it was clear that they couldn't wait nor did they want to wait to get to anyplace more comfortable.

Amanda LeMay and the programming people had praised its humanness and tenderness and appealing spirit.

"You mean you don't mind if he jumps on her bones to show the argument is over," Ned asked calmly, "but you don't like him jumping on them in the kitchen?"

Stu nodded, making a sour face.

"They can wait till they get to the bedroom, can't they?" he said.

"No!" Perry shouted, jumping to his feet. "That's the whole point!"

Archer pulled him back down.

"The charm is that they really love each other so much, and

173

they see their arguments were so silly, they can't wait," Archer said to Stu.

Sturdivant shook his head.

"The kitchen is kinky," he insisted.

"Why, the kitchen is the most wholesome place in a household!" Ned exclaimed.

"It's for eating," Stu insisted, "and I mean eating *supper*, in case you miss my point. Why can't they just kiss and then go off to the bedroom?"

"Then it's not spontaneous!" Perry exclaimed. "It ruins the whole feeling of it."

"The public won't like it," Stu said. "The people out there will think this young couple is a little bit on the weirdo side, if they have to do it in the damn kitchen."

"It doesn't show they're weird, it shows they're human!" shouted Perry.

"There's nothing to get loud about," Archer cautioned him.

Stu turned to Perry and stared.

"I understand you're from back East," he said.

"I live in Vermont," Perry admitted.

"In fact," Stu went on, "all of you people are from the New York area, isn't that so?"

"As a matter of fact, I grew up in Minnesota," Ned Gurney said. "Is that any better?"

Ned was getting hot under the collar.

"It isn't a matter of better or worse," Stu explained. "It's just a fact that intellectuals from back East don't really understand how the *real people* feel about these things. And it's our job to see that we don't offend them."

"My God, this is the nineteen-eighties!" said Ned. "You have everything on TV — you even have incest."

"Not in the kitchen we don't!" said Stu, standing up.

"Besides, I understand this may be an eight o'clock show. That's a family hour. We have to be especially careful. We have a special responsibility to the children of this country."

Archer stood up.

"We didn't know they were thinking of us for eight o'clock, Stu. We appreciate your concerns, and we'll of course cooperate in every way we can."

Ned and Perry rose glumly, murmuring, and Stu got up to walk them to the door.

"Don't worry, boys. We're not prudes over here, we'll get along fine."

He slung a comradely arm over the slumping shoulders of Ned and Perry.

"Say, you boys hear the one about the traveling salesman who stopped at the farm where the daughter kept a pet giraffe in the barn?"

Obediently, they listened.

Loudly, they laughed.

Outside, they cringed.

For the first time since he started working on the show, Perry wanted a drink. He did not have in mind a fine Chardonnay with a delicate nose and amusing bouquet. He was thinking more of a water glass filled with straight gin.

From the fuming looks of Archer and Ned, he figured they might for a moment forget their higher tastes and join him. It was only eleven in the morning, but maybe they could find one of those dark, anonymous, funky bars, air-cooled and stinky with last night's booze, and quietly tie one on. Maybe they'd decide to give it all up and go buy a small newspaper on the Cape.

They walked down the sterile hallway in stony silence, and once inside the elevator, Perry jabbed for the lobby button, anxious to get on the road to his imagined oasis. But Archer brushed his hand aside and poked the button for ten — the top floor, the executive floor.

"What are we going to do?" Ned Gurney asked, "jump?"

"We're going to get an explanation from Amanda LeMay," Archer said grimly.

"You mean about why a young married couple can't make love in the kitchen?" Perry asked.

Ned snorted.

"I'm sure as far as Amanda's concerned, they could make it on top of the refrigerator. Or in the sink, for that matter. That's not the problem."

Archer grunted as the elevator reached ten.

"The problem is," he said, "we've given them a sophisticated, adult show, a quality show for an intelligent, educated audience, and now they're planning to shove it into a family-viewing slot. It's going to tie our hands behind our back, besides giving us the wrong audience. They're going to bury us."

"We're going to nurture you," Amanda said.

Her eyes were large and warm, almost moist from the intensity of her assurance. She stood up and moved from behind her desk toward where Archer, Ned, and Perry sat facing her. She was wearing a loose dress with long, puffy sleeves, but cut low in front, showing the ample breasts that now seemed to be rising and falling with her heartbeat, her emotion. She seemed like an earth mother, strong and protective.

"A show like yours," she said, "is unique, special, a bit fragile. You need to be nurtured."

She extended her arms, and for a moment Perry had the feeling she was going to come a little closer and bury his head against her heaving breast, and he averted his eyes in flushed embarrassment, fearing if she did what he fantasized, he would hurl his arms around her waist and clutch her to him, crying, "Mama, make it all right!" To his relief, however, she turned to Archer.

"Our strategy now is to put you on after the season starts, Sunday night at eight. You'll be against 'Danny, the Golden Dolphin,' and 'Little Asian Rascals,' a new sitcom about a group of Vietnamese orphans who live on a catamaran in Newport Beach, looked after by a retired Air Force general and his deafmute daughter. Danny's been on for four years and he's starting to slip. The new show is very iffy — we don't think the Vietnamese kids will draw in Middle America."

"Still, that's traditionally a family hour," Archer argued.

"Our testing has shown that you have a great appeal to teenagers," Amanda said. "It's the old story of young people wanting

176

to know what the big kids do — what they'll be emulating in only a few years. Research shows you can build a real following in this slot — a following that will grow up with your show, mature with it, and eventually move with it into a later time slot."

"That's awfully far down the road," Ned Gurney said uneasily.

"*Exactly*," Amanda said. "That's how much faith we have in 'The First Year's the Hardest.' We see it as a slowly building staple, something that will work itself into the American grain, like 'The Waltons,' like 'Happy Days.' That's why we're going to do all we can to *nurture* it."

She not only smiled, she glowed, with the pride of a loving and dedicated mother.

Archer stood up.

"Thank you," he said.

He shook her hand and Ned and Perry followed suit, smiling and nodding as they filed out of her office. Just at the door Amanda called out "Gentlemen!" They whipped around to see her give them a big conspiratorial wink.

"Watch the trades tomorrow," she said.

Not only the trades had the story, it was the lead piece in the Entertainment section of the L.A. *Times*. It was the highly regarded annual report of Dexter, Schuman, Glass and McGillicuddy, evaluating the networks' new shows of the upcoming season, and predicting those that might be real winners in the race for the ratings.

"The First Year's the Hardest" was singled out as "fresh and appealing, the most original young domestic drama to come down the pike in many a moon." The prognosticators especially praised the "crackling dialogue" of prize-winning story writer Perry Moss, the "sensitive, nuance-rich pastoral direction of former Off-Broadway firecracker Kenton Spires," and credited the "mid-eighties aura" as well as the general high quality and production values of the show to executive producer Ned Gurney, another prestigious transplant from the East.

"This should be the first big feather in the otherwise bare

177

bonnet of young Archer Mellis, whose blasts at the Industry earned him the top job at Paragon TV. If he can keep together the talented trio that produced the summer's smash-hit pilot, he might well have a long-running ratings-buster. It's already rumored that network executives, pleased with the early series material, may up their order from the safe three shows to something more substantial."

Perry read the story to Jane as she drove him to work that morning, his voice sounding as profound and deep as a foghorn. When he finished, folding the paper on his lap and looking over at her, she said, without even smiling or looking over at him, "Oh shit."

"Hey! What is it with you? Can't you stand to hear your own husband's show may be a big hit? Is that so awful?"

"They'll want you to stay," she said.

"Don't be paranoid. They know I have to go back in September. It's all understood."

"If the show's success depends on keeping the 'talented trio' together? You think Archer's going to lose the 'writer of crackling dialogue'? When his bonnet depends on it?"

"Love, you really are paranoid. I'm going to touch up the scripts from home. I'll still be officially Story Consultant, a part of the team. Hal Hagedorn will probably take over as story editor, and do the real day-to-day work out here. All the network cares about is that I'll still be officially connected to the show. 'Put my stamp on it,' as Archer said."

"That was before this article."

"This article doesn't change any of that. My arrangement is all arranged."

There was no time for the highly praised triumvirate to dawdle over their rave from the prognosticators, since the real news that Archer revealed when they arrived that morning meant that their efforts had to be accelerated at once.

As the advertising seers had so uncannily predicted (and by the very act of that prediction helped insure that it would come true), the network already — this morning! — had commissioned another three episodes of "The First Year's the Hardest," thus doubling the original series order to a total of six hour shows following the pilot!

This meant the already frantic pace and elaborate planning of the production campaign for the new show now had to be doubled, and, like World War II fighter pilots scrambling to get airborne, the three leaders rushed out of Archer's office to get the logistics under way. But one of them was called back for a private high-level word with the commander.

"Perry!"

The writer turned, automatically straightening to attention.

"Sir?"

His young boss smiled, came forward, and gave him a comradely clap on the shoulder.

"Since when did you start calling me 'sir'?" he asked.

Perry chuckled nervously.

"I guess it just slipped out," he said.

"I know I've got to give orders sometimes, but remember, *amigo* — we're in this together."

Archer was now hugging the writer so close to him, as he walked him slowly around the room, that Perry was dizzied by his after-shave cologne.

"Let's you and I slip away for a little lunch today," Archer said. "Just the two of us."

"You mean — off the lot?" Perry asked, both flattered and confused. On this of all days there was little time for such Eastern-style decadence. Perry had counted on wolfing down a container of yogurt while in conference with Ned and the writers, if in fact there was even time to swallow while working out a strategy for a whole new set of story lines. So much had to be accomplished in so little time, not only with the new order for shows but with Perry only having another week or so before retreating back to his consultancy position in the East.

"Sometimes we need to get away for a little perspective," Archer said, giving him a squeeze and then releasing him. "Could you drop by at a few minutes after twelve?"

"Yes, sir," Perry caught himself, then laughed nervously,

blushing at the same time. "I mean — *muy bien, amigo.* And — *muchas gracias.*"

Archer winked.

"*Mon plaisir,*" he said.

The Bach Violin Partitas, as interpreted by Zino Francescatti, rang searingly, plaintively, through the quadraphonic sound system of Archer's car as he drove Perry to lunch, moving at a steady, almost leisurely pace along Sunset Boulevard. To speak would not only have been acoustically difficult, but would also have seemed, against that music, uncouth, almost irreverent. The contrast between the soul-stirring music inside the car, and the zany, superhype billboards and marquees of the bars and rock clubs and restaurants, motels and movie houses, rent-a-car lots and T-shirt boutiques, the whole glitzy agglomeration of the famous thoroughfare, which seemed even more hallucinatory in the smoggy glare of midday, gave Perry the disorienting illusion of traveling inside some kind of space capsule that preserved the essence of an ancient civilization while it slid through the fantastic surface of an alien star.

They did not pull into the parking lots of any of the restaurants along Sunset, nor did they sweep on around the curve into Beverly Hills and the hip, show biz oasis of the Polo Lounge of the famous pink hotel, but rather, Archer guided them up into the hills, on winding streets, climbing to a pinnacle topped by a quaint-looking Japanese restaurant.

Through the glass walls, the view was fabulous, even though hazed by the smog. In fact, that element perhaps even served to glamorize the prospect, adding as it did a filmic glow of unreality, like looking at the world through a brown filter that perhaps was after all a glimpse of how all life would look in the future. This *was* the future. It lay before them, fascinating in its variety, a dizzying display of sparkling glass towers and raw, scrubby hills streaked with ribbons of roads, alive with metallic movement.

"Well, there it is, amigo," Archer said, raising the tall, cool glass containing the drink he had recommended for them both, the Sayonara Sunset. Perry took a sip and nodded, momentarily choking on the emotional lump in his throat as well as the tangy concoction of citrus, saki, and Triple Sec. Hoarsely, he whispered, in affirmation:

"Hollywood."

"Magic," said Archer.

Perry felt a shiver, a thrill.

"It's impossible to explain," he said. "Isn't it? To outsiders."

"Exactly. Either you get it, or you don't. The funny thing is, I had a feeling all along that you *would*. Most writers — especially distinguished literary artists, like yourself — are afraid of it, so they simply take on the easy, condescending pose."

"Hell, I was too naive to be afraid. And then I guess I lucked out, getting on the air and all."

"And getting renewed, before the first show of the series even airs? That's more than luck. You've got the touch, the magic."

"You got it out of me. And put me with the right people. Ned. Kenton. It's like we've been working together all our lives. A team."

"It's one of those once-in-a-lifetime things."

"I guess so."

"I know. I also know it's a shame to break it up."

"But we're not! I'll probably be on the phone with Ned every day. We practically communicate in code now, anyway."

"It won't be the same."

"Archer, you know I'd love to keep right on doing what I'm doing, right here, but I can't."

"Perry, I wouldn't have the nerve to ask you to just keep on doing what you're doing for the three new shows."

"Well, thanks. For not trying to tempt me."

"It would be an insult."

"Not at all. But I just couldn't do it."

"Of course not. Postpone your obligations back East, just to continue as story consultant?"

Perry, relaxing, took a larger sip of his drink.

"You deserve a more important role in the show now," Archer said.

"What do you mean?"

"I mean I am offering you the position of *executive* story consultant, starting with production of the three new shows just ordered."

"I'm honored," said Perry, "but I can't."

He took a large gulp of his drink, then asked, "But what would it mean, exactly?"

Archer shrugged.

"More money. Another five hundred a week."

"I'd be making three thousand a week, then," Perry said.

"I know it's not much of a difference. The important thing is, once you've held an *executive* position on a series, you'd always be involved at that level, on any show you worked on in the future."

"The future?"

"It could be whatever you wanted to make it. Once you've held an executive position, in your own series, and seen it through, you would write your own ticket on anything you wanted to develop next. You could take a break, go back to teaching, then come out and get a new show launched."

"Archer, if I don't go back for this fall semester, I could lose my tenure."

"Your *academic* tenure."

"What other kind is there?"

"Well, in the sense that 'tenure' means security, I'd say that having a prime-time series on the air, with royalties coming in from every show, not to speak of reruns, is about as nice a 'tenure' as a man could want."

Perry finished off his drink. Archer ordered another round, plus the luncheon special sushi platter.

"Don't give me an answer right now," Archer said. "Play with the whole idea. See how it feels."

"I'd have to discuss it with Jane, of course."

"Of course. And remember — it's not a matter of you or her choosing this life and work out here and giving up the life you had before. The beauty of all this is, you can have both. You can be bi-coastal."

Perry, feeling giddy now, began to giggle.

182

"We could have our sushi and eat it, too. Or our Boston scrod."

Archer smiled, sweeping his hand toward the vista that lay below them.

"You can have it all," he said.

Perry brought home a dozen red roses for Jane that night. He wanted to take her out to dinner, maybe even up to the Japanese place with the fabulous view — it would surely be dramatic in the evening, a fairy-tale vista, fired by the million lights clustered in the flatland and flung through the hills. But Jane had already prepared a special favorite. The basil she had planted in her tiny, improbable garden had grown, and she had made her wonderful pesto with it to serve with linguine, along with a crisp green salad, fresh bread, and one of Perry's specially selected fine California wines. She had even lit candles, as she used to do at home, not for any special occasion, but just to make things intimate and nice. She was cheery as she hadn't been in some time, thinking now about preparations for going back home. She was in such a loving, accommodating mood, she even agreed to go sit in the hot tub with Perry after dinner and sip some more wine — not just on her lawn chair outside the tub, but right in it, sharing the experience with him as he liked her to do.

There was a Santa Ana wind, the dry, mysterious wind off the desert that supposedly spooks some people, causing migraines and melancholy, but Perry and Jane had both found the phenomenon to be enjoyable, romantic. Stray leaves and tiny sticks blew around the yard, and the air was cleansed of smog, made sharp and penetrating. You could even see some stars.

Jane said she'd like to have a little party before going back, just Ned and Kim and Kenton and his wife maybe, a closing out, a rounding out of the time together, a gracious end to the era.

That was when he told her about Archer's new offer.

She listened in silence, sipping from her wine, her expression unchanging. He told her all the implications, what it would mean to be an executive, as well as the extra money, and his obligation to see the show through to success. He explained how it didn't mean giving up the East for good; it meant they could go back for the spring semester, and then come back to L.A. the following summer perhaps. It would mean they could be bi-coastal, have the best of both worlds.

Still, she remained silent.

"Don't give me an answer right now," he said. "Play with the whole idea. See how it feels."

She didn't say anything, but slowly pulled herself up out of the tub and toweled off. Then she went inside.

Perry sat out a while longer, wondering if this was going to be a terrible scene. Finally he decided he'd better face it, whatever it was.

When he went in the bedroom, Jane was lying on the bed, nude, staring at the ceiling. He sat down beside her and put his arms around her.

"I love you," he said.

He feared she might turn away but she kissed him, fiercely, then holding his face in her hands she stared at him, intently, as if she were seeing him for the first time, or had discovered he was a stranger or some kind of schizophrenic maniac, but before he could protest or question her, she was kissing him again, pulling him to her, and wildly, ferociously, she made love to him, leading, pulling, encompassing, enveloping, smothering, leaving him drained and dazed. He dropped, blank and mindless, to a deep maw of sleep.

Perry woke a little after dawn, revitalized and ready to roll into action. Jane was obviously zonked, curled into the fetal position, and he didn't want to wake her. He was full of ideas and energy, and wanted to go in early to the office and dash off some memos for the new story lines to discuss with Hal and the other writers. He had to stifle a pleased chuckle at the little idea that was developing now in his teeming brain — Jack secretly goes to cooking school, and he and Laurie fight over who gets to make the meal for a party! Anyway, the important thing was to get as much work in as possible since he would have to spend a lot of time today on getting his other plans in order, now that he knew Jane was amenable to staying on for the next leg of the journey.

He left her a love note, suggesting they go out to dinner that night, at the dramatic restaurant on the hill, to celebrate.

California, here I come,
You're so tasty, yum-yum-yum

He sang as he drove to work, beating his palm on the steering wheel in time to the music.

Perry picked up a chilled bottle of Schwamsberg champagne on the way home from the studio, and was already undoing the foil as he swung in the door, calling to Jane on the way to the kitchen.

"Come and get it!" he crooned happily as he popped the cork, pouring the bubbly elixir into two of the tulip-shaped glasses, but there was no answer. He took a tantalizing taste from his own glass, and called again. Still getting no reply, holding the bottle by the neck, he went outside, wondering if Jane was working in the garden, but there wasn't any sign of her. He went back in the house, swinging the bottle along at his side, wondering if maybe she had taken a walk or gone to the market or resumed the photography of Santa Monica Boulevard she had once given up as too depressing. She wasn't in the study, or the bathroom, and finally, he found her, in the bedroom.

She was packing.

"Hey!" he said. "What's going on?"

She didn't even look up, much less answer.

"I asked you what you're doing."

She continued neatly taking her clothes out of drawers, folding them, and placing them in her big suitcase, which was lying, open on the bed, already half filled.

"Jane?"

She acted as if he wasn't in the room, or maybe didn't exist at all.

"Jane, I'm talking to you," he said patiently.

He had never seen her like this before. She seemed perfectly calm and composed, her movements were sure and steady, yet she continued to ignore his questions as well as his presence. It was as if she were in a trance. For a moment he wondered if she was under the influence of some kind of drug.

"Please, love," he said gently. "Won't you answer me? Won't you tell me what you're doing?"

She didn't look at him, she continued her activity, but at least she made a response, she uttered a word.

"Packing," she said.

"Why?" he asked. "Where are you going?"

"Home."

"I don't understand."

"I know you don't."

He was still holding the bottle of champagne in his right hand. He looked down at it, as if he wondered how it had got there. A few wisps of the frosty potion were still curling out of the mouth of the bottle, like smoke from a gun. He set the bottle down on the dresser, and leaned against the wall, trying to brace himself. His heart was pounding wildly, but he tried to speak calmly, without letting his voice go quivery.

"Are you leaving me?" he asked.

"I'm leaving *here*."

"It's the same thing."

"No, it's not. You're the one who's left. I want to go back to where we were."

"But we will! I explained all that. I even spoke to Al today. He's going to talk to the dean. He's sure he can fix it! I told him we'd be back for Christmas, just like you want. Then I'll teach the next semester."

He went to her, taking her by the arm.

"Dammit, don't you understand?" he demanded. "We can go back for Christmas. We can live there and teach, and come out here and do TV and movies. We can do both, live in both places. We can *have it all!*"

She shook his hand off, and resumed her packing, placing in a dress with extra precision.

"I don't want it all," she said.

"What the hell *do* you want?"

186

"I want you. Us. The way we used to be. The life we used to have."

She was still speaking calmly but there were tears coming out of her eyes now.

He went to her, put his arms around her, held her to him.

"I love you," he said.

"But you love this more."

He broke away.

"What do you mean, 'this'?"

"What you're doing. Here."

"I love it, sure, is that a crime? Do I have to choose? Between my wife and my work?"

"You have to think about the way you want to live."

She turned away, wiping her eyes, and resumed the packing.

"You really are leaving me," he said.

"No. I'll be home. You can come back anytime you want."

"But now — just when all this is breaking for me, just when I need you with me, you're cutting out, is that it?"

"You won't even miss me."

"That's crazy. Listen, you've forgot your own advice."

"What are you talking about?"

"When we first came out and *I* was the one who wanted to pack it in, after that crazy network meeting. You told me to hang in there, you told me if the people bothered me, just to pretend I was a 'field anthropologist,' doing work among the 'Dippy-dos.' Well, you can do the same. You can start taking pictures of the people here. You haven't even been using your camera, lately."

"I know. That's one reason I have to leave. I can't even *see* things any more. Everything looks the same to me. Flat and lifeless. Repetitious."

"Jane, please stay."

"You don't even know I'm here. You're living the show. You'll be able to do it more freely with me gone anyway."

She shut the suitcase and pressed the lid, snapping the catches.

Something in Perry wanted to yank the suitcase open and throw everything to the floor, fling Jane down on the bed and make mad, passionate love, make her stay. He felt paralyzed, though. He stared at her and blinked, trying to put her in focus, trying to see clearly what was happening, yet everything seemed fuzzy and unreal.

"Excuse me," she said. "I have to take a shower and change." She brushed past him.

He picked up the bottle of champagne and walked out to the backyard. He sat down in the lawn chair, next to the hot tub, and took a long pull from the bottle. His head felt bubbly and numb. He held the bottle in both hands and looked at the label.

Blanc de Blanc.

Blank dee Blank.

Blankety blank.

Blank.

He closed his eyes, put the bottle to his mouth, and tilted his head back, gulping.

Blank.

Perry woke to a feeling of emptiness. His arm reached out automatically in the bed beside him but no one was there to touch. Nothing. He had a sense of vacancy, of blank space. He jumped up, dressing as fast as if the house were on fire, and got out into the street, into the car, into a restaurant and up to the counter, where he ordered and ate a cheese omelette, toast, blueberry muffin, orange juice, coffee, and an order of fruit salad. Filling up. Trying to cover the hole he felt inside himself, the cavity.

Get busy. Take action. Take care of the things you've been putting off. Like the option on "The Springtime Women." There was a gold mine, just waiting to be used. Vaughan had called a few days ago to say Harrison Ford had actually read the story and liked it! This was no Hollywood hype, this was a real project, ready to fly.

"What about your agreement with Ned Gurney?"

Perry jumped, as if a pin had stuck him.

That was Jane's voice.

"My agreement with Ned was only *verbal*," he said out loud, as if he were answering her back.

Damn. Was he flipping out? No. This was normal, it was simply a reaction to his wife's being gone when he was used to having her there all the time.

He had never mentioned to Jane his whole conversation with Vaughan about "The Springtime Women," fearing she wouldn't understand. And she didn't! At least the way her voice sounded just now she didn't, but that of course was just Perry's imagination. He took a deep breath, steadying himself. Forget about Jane. There was nothing in the world to stop him from going ahead with Vaughan since he had nothing signed with Ned Gurney. He was simply taking a much better deal. He was simply being practical.

Perry whistled to himself as he drove to his agent's office, reflecting how, as if by the miracle of his simply being in Hollywood, that once-modest short story of his had become something of a hot property!

"I thought you told me you were going to do this project with Ned Gurney," his agent said.

Charlie Brindle was one of the old school of Hollywood agents. It figured. Perry had gone to him through the recommendation of his literary agent in New York, who himself was one of the old school of the publishing world. Clement LeMoyne had been a friend and supporter of Perry's ever since he sold his first stories, and was perfectly good at negotiating nice little distinguished literary works, but he wasn't really in tune with the pulsing new world of the bi-coastal entertainment business. He in fact had seemed almost as shocked as the faculty of Haviland College when he heard Perry was going out to work on a TV script in Hollywood. LeMoyne had warned him about "getting in too deep" or "with the wrong sort of crowd" (as if he were a kid going off to college!) and strongly recommended Charlie Brindle as the right man to handle his business out there.

"He's one of the solid old-timers," LeMoyne had said. "Not one of these flashy new shark types. You can trust this man. His word is his bond."

Charlie Brindle was an old-timer, a man at least in his seventies. He did not even look like a Hollywood agent, but with his unbuttoned vest and loosened tie he reminded Perry more of those veteran crusty city editors of newspaper legend. He had done all right in handling Perry's business up to now, but he obviously wasn't in synch with the new breed of operators, or familiar with the new way of doing things in the supercharged new bi-coastal, megabuck world of tomorrow. Perry tried patiently to explain the situation to him.

"I never signed any papers with Ned, and it just so happened that Vaughan Vardeman, who's an old friend of mine from way back, is in a far better position to make this happen. He even has Harrison Ford hot about it."

"You told Ned Gurney you and he had a deal on this. You even shook hands on it. Have you told him you want to sign this option with Vardeman instead?"

Charlie held up the option papers Vaughan's lawyer had sent over, as if he were exhibiting damning evidence.

"No, I haven't told Ned about this, but of course I eventually will, and I believe he'll understand and want me to do what I think is best for me."

Charlie tossed the papers across the desk at Perry, as if they were a bad piece of copy he was giving back to a cub reporter.

"That's not the way I've done business for forty-five years."

"Well then," Perry said, trying to keep his voice calm, "I guess I better find someone who'll do business for me the way it's done today."

"I'm sure you'll have no trouble," said Brindle, lighting up a big black cigar.

Perry grabbed the contract with hands slightly quivering from rage and stuck it into the inside pocket of his new safari jacket. He had got up and turned to go, when Charlie called after him.

"Hey Perry, let an old-timer give you a tip. A piece of free advice."

"I'm listening."

"Go home. Go back East and write your books. It sounded like a good life. Go on back, before it's too late."

Perry made a snortlike little laugh.

"I'll remember that," he said.

"There'll come a time," said Charlie, "when you will."

There are times when everything falls into place, times of being so in tune with the world and with the work you are doing that it seems instead of thrashing around to find something you need, all you have to do is think you need it and it appears, like something materializing at the touch of a wand, to the trill of the magic music, outlined by a lacing of stardust.

That's how fortuitously Ravenna Sharlow appeared.

It was the day after Perry's visit to old Charlie, and he had decided to take off an hour or two in the afternoon to call on some agents. He hated to take any time away from the lot, but this was crucial. He not only wanted to get the option with Vaughan nailed down, he wanted to have his new deal as executive story consultant negotiated, making sure he was getting all he deserved in that lofty new position. He tried to put all this out of mind while he focused on the script he was writing, but just as he began to really concentrate, a sudden knock came at the door.

"Yes?" he shouted, with a mixture of annoyance and urgency.

The door opened, and standing inside it was a tall, sun-bronzed, ravishing blond woman in a tailored, businesslike suit with a jacket, plain silk blouse, and medium-length skirt that hovered over fabulous, perfectly shaped calves, ending in high-heeled sandals held together by some sort of gossamer threads. Perry's first thought was that she must be either an actress or some powerful new network or studio executive, at least a vice-president.

"Thank you," she said.

Her voice was husky, provocative.

She must be an actress, he figured.

"For what?"

"The fabulous show you've created."

She must have just read for a part — they were casting for a teacher friend of Laurie's, and though this woman was far more glamorous than Perry had imagined for the role, she would certainly be an attraction for the show. Might even be worth tilting the story a bit to make it exactly right for her.

She stepped forward, extending her hand with a jangle of bracelets, and shook Perry's hand, gripping it firmly, looking him squarely in the eyes.

"I'm Ravenna Sharlow," she said.

"Perry Moss."

"I know. I'm a great fan of your work."

"Why, thank you. Are you here to read for a part?"

"Oh, no! I brought in a client of mine who's reading for that juicy role of Laurie's new teacher friend. It's a gem. Like everything you do."

"Thanks, but I can't take credit for that. Hal Hagedorn wrote that particular episode."

She shrugged off that information with a toss of her blond mane, throwing her head back proudly.

"It's your show — it's all your creation, no matter who develops little variations on the theme."

"Well, that's very generous of you. Please sit down."

She sat with smooth grace on the little folding chair, making it seem like a throne. She crossed her legs, and the skirt rode up to the lovely, shimmering knee.

"So, you're an agent?" Perry asked.

"Partly that. I'm also a business manager for my clients."

She smiled.

"I have a degree in business administration, as well as drama. I'm a full-service agency."

He felt his throat go dry.

"I believe it," he said. "Well, you represent actors. Do you know anyone like yourself, but who handles writers?"

"Writers," she said, "are my favorite."

"This is amazing," he said. "Uncanny. I was just about to go looking for a new agent."

"I'm sure the top people in town would be happy to have you. You could take your pick. I'm only a small operation, myself—just me and my secretary — but let me confess that representing you would be the greatest thrill of my entire career. It would be like — well —"

She shifted her legs, recrossing them, and smoothed a hand over one radiant knee.

"— like having my most outrageous dream come true."

He felt himself swell, grow expansive. Here was this gorgeous, no doubt brilliant woman sitting before him, herself a fantasy of flesh and brain, and he, Perry Moss, had the power to make her dream come true!

"Are you free for lunch today?" Perry asked.

"On two conditions."

"Name 'em."

"One, you let me use your phone to cancel the lunch date I had till just now. Two, you let me take you to my own favorite spot."

Perry leaned back in his seat, smiling.

"You got it," he said.

The place was suffused with gold.

You followed Sunset Boulevard to get there, passing through the flashy vulgarity of the Strip, curving down into the lush, palm-lined precincts of Beverly Hills, the famous pink stucco hotel that was paradise for fortunate, important pilgrims from the East, past the fairy-tale mansions of tropically inspired imagination, down and up and around the hills but still coursing west through the lesser pastel apartment buildings and subdivision homesteads spread through Pacific Palisades, and finally, plunging headlong toward the ocean itself, crashing right up against the thin line marking the edge of a world, the Pacific Coast Highway; and there it was, not just a symbol or phrase but the real smashing surf and bald rock and enormous hot sky of it, reminding him again with a thrill where he was: *the Coast.*

If you kept careening down Sunset through the traffic light on the highway you'd smash right into the restaurant, but you stopped, slowed, took a dogleg jog across the highway and into a parking lot, then crunched on foot across the gravel and into the nautical entrance (lobster nets, cork floats, life preservers) where, as the door shut behind, you at once were bathed in a brilliant intensity of sunbright light and deeply chilled air. Blinking, looking down at the sawdust floor softens the glare, and soon, seated at your smooth wooden table of butcher-block wood, you become accustomed to the juxtaposition of natural and artificial elements, sunlight and ice-cold air-conditioning, everything intensified, colors as well, deep sea blue reflected through the plate-glass view, but above and behind and over all, the radiance of sun, the sense of gold, its elemental presence.

The gold reverberated in the frosty glass mugs of beer, the fluted glasses of wine, those liquid shades of sun, and the customers consuming them, absorbing them, taking them into themselves, letting them circulate, being lifted by their magic, taking on their glow, so the gold of the place was inside the people as well as the room, and Perry felt a part of it, felt it a part of him, not just a visitor now or a tourist, but participant. *One of them.*

To make it complete was Ravenna, across from him, golden girl, or once a girl grown into goddess now, of this time and place, rising queen resplendent as the light glistened from her long gold hair and smooth gold skin, and she fluently spoke the eloquent, lullaby language of the realm.

"Two hundred thousand, maybe two-fifty, for an overall deal in television with a studio, for a year, I could get you that tomorrow, whenever your own show's over or your contract is up, whenever you want."

"Wow."

The innocent word popped out before he could restrain it.

"But you wouldn't want that," Ravenna revealed.

"I wouldn't?" he asked, wondering. "I mean — well, it sounds OK — but hey — how would I know?" he asked, fumbling.

"You'd have to be 'exclusive' to that studio," she explained. "You wouldn't be able to entertain offers from anyone else, so your hands would be tied for a year, just for the guarantee of two-fifty."

"*Oh* — well, hell," he sniffed, shook his head, sighed at the narrow escape, the seemingly golden trap that would have closed on his God-given, constitutionally guaranteed freedom to make more than a mere quarter million in one precious year.

"I don't want to jostle the Vardeman deal, let's leave that stand as is."

Ravenna had of course immediately understood and approved Perry's decision to give the option to his story "The Springtime Women" to a proven producer of power like Vaughan instead of risking it with Ned Gurney. She was happy to handle the whole matter, including, if need be, explaining to Ned why he wasn't going to get the rights, when the time came. She was also dying to meet the Vardemans.

"If Vaughan gets that off the ground," she said, "as I'm sure he will, and you have that credit under your belt, we'll be talking two-fifty, three for your next feature script."

Two-fifty, three?

Let's see. It took two months to write a two-hour pilot, which is about the length of a regular feature film, so — well, figuring it would take more time, a feature after all was an art form, a goddam *film*, you wanted a little leeway, a little creative breathing space, so double that, say it took four months to do the script, well, you could turn out three a year, which at two-fifty, or three —

Wheee!

Three-quarters of a million, or better still, at the higher rate, which by then would be only deserved, $900,000, or almost a mill —

million a year —

meant —

millionaire —

me!

He raised his glass, the cool gold kissing his lips, gold reflecting back from her shimmering hair, gold pouring in through the windows, shining in the glasses of wine and beer, paving the sawdust floor, golden, gold, up and down and all around, everywhere.

A millionaire needs a staff.

Poor old Charlie Brindle didn't understand such things. Ravenna not only understood it was necessary, she understood how to do it, whom to hire.

The best.

Reg Melman, the powerful young attorney whose silk shirt unbuttoned to the waist and array of gold chains around his neck made him seem to Perry as if he might be able to grab a microphone and entertain a Vegas nightclub audience with ease, was way overbooked with clients, but as a favor to Ravenna was willing to take on Perry, not even charging a fee but simply taking five percent of all entertainment earnings. That meant Reg had confidence in Perry's earning potential, or the five percent would hardly make the paperwork worth his time.

Stu Sherman, the suave accountant whose office in one of the towers of Century City on the Avenue of the Stars reminded Perry of an elegant art gallery, served Perrier in fluted glasses while discussing the new client's overall financial picture.

Perry was grateful that Ravenna had come along to literally hold his hand. She helped translate. When Stu wanted to know if he had his liquid assets in T-Bills or money market or stocks and bonds, Perry looked blankly at Ravenna, who, through a series of gentle questions, was able to ascertain that Perry had $53,000 from his earnings in television thus far in a savings account in his local bank. Perry realized this was like admitting he had put the money in an old sock and hid it under the bed.

"Don't worry, darling," Ravenna reassured him, "Stu will get into something useful right away."

Stu thought the most important thing was to get Perry into a nice little condo that would serve as a shelter against taxes as well as the wind and rain.

"Can I afford that?" Perry asked.

"You can't afford not to," Stu advised.

"We'll see Clarice von Grebhart right away," announced Ravenna.

"Perfect," Stu Sherman said.

"Who's she?" Perry asked.

"The best realtor in Beverly Hills. *And* the most adorable."

Clarice was an absolute dream, a puckish, gaminelike, long-legged creature with short, charmingly mussy hair, clad in a thrift-shop Girl Scout uniform and high-heeled red sandals and intriguing dark glasses. She looked more like a movie star than a realtor, but Perry was beginning to observe that many of the women who worked here in everyday jobs, secretarial and sales and clerical, perhaps in defensive reaction, looked more glamorous than most of the actual movie actresses he met.

Clarice, gunning her cute little red convertible all over town, found Perry a terrific little bargain — not in Beverly Hills, of course, which he hardly could afford, but near the little place he and Jane had rented for the summer in the flats of Hollywood. It was a new high rise, a good investment property, and Clarice was able to get the owner down a little so that Perry could pick up a handy little one-bedroom for $249,000. Ravenna whipped out her pocket calculator and figured it would mean Perry would be paying about $3200 a month for his mortgage, but with all his prospects this was quite within reason, especially since it was a tax write-off.

Clarice buzzed them over to the Polo Lounge and they had Mimosas to celebrate. Perry panicked for a moment, realizing he had no furniture and didn't want to spend the time — that was now more important than the money — to go out and buy it, but Ravenna assured him that was no problem, he could get whatever he wanted through Abbey Rents.

It was easy.

Everything here was easy.

He wondered if Clarice and Ravenna were easy to have, but the truth was Perry was quite happy being with them, being seen with them, without any desire to go to bed with them. In fact, the show was still taking up all the energy he might ordinarily have for sex, which was just as well. That made everything easier, too.

X

AT FIRST PERRY didn't notice anything.

He had come in late to the office after stopping at the escrow company to sign the papers for purchasing his new condo, and was so absorbed in thoughts of his burgeoning personal empire that it wasn't till he nosed his car into his parking space that he realized something was wrong.

People were running.

Perry's immediate fear was that the building must be on fire, but as he swung out of his car and looked around he saw no evidence of flames, or even smoke. Besides that, people were not only running out of the building, others were running inside. Everyone looked purposeful but grim, evidently exercising control over some kind of generalized panic.

What the hell could have happened?

Had the series been canceled even before it went on the air?

Had Archer Mellis resigned his post at Paragon in order to take over the Chrysler Corporation?

Had additional restrictions from the network's Department of E. and A. provoked Ned Gurney into threatening the life of Stu Sturdivant?

Damn. You couldn't leave the lot for an hour without missing out on some life-or-death crisis. Striding toward the building, but restraining himself from running until he knew what the hell was going on, and whether such panic was only an overreaction,

Perry swore to himself he would never again stray off on his personal empire-building business during working hours. Just before he got to the building the cute little ten-year-old actress who was playing a neighbor of Jack and Laurie's burst out of the building and started to dash past him, her pigtail flying. Maybe some tragedy had occurred on the set! Perry yelled after the little girl and grabbed her arm.

"Hey, what's going on?" he asked.

"Christ, man," the precocious tot piped up, "didn't you read the trades this morning?"

"No, I didn't," he admitted shamefully to this ten-year-old who had probably memorized the entire contents of *Variety* and the *Hollywood Reporter* over her Cocoa Pops that morning. "Why? What did they say?"

"We're going on Friday night against 'Dallas.' "

"You mean this show? 'The First Year's the Hardest'? "

"I don't mean 'The People's Court,' " sighed the little girl, as she turned to run off toward the set.

"That's impossible!" Perry yelled after her. "We're an eight o'clock show!"

"Read it and weep!" the little tyke called back over her shoulder.

This was absurd. The kid must be pulling some kind of sick joke on him. Perry stood watching her receding pigtail a moment, then turned and ran full tilt toward the office.

"Where's Ned?" Perry demanded in a kind of shout-screech, as he saw that the door to Gurney's inner office was flung open and the room was empty. Ned's secretary, looking so pale it seemed she had lost her suntan, said, "They're all at Archer's."

Perry took off in a sprint.

It looked like rehearsal for a new Samuel Beckett play, or a civil defense emergency room. Ken Spires was lying on his back on the floor, with his feet propped up on a chair at a forty-five-degree angle. Ned Gurney was sitting in a corner with his legs drawn up close to his body and his head resting on his knees, murmuring in a trancelike chant, "It's genocide, it's genocide, it's genocide . . ." Archer was pacing the room with the cordless phone cradled in his neck, saying, "Tell him I'll be there anyway. I'll be in his office waiting for him. If he's not in his office I'll be at his home. If he's not at home I'll be at his club. If he's not at his club —"

Archer's voice was extremely calm and modulated, and it was only his contrasting garb that seemed out of kilter. He was fitting gold cuff links into the starched striped dress shirt he wore with a regimental tie while he kept the phone receiver locked against his neck with his chin, but below the waist he had on only bikini undershorts, knee-length yellow sweat socks, and a pair of his hand-tooled cowboy boots. When his secretary rushed in with his darkest London suit, still in a cellophane cleaning bag, and a pair of highly polished black wing-tip shoes, Archer, still speaking into the phone receiver, hopped onto the edge of his desk and stuck out his legs. His secretary pulled off his cowboy boots, peeled off the yellow sweat socks, and handed him his black shoes and socks just as he was finishing his phone conversation — or rather, what seemed more like his monologue-edict to whomever he was speaking.

"You'll never find him," Ken Spires moaned fatalistically from the floor. "He's hiding from you."

"I'll find him," said Archer, slipping on the heavy trousers with the quick, certain facility of Clark Kent transforming himself into Superman in a phone booth.

"Find who?" Perry asked, drawing the first slight notice to himself from the others.

"Max Bloorman," groaned Ken from the floor. "Who else would put us up against Dallas?"

"It's genocide, it's genocide, it's genocide . . ." Ned continued chanting.

"What the hell happened to Amanda LeMay?" Perry shouted, hearing his voice crack. "She said the network was going to 'nurture' us."

The word *nurture* seemed to snap Ned Gurney out of his trance. He uncoiled from his fetal crouch in the corner, sprang to his feet, and waved both arms in the air.

"Nurture!" he yelled. "I'll show you what they mean by 'nurture'!"

He grabbed Perry by the arm and led him to Archer's desk, pointing to an empty spot on it.

"Look there. Imagine there's a fly sitting there. OK? Now, we're going to 'nurture' that fly. Just watch how we do it."

Ned raised his right hand, sticking out the thumb, like a weapon, and, gritting his teeth, smashed the thumb down on the imaginary fly, pressing and grinding until it would have surely been obliterated into dust.

"We have just 'nurtured' that fly!" Ned exclaimed, then cackled wildly before returning to resume his crouch in the corner.

"But what about Amanda?" Perry persisted. "I really thought she cared about us. About the show."

"That may have been her downfall," said Ken.

"You mean she's been demoted?" Perry asked incredulously.

"She's gone into independent production," Archer said, buttoning up the vest to his suit with sure, determined steadiness, like a knight putting on his armor.

"You mean she left us in the lurch to produce her own shows?" Perry asked with indignation.

A harsh, wild laugh came from Ken, who was still in his shock position on the floor.

"It means she's been fired, you rube," he said.

Perry didn't even mind the put-down from the usually gentle Ken. In fact, he felt it fit. Who else but a rube would have sunk all his cash into a new condo with a mortgage of $3,000 a month, assuming his new series was going to be that one-in-a-million hit before it even went on the air — before it even had a specified time slot?

Not even live coverage of the Second Coming could compete against "Dallas" on Friday night at nine.

Perry slumped to the floor, joining his colleagues.

"Poor Amanda," he said, for some reason finding it less painful to think of someone else's ill fortune.

"Don't worry about Amanda," said Ned. "She's swamped with offers."

He moved out of his crouch and stretched out full length on the floor.

Only Archer Mellis was grimly functional. He poked his arms into the suit jacket his secretary held for him, grabbed his attaché case, and swung toward the door, glancing back to point a pistol-like finger at his fallen troops.

"I'll try to get us shifted to a better slot," he said, "but in the meantime, we're on Friday night at nine, and let me remind you that J. R. Ewing is not just lying around on his butt right now. Let's go!"

Like boxers trying to rise before the count of ten, the three men dizzily struggled to their feet.

"Don't think poor."

Ravenna was squeezing Perry's hand and staring into his eyes like a hypnotist.

When he frantically called her to lament, with quivering voice, the terrible news of his show being matched against "Dallas" and ask if it was too late to get out of his purchase and sale agreement for the condo, Ravenna ordered him to calm down and meet her for dinner. She wielded her growing influence to get them a reservation at *Le Duc*, the newest and suddenly most chic French restaurant in Hollywood, whose cachet was matched only by its prices.

"Dallas" was all that Perry could say, as if that explained everything.

Perry felt a sudden lust for a double martini, straight up, as dry as the most malevolent Santa Ana wind in history. Luckily, when the waiter came to take their order for drinks, Ravenna shot a glance at Perry's troubled countenance and ordered for both of them.

"Bring us each a Kir Royale," she said with a sparkling smile and a wink to the waiter, as if they were there to celebrate some amazing stroke of fortune.

It was of course just the right thing — zippier and more festive than a plain glass of wine, and yet keeping Perry to his pledge of staying off the hard stuff. It was made of crème de cassis and that magical potion Perry still associated with the glow of his first happy days out here with Jane, that greatest of all elixirs, champagne.

By the end of the second drink, Perry realized he was crazy to even consider backing out of the condo deal. Ravenna reminded him that if the very worst happened and the show was canceled, he would simply move right onto the big deal for a feature film of his next story, produced by the powerful and popular Vardeman.

Perry's only danger, Ravenna clearly showed him, was in panicking, in imagining any kind of defeat, in even allowing himself to think of a circumstance in which he had to worry about such minor matters as a $3,000-a-month mortgage. Defeat was self-fulfilling; think poor, become poor.

The food was reassuringly rich. After the morels, flown in fresh from France, after the *Volaille à la Vapeur de Truffes et Puree de Christophines*, after the *Sorbet Maison aux Fruits Exotiques*, Perry felt much more optimistic. When the coffee and brandy arrived, so did an impeccably dressed, slim gentleman named Scotty Shearson, whom Ravenna had invited to stop by and join them for a drink. Scotty had done some acting off and on, but now he had his own business, in the area of personal public relations, which involved getting his clients' names mentioned by the right people, in the right way, in the right places — newspaper columns, for instance, even radio and television shows that dealt with the world of entertainment and its personalities.

A "personality," Perry gathered, was someone who, with the right professional attention, might become a "celebrity." He of course admitted to no such self-seeking aspiration for his own sake, but Ravenna pointed out that any public attention that came his way right now could only help the show — just when it needed all the help it could get. Furthermore, Perry was impressed with the positive way in which Shearson viewed what only hours before had seemed the unmitigated disaster of the scheduling of his fragile new program.

"I love it," said Shearson. "It's the old David-against-Goliath plot — and you know who won!"

As if to help celebrate the upset victory in advance, the restaurant owner himself sent a round of cognacs to their table. Scotty raised his glass in a toast to Jean Paul, evidently a close friend, which explained how Ravenna had been able to secure this choice table at the last moment in such a hot new dining spot. Among Scotty's many services, he aided his clients in securing the right tables at the right places, so they could be viewed by the right people and later be reported in the right columns as having been seen there. As if all this weren't enough, Scotty revealed (*sotto voce* of course) an exclusive bit of info he had heard from sources deep inside the network, so dangerously new that its reverberations had not yet even been reflected in the ratings:

" *'Dallas' is slipping.*"

Ravenna gave a squeeze to Perry's knee.

"And *you*, darling," she whispered, "are on the way *up*."

Perry went home feeling like a million dollars, justifying his addition of a personal public relations counselor to his growing staff with the age-old logic that it takes money to make money. Besides, Shearson's retainer was only a token $250 a week, and it was, anyway, as Ravenna pointed out, tax deductible, which in Perry's thinking had come to seem like the same thing as free.

"Welcome to kamikaze time," said Ned.

He was holding a beer, trying to seem jaunty. Perry was glad that Ned at the last minute had invited the "First Year" inner sanctum to gather at his home to have dinner and watch the show, as they had done for the pilot, but this of course was quite a different circumstance. Instead of excited anticipation there was simply nervous tension, a sense that if you accidentally bumped into someone you might get a nasty little electric shock. Kim, who looked bleary-eyed and bedraggled in baggy blue jeans and one of Ned's old button-down dress shirts, had not made one of her wonderful curries but ordered out an assortment of deli stuff from Greenblatt's — sandwiches, deviled eggs, chicken wings. Instead of a snappy, red-coated bartender there was simply a variety of bottles arrayed on a card table, but most people seemed to be taking cans of beer from a big cooler on the patio.

The cast of guests was different, too.

The main difference for Perry was that Jane wasn't there. He had waked that morning missing her more than usual, feeling her absence like an ache. He thought how nice it would be to have her comfort, her hand-holding, her support. He had called her, hoping to get some of that on the phone, but he realized at once it was a mistake. She didn't seem to understand the do-or-die nature of the coming evening's crisis. She actually complained that Perry hadn't asked how she was doing herself, how things were going in Vermont. (*Vermont?*)

Oh well. Kenton Spires's wife was missing, too, off on some therapeutic shopping spree in New York. Perry was just as glad. They wouldn't have to put up with her whining over how she missed Bloomies.

Unexpectedly, Kim's buddy Liz Caddigan, the actress, was there, looking crisp and fresh, perhaps because she had nothing to do with "The First Year's the Hardest." Perry was a bit unnerved to see her, feeling this gathering should have been limited to "the family," those directly involved with the show, as if tonight's airing were a private and intimate affair. Against "Dallas," it might in fact be just that.

Watching was pure agony, knowing that at the same time, just a channel away, the flash and flesh of "Dallas" was being offered. "The First Year" seemed now too slow, too gentle, too wispy to survive in this real world. If only they had known, if only they had designed it for sophisticated, late-night viewing! If only the censors hadn't prevented them from at least having that last scene of lovemaking in the kitchen!

At one point they flipped to Dallas during a commercial, only to have their worst fears confirmed by watching the fascinatingly evil, magnetic J.R. in bed with some exotic young beauty, with an ice bucket of champagne at their side!

"Well," said Ned, "at least he's doing it in the bedroom. At least they didn't let *him* do it on the kitchen floor."

205

"Of course not," said Kenton. "J.R. may be ruthless, but he's not kinky."

At the end, Perry felt bloated, yet had another beer. Everyone decided it was best to get to bed early. There was nothing much to say.

Perry gave Liz a ride home and she invited him in for coffee

"Do you have any of that brandy left?" he asked.

She smiled.

He settled himself on the couch this time, feeling an anxious, aching mixture of anger, frustration, and lust.

It was the first time he'd been to bed with any other woman since he met Jane more than five years before. He told himself that she was the one, after all, who had left him, had physically left his bed and living quarters and gone back clear across the country by her own choice. He had nothing to feel guilty about, he assured himself.

Still, he was clumsy and inept in bed, and finally, inadequate.

Liz lit a cigarette. She was coolly comforting, in a detached, almost clinical sort of way.

"You have the show on your mind," she said. "I understand."

"Hell. I'm sorry."

"Listen, that's what it's like when you're doing a series."

He dressed quickly, sheepishly.

"Call me when you're on hiatus," she said.

"When I'm what?"

"When the show is *on hiatus*. You know. That's the break between production orders."

"Oh," he said. "Sure. Thanks."

"Believe me. You'll be relaxed then."

"You're too soft."

Archer Mellis stood ramrod straight. His hands were clasped behind him and his feet were planted apart in the military position of at ease, yet his manner was one of full attention. He was wearing one of his khaki shirts with epaulets, and khaki pants tucked into paratrooper boots. He looked as if he might be about to order his men to jump, whether they had any parachutes or not.

Perry glanced over at Ned, wondering if he, too, was feeling lonely.

"Shouldn't Kenton be here?" Perry blurted out.

"Kenton's out," snapped Archer.

"I know he's out shooting," Perry said, "but they're just over at stage three, it's only a few minutes to —"

"He's out of the show," Archer said firmly.

Ned jumped up.

"Surely," he said with disbelief, "you're not going to yank him in the middle of —"

"He can finish this episode," Archer said.

Ned winced, and sat down.

"My God," he said, "were the ratings *that* bad?"

They had decided not to check the overnights on the weekend, figuring Monday morning would be plenty soon enough. Before anything else, they had been summoned to this meeting in Archer's office.

"You got a ten," Archer said.

Ned grabbed his head.

"A *ten*," he said. Then he burst out laughing. "It's too bad a ten doesn't mean what it meant for Bo Derek."

Perry, catching Ned's hysteria, said, "Does that mean there were only ten people watching? You know, I kind of had that feeling — that only about ten people in the whole country were watching our show."

"I'm glad you gentlemen are amused," Archer said.

Ned sat back down and Perry bit his lip again. He felt lightheaded.

"All right, in all seriousness," Ned said, "it's not fair to make Kenton the fall guy. We're all just as responsible. Why pick on Kenton?"

"Max thinks Kenton's direction is too pastoral," Archer said.

Perry remembered that was the very word that Archer had originally used in praise of Kenton's direction — its "pastoral" quality, which he said was so classy, so class-*ic*, so superior to the jangled junk of network television, a distinguished "style" that would put a distinguished stamp on "The First Year's the Hardest," set it apart from the run-of-the-mill stuff.

By now, however, Perry had his mouth under control. He bit his lip and did not mention any of the above.

"Pastoral," was all Ned Gurney said, rolling the word around with a kind of nostalgia.

"And I happen to think Max is right," Archer said.

"Do you think he was right to throw us on at nine Friday night against 'Dallas'?" Ned asked.

"Listen, Ned, this is not Broadway, this is network television. We have to be ready for everything. Max explained to me certain factors that overrode earlier considerations."

"You had a long talk in New York with Max himself?" Ned asked.

"I spent a great deal of time with him," Archer said. His chin jutted slightly forward, with pride. "Max and I watched the show together Friday night."

Awesome, as the kids would say. It was sort of like a bishop coming back from Rome and telling the priests he had spent an evening in prayer with the pope. Max of course wasn't the head man of the network, but he was the highest one that mortals could commune with; the head man was unseen except by divine visitation, like God.

Archer, perhaps feeling more relaxed and comfortable merely by the recollection of his private audience with the powerful man, leaned back against his desk, folding his arms across his chest.

"The important thing is," he went on, "Max believes in your show. He wants to hang in there with you."

"If Max is so committed to us," Ned asked, "is he going to take us out of the most suicidal time slot a new show could have?"

"He's going to personally keep an eye on your show, decide what's the best way to go with it."

"I might suggest, as executive producer, that I think the best way to go might be to the eight o'clock time slot we were promised in the first place, and that we designed the show to fit."

"There's no use going backwards," Archer said.

"It's not a matter of 'back,' for God's sake," Ned said. "If he keeps us on Friday at nine it's a matter of *down*."

"Not if you get stronger," Archer said.

"How? What are you talking about?"

"Max thinks your future lies in becoming harder."

Perry could feel his ears getting hot and his heart beginning to pound.

"In all due respect," he said, "we've finished shooting three shows, all approved by the network, on the following stories: Jack takes cooking lessons, Laurie takes karate lessons, and the two of them buy a home computer. Those subjects were conceived and designed for an eight o'clock family-viewing hour, which is soft, as I understand it."

"Correct," said Archer.

"Now," Perry continued, "we have developed outlines for three new shows that have just been approved by the network as well. These scripts involve Jack and Laurie joining the town bowling league, Laurie getting angry at Jack when he takes *her* side in a fight she's having with her father, and Jack's old friend who was a football hero coming for a visit to try to borrow money. None of these, either, can by any stretch of the imagination be thought of as hard shows, and our writers are already at work on them."

"Stop them," Archer ordered. "We'll eat the payment for the outlines and have those writers begin on three new tough, solid, hard stories."

"My God," Ned moaned, "we have to recycle our brains! Off the top of my head I can't even think of what hard stories our nice young couple could get involved in. Do they hold up a liquor store to solve the financial problems besetting a young married couple today? Is that the idea?"

"The idea," Archer said patiently, "is to deal with hard, real, topical subjects from today's headlines."

"Like what?" Perry asked, feeling reckless now. "Jack goes to join the rebel forces in El Salvador?"

"Since you gentlemen seem to be having difficulty with this," Archer said with heavy irony, "I'm sure you'll be pleased and relieved to know that Max himself has come up with three ideas for episodes that he expects you to carry out."

"Amazing," said Ned. "Is he going to tell us in person?"

"Lou Simmell is going to tell you."

"Who's he?" Perry asked.

"*She* is the new head of West Coast programming," Archer said, "and she'll be here to meet with you in half an hour."

Archer grabbed a pair of goggles off his desk and slipped them onto his forehead, just above his eyes.

"I take it you aren't staying for the meeting?" Ned asked.

"I'm flying to Tijuana for lunch with *La Pasionara*," the young executive said. "I hope to sign her."

"Isn't she rather ancient by now, if she's still with us?" asked Ned.

"You're probably thinking of the one from the Spanish Civil War," Archer explained. "This is the female matador out of East Rutherford, New Jersey. She's a natural for a two-hour movie, maybe a series."

"If you don't sign her," Perry said, feeling dizzy now, "maybe we can use her experience as a hard plot for Laurie."

Ned laughed, then extended his hand to Archer.

"Good luck, *amigo*," he said.

"I'll need it," Archer told him. "*La Pasionara* cut two ears and a tail yesterday. She's hot right now."

He quickly transferred some papers from attaché case to duffel bag and swung from the room, turning to give a quick salute and a "*Ciao*."

Lou Simmell was a brilliant young sociologist whose tough-minded ability to relate cultural trends to economics accounted for her meteoric rise at the network. She bristled with opinions, ideas, and proposals. Even her hair bristled, sticking out not in curls or ringlets but straight, like needles, giving a kind of porcupine effect. Her voice, cutting and quick, seemed to bristle as well.

"Your show has a unique potential," she told Ned and Perry. Somehow, she made that good news sound threatening.

"You have a chance," she continued, after a teacherlike pause to make sure her message had sunk in, "of capturing the most demographically desirable audience out there today — the YUMMIES."

" 'Yummies?' " asked Ned. "Are they the ones who buy the most food products?"

"They're the Young Upwardly Mobile Marrieds," Lou explained.

"I thought they were called 'YUPPIES,' " Perry said.

"Those are by definition *professional*. There are many upward mobiles out there who aren't in the professions, but who enjoy great earning power — people in sales, production, marketing, even small-business development."

"But you don't think they'd like our show the way it is?" Ned asked.

"There's a general recognition by all of us that you're too soft. The ten share proved it."

"I thought it proved we were up against 'Dallas,' without any previous promotion or advertising," Ned said.

"Advance promotion and ads would have only accounted for a change of a few points at most."

"What accounted for the forty share we got for the pilot?" Perry asked.

"You were only up against second-division baseball and stale magic."

"As you may know, Lou," Ned said pleasantly, "we originally were told we were going on at eight, to appeal to a younger audience."

"Max thinks that would be a waste of your potential to get the YUMMIES."

"Okay," said Ned, "we're supposed to go hard. How do we do it, and still maintain the premise and tone of the show?"

Lou pulled a paper from her attaché case.

"These are the topics you'll deal with in the next three shows —"

She looked up in such a way that Perry pulled out a notebook and pencil so he could write them down.

"All right," Lou said. "You'll deal with AIDS, toxic shock, and acid rain."

"My God," said Ned, "we'll kill off our entire family!"

The once ebullient family of "The First Year" company seemed itself stricken with some contagious malady.

A new and different mood set in, a gloomy sort of resolve that permeated the offices and suffused the set itself like a sort of odorless gas, an insidious chemical that set people's teeth on edge and bent them slightly forward as they walked, as if they were bearing some invisible burden.

Some people said it was only a natural reaction to the ratings. Getting a ten share, no matter how powerful the opposition, was bound to be demoralizing. To try to combat this defeatist mood, Perry took it on himself to prepare a memo citing statistics of how badly *all* shows had done against "Dallas" in the past season. The second-place show in that time slot usually didn't rise above the high teens, rarely hitting even a puny twenty, and the third-place spot was usually not much higher than the pitiful ten that "First Year" had garnered. Why, one two-hour special of a series, heavily promoted to try to make some inroad against J.R. and company, had come away with a thirteen! That was like egg on the face. And "First Year" had gone on unheralded, without fanfare. Their ten was nothing to be ashamed of!

Perry was proud of his morale-building memo; he even got a personal memo from Archer praising his memo. The elation lasted about as long as it did for the others on the show who read it — about a minute and a half. Maybe two full minutes if accompanied by a hit of black coffee.

Rumors now were rife, including assorted opinions on why the once-peppy company seemed to have lost its zest. Some said it wasn't the ratings at all, but the demise of Kenton Spires, whose gentle, supportive handling of cast and crew had created a benevolent spirit that everyone from the beginning had told Perry was rare on a set, almost a miracle. Archer, however, assured Ned and Perry in retrospect that Kenton's manner had really been a negative factor, subtly contributing to the essential softness of the show.

By hallowed show biz tradition there was a wrap party at the end of every production, whether it was a multimillion-dollar feature film with a star-studded cast, or merely an hour episode of a TV series. When the final take of the final scene was shot and the director had passed the word to print it, the first assistant director — in this case Rod Sampson — intoned the traditional words that ended production — "That's a wrap!" — and everyone would head for the beer and wine and crackers and cheese for an hour or so of comradely fellowship, a kind of family love feast of celebration and mutual congratulation for having done the job.

At the end of the last show that Kenton directed, however, there was no wrap party. A memo came down from Archer Mellis banning such an event, on the grounds that it was too "dangerous," citing the fact that after the last one, one of the actors had had a little too much wine and tripped and fallen on the gravel on the way to his car, causing a cut on his forehead that had to be bandaged, necessitating postponement of a scene he was in. Such hazards could not be tolerated, the Mellis memo said.

Of course the real reason was that Archer wanted to prevent the outpouring of sentiment that would naturally accompany the much-loved young director's departure from the show. But, like all such attempts at suppression of natural emotion, it only sprang up surreptitiously. One of the cast held a secret wrap party for Kenton in one of the trailers used for dressing rooms. There wasn't room for everyone, so people huddled around outside, speaking in hushed voices and sipping from paper cups of wine in the cool California night. Perry had the feeling he was in occupied Poland. He and Ned, after making an appearance to show their solidarity with Kenton and the cast and crew, went back to the office and invited Kenton to stop in for a final toast on his way home.

Kenton was calm. He was pale, but not perspiring. He confided in Ned and Perry that he had made a decision about his future. Or maybe it had been made for him. He knew the word was already around that he'd been dropped from the show. Since this was his first job on network television and he hadn't cut it, he knew it would be a terrific handicap to overcome out here. He was going back to New York. He was going to direct in theater and try to supplement it with teaching. Maybe some low-budget film work would come along. Whatever, he was leaving L.A. He made a little joke about his wife being pleased; she could go to Bloomingdale's every day now. Ned and Perry laughed. The sounds came out thin. The scary part was that they knew this bright and talented young man had done a terrific job, that he was not getting cut because of poor performance, but rather because the ratings were poor and a scapegoat was needed. It could have been any of them.

It was show business.

It was war.

After two weeks of preemptions for specials ("The Miss Tap Dancing America Pageant," and "The First Annual Husbands and Wives Weight-Lifting Competition Live from Las Vegas"), the second of the soft versions of "First Year" was sent like a poor sacrificial lamb against the all-devouring mastodon that was "Dallas."

Oh God. This "First Year" episode was the one about Jack and Laurie buying their first home computer.

Astonishingly, "First Year" got a fifteen share, improving by almost half! After another week of being preempted (a network news investigation of sexual abuse in the social-work profession), the final soft show (Laurie takes karate lessons) crept up to a sixteen, only two points behind the second-place show in the time slot.

Maybe Perry's show was actually "building." Maybe it was slowly, magically, against all odds, attracting an audience that would grow, perhaps even after a full season make some significant inroad against the most popular show in the known world. Maybe the phenomenon of "The First Year's the Hardest" would signal a shift in mass taste, a ground swell of yearning for subtlety and quality!

There was never a chance to find out.

The next episode of "First Year" was scheduled at a new time. The network announced, with considerable pride — not only in the show, but in its own courage and conviction on behalf of innovation and quality — that it was sticking to this new show despite its poor ratings, and was putting it into a new time slot, where it was more likely to "find its audience."

The new time slot was eight o'clock Sunday night.

That was the soft time of family viewing and family-type competition that the show was originally promised for.

But the first episode scheduled was the first of the hard shows, the controversial epic of AIDS.

The network cautioned families that the material might not be deemed by some parents as appropriate for young children.

The National Committee for Clean Television, a powerful volunteer organization based in Wyandotte, Tennessee, protested the subject matter of the AIDS show and warned its members as well as its friends in Congress that this episode was not suitable for family viewing.

Still, it was a better shot than going against Dallas.

The AIDS episode scored a twenty-six share, the first time out of the teens since the pilot! That at least was respectable.

Maybe Max Bloorman had been right after all in demanding the hard subject matter, and then in seeming contradiction putting the show in the family time slot just to stir controversy. Maybe the seemingly arbitrary and contradictory network moves were not really blunders but signs of strategic genius. On the other hand, maybe the quality writing and production of the show were at last finding an audience that appreciated good, adult entertainment.

None of that really mattered. The bottom line was that the show had a chance. If the "First Year" company could not enjoy the luxury of confidence yet, at least the many workers whose livelihoods depended on it now had legitimate rights to harbor that most basic ingredient of show business survival: hope.

XI

T HE WORD WOULD come down today.

Either the show would continue to be, or not to be.

Perry could only pick at his spinach salad. He didn't even have the appetite of a rabbit. How nice it would be, how comforting, to be walking the beach in Venice right now with Jane, listening to the surf, thinking of the moment's problems in some kind of perspective, and knowing no matter what happened he had his mate beside him. Instead, he was having lunch in the commissary with Ned. They were like a couple of old Kremlinologists, trying to assess the signs and portents that might be found in the behavior of the network brass.

Up to now, they had continued to hedge their bets. After the AIDS episode got a twenty-six share, the network gave the show two more script commitments, but hadn't ordered the actual production yet, or hinted at whether there would be a real renewal, a significant block of something like seven more episodes that would mean a fighting chance for the show to establish itself as a series. Now, with the second hard hour scheduled for next week and the third now finishing shooting, the powerful "they" of the network had to reach a decision. It could go either way.

Only last week, a series that Perry and Ned, no doubt in their elite/effete Eastern snobbery, considered a real turkey was renewed for a whopping thirteen hours, even though it had never got above a twenty-three share — less than the last episode of

"First Year." So why was the network sticking with this lackluster sitcom tale of two divorced women who start their own limousine service? Because, as Archer explained to Ned and Perry with a shrug, "Somebody up there likes it."

Somebody up there in Valhalla, the brass heaven of power and decision, had taken a fancy to the concept. Or maybe someone's wife liked it, or teenage daughter, or girlfriend. God only knew. Whichever God it was. Maybe Max Bloorman himself. Maybe the head man above him.

"Don't worry," Archer said suddenly, winking at Perry, "I think you'll get renewed."

Then he was gone.

Perry and Ned looked at each other, trying to ascertain what *that* meant. Was the young executive simply trying to perk up their flagging spirits? Did he know something he wasn't telling? Did the fact he looked at Perry directly and not at Ned when he said it have any significance?

"Let's go back to work," Ned said finally, "before we go crazy."

Perry tried to work on one of the newly commissioned scripts in which Jack has a recurrence of an old herpes infection and Laurie suspects him of having picked it up from some recent extramarital sexual encounter, but he couldn't concentrate. As well as worrying about the fate of the show, he was distracted by thoughts of the upcoming Thanksgiving holiday.

Even out here in Southern California some traditional ambience, a hint of roasting turkey and cranberries, seemed to leave a trace in the air, maybe only a vestigial memory, but still it was there, causing a twinge, a restlessness, a distraction. Perry got up and dropped down to Ned's for a break after an hour or so, but he was not in his office.

His secretary said he'd been summoned by Archer.

Maybe this was it.

Perry decided to wait and find out. He sat down in the little waiting room outside Ned's office and leafed through the day's copy of *Variety*, not really seeing the words, just for something to do. The moment Ned walked in he could read the disaster in his face.

Perry stood up, feeling dizzy.

"They dumped us, huh?" he asked, wanting to know the worst at once.

"No," Ned told him. "You got renewed. I'm the only one who was dumped."

Perry followed Ned into his office as the former executive producer began to empty his drawers, stacking papers on top of his desk, sorting and throwing some things in the wastebasket.

"This is crazy," Perry said. "There can't be any show without you."

"The network thinks otherwise. They think I'm not cut out to produce hard stuff."

"Bullshit! You're the only one who can do it and keep some quality, too. If you go, I go."

"Don't do anything rash. After all, it's your show."

"Not anymore, it's not. It belongs to Archer Mellis and the network as far as I'm concerned. And I'm going to tell him so right now!"

He told him so.

Archer told Perry to sit down.

"You can't leave the show," Archer said calmly. "You're the new producer."

"Are you kidding?"

"Who else knows the show as well as you? Who else could step in and take over?"

"But I'm a writer."

"Now you'll be a writer-producer. What the Guild calls a 'hyphenate.' "

Yes, Perry had heard about multitalented men who rose from the ranks of mere writers to become writer-producers or writer-directors. It was like being a double threat. And of course it meant more money. More power.

"I guess I'm shocked," Perry said. "I wasn't expecting this."

"Think it over."

"Yes, I'd like to do that. Can I have a little time?"

"You can let me know first thing in the morning."

"Thank you," Perry said.

Perry stuck one hand casually in the pocket of his silk-lined safari jacket, turned slightly to his left and lifted his chin.

Snap.

What a picture.

It was only his image in the full-length mirror in his bedroom, yet it seemed so perfect, so *apropos*, that he heard in his mind the quick snap of a shutter, imagined the photo, black and white and grainy on the printed page of a newspaper — the Entertainment section, say, of the L.A. *Times*, with identifying caption: THE PRODUCER.

He turned again, full profile now, and sucked in his gut. There was still a bit of a bulge, a reminder of his past, undisciplined life as a civilian. He would have to work on that. He was a leader now. He had to set an example. He smiled, wryly, not at all displeased, seeing himself now in full color on a slick magazine page — *People*, perhaps?

He was, after all, quite a story.

"The Transformation of Perry Moss."

From wimpy academic to powerful producer. In less than a year. Perry pictured a comic strip showing shy Professor Grimsby surreptitiously ducking into a telephone booth, quickly changing out of his ragged tweeds and rep tie into a silk-lined combat suit with a gold chain and emerging tan and trim as Darryl diLorenzo, movie producer.

Perry turned back full face to the mirror and crossed his arms over his chest, cocking his head and admiring who he was, what he had become.

A Hollywood Producer.

"Betrayer, you mean."

It was Jane's voice, clear as a bell. It was so real that Perry went out and looked around the living room, just to make sure she hadn't flown in to surprise him as some kind of joke, or maybe to express her anger about his replacing the man he once so esteemed. That's how she'd feel, of course, simply because she refused to understand how things worked out here. Perry went back and looked in the mirror again. He took a deep breath and stood up tall, taller, staring in his steely blue eyes, direct and unashamed.

Of course he felt badly about taking Ned Gurney's place, but if he didn't somebody else would. They could still be friends. It was nothing personal, it was business. Show business. It was dog-eat-dog and you better watch out for yourself. Perry gave himself a knowing wink in the mirror, then said aloud the simple slogan that was all he needed or wanted to live by in his powerful new incarnation as a hyphenate, a Hollywood writer-producer: "Go for it."

Off and running.

Archer announced over coffee in his office that he and Perry were due at the network later that morning to view the last episode of "First Year" with none other than Max Bloorman and the East Coast brass! They were out here making heavy decisions and thought so much of this show's potential they were willing to take an hour out of their valuable time to give the producers their own notes and comments *while they watched*. It was a unique opportunity. Archer suggested they take along Hal Hagedorn, whom he'd promoted to the post of story editor, now that Perry would not have time for his work with writers in his old role of story consultant. Perry agreed that Hal was the ideal choice, though he kind of wished Archer had asked his opinion first. No use nit-picking, though, things were rolling now. The East Coast brass would be waiting.

Perry assumed that the New York executives probably enjoyed their sorties to the Coast, and perhaps had worked this one in as part of their Thanksgiving holiday. He figured they would be in that kind of mood, shedding some of their Eastern burdens along with their three-piece suits for a week or so to relax and refresh themselves in this brighter and lighter landscape.

He was wrong.

It may have been the day before Thanksgiving, but Max Bloorman and his men were not on any kind of holiday. They wore dark suits with plain, dull ties, and reeked of cigar smoke, cologne, and power. Jowly and glowering, they spoke in growls, reminding Perry not so much of New York businessmen as members of the Soviet Politburo.

Bloorman himself, with his shiny bald head looming above his black suit, his bushy steel-gray brows hooding blank eyes underlined with deep purplish folds of flesh, might surely have been cast as a senior official of the KGB. His principal sidekick, Otis Runcible, was a small, immaculate man with black hair slicked straight back from his brow and an expression of grim deliberation reminiscent of the late Lavrenti P. Beria.

Perry was relieved when the grumbled introductions were over and the lights went out in the network's executive screening room. He figured if this episode on Jack and Laurie battling acid rain could get a human sigh out of these guys it could be subtitled "The Miracle Worker." He was not surprised when the only sound that came from the executives during the show was sporadic outbursts of coughing brought on by the inhalation of their heavy cigars.

When the lights went on, Max Bloorman and his men, who were seated at the front of the screening room, did not even bother to look back at the film's producers when they delivered their devastating notes. Hal, Perry, and even Archer had to lean forward to hear the snide and cutting comments that came from the powerful men down front, aimed at the ceiling like some of the smoke they blew. The show seemed to them "too soft," too "candy ass," there were scenes that were "chickenshit" and lines of dialogue as well as performances and direction that were "half-assed" and "pissy-ant."

"Too many eggheads," said Bloorman. "Especially that faggy professor."

"You mean Laurie's father?" Perry asked.

Lon Ridings, the actor who played that role, was a former Broadway cohort of Ned Gurney's, and probably the finest, most brilliant actor on the show.

"Her husband's one prof too many as it is," said Bloorman. "You should make her pop a cop. Get some guts in this show."

"Well, he can't give up his tenure now and join the town police force," Perry said.

"Why not?" asked Bloorman. "It would give him some balls."

"Max, I think the cop is a great idea," said Archer Mellis. "What if Jack's father is a cop?"

"Jack's father is a lawyer," Perry said.

Archer gave him a dirty look.

"We haven't seen him yet. He could be a cop, and move into town — maybe even move in with his son and his daughter-in-law and her family."

"Go for it," said Bloorman.

He stood up, got out a handkerchief, and blew his nose. He looked at the handkerchief, stuffed it back in his pocket, and walked toward the door without a word, his henchmen following.

"Thank you so much — this was invaluable," Archer called after them.

Perry, in despair as well as anger, called to the powerful executive.

"Excuse me, Mr. Bloorman, but is there anything you like about our show?"

Bloorman turned and stared at Perry, looking him up and down as if he were a street bum who had just begged for a dime.

"We renewed it," he said, spitting out the words like the annoying bits of cigar tobacco that flecked his big, fleshy lips. Then he pushed on out the door, his troops following.

Perry was happy to accept Ned Gurney's gracious invitation for Thanksgiving dinner. He felt he could use a little of Ned's style of "civilization" after that session with Max Bloorman and the East Coast brass. Jesus. They sounded like a rock group. Heavy Metal. Perry wished Ned had been there, had got red in the face and given those guys a piece of his mind. Perry had the producer's outfit but he didn't yet seem to know how to wield what should be his power. He was already feeling lonely without Ned out there in front of him.

It was a bright, warm day in the seventies, so Kim served the buffet of turkey with cranberries and all the trimmings right out on the patio. They had decided at the last minute to put on this spread and have people over instead of going into hiding after Ned's shocking dismissal.

Mostly there were actor and actress friends. Evidently Ned felt now that he was not doing the show he could socialize with them, including Lon Ridings from the "First Year" cast. Lon needed the company, and some good holiday cheer, having already been informed by Archer that he wouldn't be renewed for the next block of shows since the role he played was being written out. Perry was also pleasantly surprised to see Ronnie Banks, the talented young actor whom they all had wanted to get the role of Jack but was vetoed by the network. They had had him back for a one-shot role as a grad student friend of Jack and Laurie, and he did beautifully with the small part. Evidently Ned wanted him for a role in *Spoons* if that fantasy movie ever became a reality.

Perry felt a sudden wrench, like a blow in the side, thinking of Jane. Their last Thanksgiving was the best he'd ever had. All his adult life he'd complained about the programmed nature of the turkey-with-all-the-trimmings traditional meal, lamenting that he couldn't give thanks by having his own favorite fare of steak and baked potato, and last year Jane had surprised him by serving a fabulous porterhouse with baked potato, sour cream and chives, a Waldorf salad, chocolate mousse, and a bottle of Valpolicella, his favorite red wine (that was a year ago of course, in his pre–Napa Valley era). Having this hoary wish come true had of course put Perry in a wonderful mood, and they spent a lovely day and night, eating and looking into the fire, and making long, slow, affectionate love. He wondered where Jane was now, today. Probably at the Cohens'. Would they have any guests? Any spare men, perhaps? A visiting lecturer of some sort, one of those fey, lonely chaps from the British Isles?

Perry finished off his first glass of wine and got another. He was just as glad Liz Caddigan was in New York for the holiday with her bicoastal lover. He had the feeling that being with a woman today would simply make him sad.

Ronnie Banks and Lon Ridings got into a funny, improvisational dialogue of an Indian and a pilgrim that had everyone in stitches, and then Lon started joking about being replaced by a cop. At first it was funny but as he drank more it got a bit maudlin. Kim went over and talked with him and he quieted down.

Perry confided to Ned his fears about doing what he was doing, and how he missed his influence already. Ned was very supportive and mellow about the whole thing.

"What the hell, it's television," he said. "Those guys are all up against the gun. It's like Russian roulette with the damn ratings. No wonder they make wacky decisions. Their own jobs are on the line."

"Still, that's no excuse for doing what they did to you," Perry said righteously.

Ned patted him on the shoulder.

"Hey, when this thing's over we'll work together on something civilized. I haven't forgotten about that option we talked about on your beautiful story. 'The Springtime Women.' "

Perry flushed. He had somehow hoped that Ned would forget about their little informal agreement. He had never told him he had actually signed a deal for it with Vaughan Vardeman.

"Ned," he said, screwing up his courage, "I've been meaning to talk to you about that."

"Sure — just let me check on Lon for a sec. I'll be right back."

Ned got up and strolled over the little strip of earth that ran along the patio at the side of one wing of the house. There was a border of assorted flowers planted there but none of them was in bloom now. Lon had gone over and lay down there, on his stomach, his head resting on his arm. It was a sleeping position but his eyes were open and he had a wineglass next to him that he picked up and sipped from. Ned bent down and spoke to him, and then came back and sat down again with Perry.

"Is Lon OK?" Perry asked.

"He will be. Right now he's taking it hard. He'd counted on this series going. Put the kids through college — that's what everyone hopes for."

"Wow. It's rough. He's not sick, though? He just wants to lie down?"

Ned sighed and rubbed hard at his forehead.

"He said he just wants to 'get close to the earth.' "

Close to the earth. My God. Perry felt little prickles along his arms, as if an electrical current had passed. He imagined himself lying that way on the ground, brought low, feeling desperate. There was a grown man over there, an accomplished and talented man, driven to such a state. It might happen to anyone out here, anyone on this roller coaster of a business. It might happen to Perry himself. He tried to shake off the thought.

"Oh well," he said, "listen, Ned. About that story. I kind of forgot about it. I mean, you didn't mention it again. And since we didn't have anything in writing, well, when Vaughan Vardeman got interested, and he gave it to Harrison Ford, well, I just thought — it would be OK."

"I see," Ned said.

"I'm sorry," said Perry.

"I wish you'd have let me know. I thought we had a deal."

"Well, hell, we'll do something else. Really. I really want to."

"Sure," Ned said. "If you'll excuse me?"

He went to talk to some of the other guests.

Perry felt rotten. He downed his wine and then got some more. He noticed Lon Ridings had taken off his shirt. He was now removing his trousers. A few people glanced over at him but no one said anything. He was wearing jockey shorts. Perry went over to him.

"Can I get you a drink or anything?" he asked.

"All I want," Lon said, "is to get close to the earth."

He lay down, flat, on the ground, digging his fingers in the dirt.

Perry turned away. There were tears in his eyes. He wasn't sure if he was feeling sad for Lon or for himself. He wanted to get out of there. He didn't want to feel this way. He wanted to feel strong and hard and upbeat, like a real hyphenate should, a successful writer-producer. He put down his glass and fled, without even saying good-bye or thanking anyone.

It was a new day, a new beginning. Perry was rested, fresh, eager to get to work.

"Come in, come in!" Archer Mellis called with a welcoming wave. "I want you to meet your new producer!"

Perry threw back his shoulders and smiled, looking around the office to see who it was Archer wished him to greet. When he walked in he hadn't noticed anyone, but now he saw, hunched in a corner, a large form, a massive hulking shape that stirred, moved, stood, and came slowly toward him.

It was a man. A large, bulky, hirsute man with wiry, tangled, gray-black hair that cascaded over his ears and grew wildly below his nose and around his mouth, bristling down his chin in the form of a great Brillolike beard.

Archer stepped out from behind his desk and clapped an arm on the hairy man's broad back, seeming to help guide and propel the creature's slow, tanklike progress across the room.

"I want you to meet your producer!" Archer said in a tone of jubilation, reaching for Perry's arm that was already moving outward and bringing it forward like a referee uniting two contending fighters before a match. Perry took the man's hamlike hand, bracing for some bone-crushing squeeze, yet he felt only a slight, bloblike tremor.

"Perry Moss, this is Donn Gunn!" Archer announced, as if to a cheering crowd.

"Glad to meet you!" said Perry, trying to match Archer's enthusiastic demeanor.

The blank gray eyes of the man called Gunn seemed to roll away from Perry's gaze, and he made a sound without moving his lips, a kind of half gurgle, half grunt.

Perry wondered who the hell the guy was, and what in the world he was going to do on the show. Maybe he was some kind of stuntman. He could have passed for a walking special effect all in himself. Well, whatever, Archer seemed to want to impress the guy, and Perry wanted to live up to his new role as producer with full flair.

"Welcome aboard!" he said, and the man made his grunt again, then turned and went back to arrange himself in the corner.

"Donn here is practically a legend in the Industry," Archer

said. "Been with some of the best shows of their kind — from 'Badge 465' to 'Krako, Special Investigator.' "

My God, maybe he was the cop! The actor who the network wanted to play the role of Jack's cop father! But surely not. Surely they could get at least a *charming* cop, an Irish cop with a lilting brogue instead of a Neanderthal with a grunt! Jesus, with this guy playing the part they'd even have the policemen's unions down on them, protesting the portrayal of decent men in blue!

He must be some sort of stuntman after all. Or maybe he was an ex-con who served as a technical advisor for TV cop shows in matters relating to theft, extortion, murder, and general mayhem.

"Well, I'm delighted to have someone of your experience," Perry said cautiously.

"Beautiful!" Archer exclaimed. "That's exactly the attitude I expected you to bring to this."

Like a proud teacher showing off his best student Archer turned to Gunn and said, "Didn't I tell you what Perry's reaction would be? He's a team player, all the way."

Gunn shrugged and belched.

"Long's he knows who's the boss," he mumbled.

Boss?

"Excuse me," Perry said with a forced smile, "but I'm afraid — not being a veteran in the business — I really don't know what it is, exactly, you do."

"I do it all," grumbled Gunn. "That's the only way it gets done."

"Perry, you must have been daydreaming," Archer said with a nervous laugh. "When you walked in the room, I said I wanted to introduce the *producer*."

"I heard you," Perry said impatiently.

"Well — if I have to repeat myself — he's your producer."

"I don't get it. I thought you meant *he* had to meet *me*. I'm the producer. I just signed papers that said so."

"Of course you are!" Archer assured him.

Perry stood up, felt his head beginning to ache, the room starting to tilt.

"If I'm the producer, how can *he* be the producer?"

Archer came and clapped a hand on Perry's shoulder.

"*Amigo*, he's the *executive* producer."

Gunn hefted himself to his feet, and said, looking past Perry, "Like the man said, I'm the boss." Then he lumbered out of the room.

"You're kidding," said Perry.

"You're going to learn things from Donn that it would otherwise take you years to learn," Archer said. "He's the best. We were lucky to get him."

"I thought this was my show."

"Of course it is. You want it to succeed, don't you? Donn Gunn's the man to make it happen."

"Holy God."

"You're a writer-producer. You'll learn from him. He can carry the burden. *You* can make it sing."

Perry opened his mouth, but nothing came out.

Sing, hell. He couldn't even speak.

Perry was going to hang tough. He was not going to let Archer Mellis, or Max Bloorman, or even that incredible hulk who was now his immediate boss, Donn Gunn, keep him from the sole purpose of making his show a hit. That was his only concern.

"Keep your eye upon the doughnut, and not upon the hole," he recalled from the wisdom of his childhood. Right.

For the role of the cop who was Jack's father they cast a terrific, magnetic actor named Shaun Farragan, the charming type with the Irish brogue who Perry himself had hoped for in that awful moment when he imagined Donn Gunn was going to play the part.

Shaun Farragan was perfect as Dan, the likable cop father proud of his teacher-son, Jack, and his daughter-in-law, Laurie, and pleased as punch to be able to move right in with them.

Shaun, in fact, was so good that when the network tested the audience reaction of the first episode he played in at Preview House, Lou Simmell called up to report enthusiastically that he tested higher than any other actor on the show!

"We want him in every scene," she happily told Perry.

"In every scene? That doesn't make sense!"

"It does if we want good numbers," she said.

"I mean, in terms of the story. It won't be about a young married couple any more. It will be a show about a cop. Is that what you want — another cop show?"

"We want a show we can keep on the air," Lou Simmell said.

So "The First Year's the Hardest" became a cop show.

All right, goddam it, it would be the best cop show that TV ever saw, the best one, anyway, that Perry Moss could make it.

He wrote the first script that was built around Dan himself. He even wrote a car chase. Hal Hagedorn, who had done this kind of thing many times before, helped show him how to do it. He gave it proudly to Donn Gunn, who probably didn't believe he could do it. He not only did it, he gave him the best cop show that was in him.

"This scene where he catches the kid who robbed the laundry?" Gunn said.

"Yes?"

It was one Perry was specially proud of — tough but poignant.

"This sucks," said Gunn.

"What the hell are you talking about?"

"Any good cop would kick this kid's ass about now."

"This cop is our hero — he's a decent cop."

"He's a bleeding heart if he doesn't cuff this hood around a little here."

"You don't know your ass from your elbow."

"I know I'm the boss around here. You know what you are?"

"Yes, I know exactly. I'm the writer-producer on this show, and I'm also the creator."

Gunn belched.

"That's a lot of horse hockey. What you are is, you're a serf. You work for me. You do whatever I say, whether you like it or not. I say write tough, you write tough. I say the cop kicks ass, you write he kicks ass."

Perry went straight to Archer Mellis.

"I'm afraid Donn Gunn is the boss," Archer said.

"I am not going to write stupid violence, especially when it makes our hero look like a jerk."

"I was hoping you could learn from Donn Gunn."

"He's a slimy sonofabitch. He's the dregs."

"He's your executive producer. That's the bottom line."

"Fuck you, Mellis. *That's* the bottom line."

"I think you'll be happier in the classroom, when all's said and done."

"You'd like that, wouldn't you? Well, I'm not running back to Vermont. I'm leaving this lousy show, and this lousy studio, and now I'm free to do some quality kind of stuff out here — the kind of stuff you promised instead of this junk!"

Archer stifled a yawn.

"Lots of luck, *amigo*."

XII

THE CHRISTMAS TREES on Hollywood Boulevard were blond. Kind of a peroxide color.

Perry smiled, shaking his head in wonder and appreciation. The amazing thing about this crazy, fabulous place was that you couldn't honestly satirize it, even in your imagination, because before you did, it always beat you to the punch, coming up with something so flagrant that it parodied itself far more effectively than any outsider could manage to do.

Peroxide blond Christmas trees!

He loved it.

He still loved Hollywood, even after the ugly battle with Donn Gunn, the pain of leaving the show, his feeling of being betrayed by Archer Mellis, and, even worse, his own betrayal of Ned Gurney.

All that was over now, past, done, *finito*. Not only that, but better still, in the incredible time trick of Southern California, the superacceleration of everything, yesterday was already prehistoric. An hour ago was dust. The present was already passing, before your startled eyes; only the future seemed real, glittering just ahead, promising and vast as the great Pacific.

The future was the deal with Vaughan Vardeman to make "The Springtime Women" a feature film, a modern classic. Harrison Ford in his first heavy dramatic role, maybe Meryl Streep and Teri Garr as the women. Of course the women in the story were older, more drab, but this was a film translation, a romantic dramatization. Not only the gold of the box office but also the gold of Oscar statuettes glinted off the project in Perry's imagination. As soon as the holidays were over Vaughan planned to try to get the whole thing launched; in fact, one of the top executives of Unified Films, where Vaughan had done his last movie and wanted to pitch this one, would be at the Vardemans' annual wassail buffet on Christmas Eve and Perry would meet him. The seed would be planted. This was how the real magic was worked. Informally. Casually. Among colleagues and friends.

Deck the peroxide Christmas trees!

Perry thought it might be a gas to get one of these evergreens dyed blond for his living room, but he feared Jane wouldn't appreciate the joke. No, he was playing this safe, traditional. He found a lot on Melrose Avenue with fir trees as green as Vermont, and bought the old-fashioned kind of colored lights and ornaments at Bullocks Department Store. He wasn't even taking a chance on getting any glitzy, expensive decorations in Beverly Hills, he was sticking with down-home values.

Gifts, though, that was something different. He really wanted to lay it on. For the first time in his life, he had the money (the power!) to give his beloved wife the finest, the best, without stint, to shower her with everything he saw that he thought would please her.

And oh, he wanted to please her, surprise her, make her smile and glow, atone for all the hurt he had unintentionally caused her by steering this new course in his career that even temporarily set them apart, put them against each other. One of the positive side effects of the break with Gunn and Archer was that it allowed him again not only to *think* about other aspects of life but even to experience emotions about matters other than the show. As he'd poured himself heart and soul into the series, spent every mental and emotional asset he had on it, he had simply put his other feelings on hold, especially the ones concerning Jane.

The only flaw in this practical if cold-blooded solution had been that Jane kept intruding into his consciousness. The most disconcerting part was the whole business of hearing her voice —

that is, *imagining* he was hearing her voice — telling him what to do or not to do, what to think or not to think. The voice was so clear, so immediate, Perry had to take a moment or so to reorient himself whenever he heard it — dammit, when he had the *illusion* of hearing it. And after those occasions there was a kind of lingering sense of her, like a trail of perfume, an ineffable presence. He had to fight it off, close his mind against it as best he could, simply because the aura of Jane was too distracting, it got in the way of what he had to do here to achieve his goals.

Then almost the moment Perry freed himself from what had become — as Gunn himself called it — his serfdom, the feelings about Jane he had struggled to hold at bay came flooding back, with all the force of a dam breaking. In a way, the timing was perfect, coming as it did just before Christmas. He still didn't want to go back to Vermont, afraid it would break the spell he was in, the concentrated effort to succeed in this new scene.

Shopping for Christmas presents for her was a fabulous high, a joy, a tangible way of expressing in action the powerful love he felt for his wonderful wife, the woman who, he now remembered with electrifying force, was the one he had felt from the first was his preordained, predestined mate for life.

He was clever enough to restrain himself, of course, respecting her taste for simplicity, her natural aversion to the very sort of treasures that spilled so seductively over the velvet displays of the exclusive shops and stores of Beverly Hills. He wished he could buy her something gold, something lavish, but knew it would only turn her off, so in the field of jewelry, he held his flagrant instincts in check and purchased for her only a simple string of pearls, whose elegance was in their very purity, the unadorned naturalness of their beauty, as opposed to any sheen or shine of flash and glitter.

He tried to keep that principle in mind in all his selections of other-type gifts as well — the softly beautiful but practical quilted bathrobe, the elegant but plain white silk blouse, the long, chocolate-brown, Italian-made leather coat, the stunning but simple three-piece fawn suede suit, the sporty Swiss watch designed for outdoor use, the powerful German binoculars she could use to intensify her viewing and appreciation of nature on her hikes and camping trips, the good telescope of a kind she had always wanted for studying the stars.

He spent a little something more than $7,000 on Jane's presents, signing the slips with the power of the new Gold American Express card his accountant had secured for his greater convenience. It would simply come out of his money-market funds and soon be replenished with the flow of new fortune that would soon be flooding in from the sale of the "Springtime Women" project as soon as the holidays were over.

The presents, gift-wrapped by the stores in glorious colors set off by bright silken ribbons and glorious bows, further spangled with bells and stars and decorative toy figures of reindeer and elves and angels tied on for extra, dramatic effect, were artistically stacked cornucopia-style beneath the tree, looking like some ultimate symbol of lushness, largesse, the plunder of love.

Staring down at them, Jane looked out of place in the picture that Perry was about to flash with the new fully automatic camera he had given himself for Christmas. Holding her small armful of home-wrapped presents, bending down and placing them tentatively against the glistening flood of the others, she seemed like some Parisian match girl brought into a wealthy home to share Christmas.

She looked good, but a little gaunt, though maybe it was just her new hairstyle that produced that effect. It was hard to get used to — the shorter trim, cut straight at the chin line, parted in the middle, and combed straight down on the sides. It looked nice, damned attractive even, but it didn't look like Jane. It didn't look like the woman he had fallen in love with on the spot almost six years before, the woman who became his wife, mate, best friend, and lover, all rolled into one. He was disappointed with the subtle but significant transformation, and felt in some vague way he'd been duped, yet he tried to concentrate on the main, the real point of wanting her to come here: renewal of love, reconciliation of differences.

She gave him a pipe, a sweater, one of her new photographs,

a pair of fur-lined moccasins he used to like to wear when he worked in his study, a first edition of Flannery O'Connor's essays, a jar of his favorite Vermont maple syrup. He made the appropriate oohs and ahhhs of appreciation (as she had done when she opened her own presents) but there was something odd, out of kilter, about this whole transaction. It were as if each was making a silent statement by bringing to the other the treasures of the two distant lands they had come from — Marco Polo exchanging gifts with Pocahontas.

Perry knew she wouldn't want to go out to some fancy restaurant for Christmas dinner, yet he didn't want her to have to cook in his tiny kitchenette with its all-electric appliances (like all real cooks, she preferred gas burners). He even considered making the stew she had taught him how to make when they met, yet felt it wasn't festive enough.

Ravenna had of course been the one with the answer to solve this culinary dilemma as she had all others: she knew a gourmet caterer who made up a splendid dinner of duck à l'orange with wild rice and puree of chestnut, and apple tart for dessert; all you had to do was heat it up.

They drank two bottles of fine Chardonnay with dinner and had brandy after, and when they went into the small bedroom to lie down for a nap, their hands met and fingers interlocked. When Jane arrived the night before, she was too exhausted and too tense to make love, and besides, they still felt awkward with each other. Now, in the darkened bedroom, full of food and spirits, they moved toward one another, explored each other as if renewing acquaintance, rephrasing their bodies' rapport, and joined, a bit awkwardly, after all that time of separation, but tenderly.

They didn't talk about "it" till the next day. Their future.

They walked the water's edge of the beach in Venice, as they had when they first came out. That was almost a year ago now. More like a century it seemed.

"I miss you," he said.

"Seriously?"

"Like fury."

"You managed to hide it pretty well. I mean, I didn't hear from you much, till the last few weeks."

"Well, I was all tied up with the show till then. All the up-heavals. The whole mess."

"So you really mean you missed me when you didn't have the show any more."

"Dammit, Jane. I don't want to argue. I love you."

"I'm sorry. I love you too. I miss you all the time."

He stopped and hugged her to him, stroking his hand on her back.

"Let's be together."

"That's what I want."

She took his hand and they began walking slowly again down the beach, in step with each other.

"You know what my fantasy is?" Jane asked, pressing his hand.

"Let's see — that I throw you down in the surf and ravage you to insensibility as the tide comes in."

"Not *sexual* fantasy. I mean the 'daily life' kind."

"Whatever turns you on, love."

"Seriously. I was thinking, maybe you could get together on some project with Mona Halsted. She loves your stories, and I bet she'd love an excuse to come out and stay awhile."

Perry stopped walking and stared at Jane. She turned toward him and smiled as she continued, eagerly.

"You could work at home, and Mona would come out and go over the script with you, and then you could fly back here for network meetings if you needed to."

"What in the world are you talking about?" Perry asked.

"I'm talking about the possibility of your working on a television project with Mona Halsted."

"Who's she?"

"Don't you remember? That wonderful woman producer we met at the Vardemans' party. She went to Middlebury, and she loves Vermont. I know she would jump at the chance to come out on business, and besides, she's a real fan of yours."

"Darling. That really is a fantasy, I'm afraid."

"Why? Why can't it be true?"

236

"There's about a million reasons, believe me. I'm trying to do a feature right now, not television. Mona Halsted is nobody."

"She's a bright, sensitive woman."

"I'm not going to argue with you about Mona Halsted's virtues. That's beside the point — *she's* beside the point."

Jane turned and started walking again, faster now, and Perry kept up alongside her.

"What is the point?" Jane asked.

"The point is I need you here. I want you to come back and stay with me through the spring. To the end of summer at the latest. Then I guarantee we go back to Vermont for the fall semester."

Jane stopped again and folded her arms across her chest, looking at Perry with a squint.

"I can't believe you," she said.

"You don't think I'm telling the truth?"

"Oh, I know you are. I just can't believe your proposal."

"What's so weird about it? That I want my wife to be with me while I finish some important work?"

"Important enough to give up your tenure for? This is it, you know. They won't extend you any longer, and I don't blame them."

"Love, this is the script for the Vardemans. This is *real* tenure — more money, in one lump, than I'd make for teaching for the next five years!"

"So to hell with your obligation to Haviland. All the stories you told me of your loyalty to them, how they took you in when no one else would, gave you a home."

"I'm going back there next fall. Even if I only teach one course. I'll be much more valuable to them."

"Because you'll be rich?"

"Because I'll have done more, accomplished more, and in a way that will bring national acclaim!"

She looked at him as if he had turned into Dracula's nephew.

"My God," she said.

She turned and started running down the beach. Perry ran after her, angrily, tackling her on the sand. Both of them were

237

heaving, puffing, glaring, wanting to pound each other. Without a word, they stood up and brushed themselves off. They drove back to the condo in silence.

That night was the Vardemans' annual wassail buffet.

Jane refused to go.

Perry explained that he had no choice; it was business.

"I understand," Jane said.

He left her lying on the couch, reading the Flannery O'Connor essays she had given him for Christmas. He kissed her on the cheek and promised to get back as soon as he could. He wanted to try to pick up the pieces, see if they couldn't work something out, now that they'd had the explosion and got the hysterics out of their systems.

The Vardemans' wassail buffet seemed very restrained; there was more talk of deals than of Christmas. Vaughan introduced Perry to Evan Shurtleff, the Unified Films mogul. He was a crisp, pale-looking man with thin lips and piercing eyes.

"I understand you worked with Archer Mellis," he said.

Perry felt the tips of his ears go red.

"Yes, I did. Unfortunately, we didn't part on the best of terms."

"So I understand."

"Still, if it weren't for Archer, I wouldn't be here. He's a brilliant guy, and I owe him a lot."

"Of course."

Perry was going to change the subject to "The Springtime Women," but Shurtleff turned his head slightly and smiled at someone who waved at him.

"You'll excuse me?" he said to Perry.

"Of course."

Perry chugged his cup of wassail and got another. Damn. He wondered if Archer Mellis was bad-mouthing him around town. The arrogant prick. To hell with it. If this cold cucumber from Unified didn't like him there were plenty of other places to go with a hot project like "The Springtime Women." Especially with Harrison Ford wanting to do it. He looked for the popular star but didn't spot him among the wassailers. He saw Meryl across the room and decided to go over and introduce himself

238

and mention "The Springtime Women." Maybe Vaughan had an extra copy of the book upstairs and could lend it to her.

Perry started edging his way through the crowd, shoulder first, when he bumped into the last person he wanted to encounter right now.

Cyril Heathrow. He was wearing a tweed suit with knickers, looking like some damn Dickens character.

"Ah, Mr. Moss," he intoned, lifting his chin. "I understand you've bid adieu to the world of television. Or it, to you?"

"The parting was mutual."

"What a loss," Heathrow said brightly, lifting his wassail cup, "to your country's culture."

"Why don't you take a flying fuck at a rolling doughnut?"

The Englishman whipped out a pad and pencil.

"I adore you people's colloquialisms," he said.

Perry went off in the crowd.

This was not his night. He had two more cups of wassail, and didn't even try the buffet. The combination of Shurtleff and Heathrow had obliterated any trace of his appetite. He was left in the crowd, without even being noticed, wanting urgently now to get back to Jane, to try to talk some sense into her. He rehearsed his arguments in his mind, went over his reasoning and logic, and decided the most important thing was to emphasize how damn much he really loved her.

When he got back home, the lights were off in the condo. Maybe Jane was taking a nap. She was not in the bedroom, though. Or the living room. She had taken her suitcase. She had left the presents he gave her under the tree.

She was gone.

Perry needed a drink. He went to the fridge but the wine was also gone and the only thing he had was the bottle of champagne he had planned to use for making Mimosas for him and Jane the next morning. He opened it, and poured the bubbly into a tumbler. He sat down in the living room and tried to think what to do.

Should he follow her home? Should he pick up the phone and book the next flight? He could probably get the red-eye to

New York that was popular with show biz insiders, winging into the Big Apple at dawn. Then he could take the first shuttle up to Boston, rent a car at the airport, and drive north, maybe through a snowstorm, mushing himself on till he dropped in the driveway at home and was hauled inside by a loving Jane, bearing a cask of brandy around her neck.

No. He was not going to run. He was not going to put his tail between his legs and slink away in the night. Sure, it might be fine that first night or two, making love in the big bed under the comforting pile of covers, sitting by the fire in the arms of his beloved and lovely wife. But then he'd have to face reality. His colleagues. He'd have to look them in the eye and admit defeat. He'd have to bear up to the dean's smug sneer, the sympathetic coos of the faculty wives, the pats on the back of professors whose welcome was tempered with an unspoken "I told you so."

No. He was going to stick it out. He was going to hang in there until he got at least one picture made — "The Springtime Women" was just around the corner, for God sake — and then go back in triumph, in his own good time.

In the meantime, he ought to call Al Cohen and just ask him to check on Jane when she got back, make sure she was OK. The trouble with that was, he'd have to tell Al he wasn't coming back — yet again — for the spring semester. And that would bring up the whole ball of wax about tenure.

Perry knew the dean would never give him another period of grace, that in effect he'd be giving up his tenure by failing to go back this time. He had already thought it through and was ready — even committed — to gambling on the greater kind of tenure that awaited him with the gold rush of his entry into feature films. Al Cohen would never begin to understand that, though, and he didn't want to try to explain it or defend himself.

He took several gulps of champagne and sat down right then and there and wrote to Al. He said he realized he was forfeiting his tenure, but his commitments in California prevented him from returning to Vermont at this time. He fully planned, though, to return for the fall semester and looked forward to teaching —

if not his regular class load, at least his writing seminar, and perhaps, with department approval, beginning a new workshop on the craft of film writing. He felt sure it would be popular with the students, and in fact when word of it got around New England (there should be no problem getting a feature on it in the Boston *Globe* when the time was ripe), it might very well attract new students to Haviland. It would, in a sense, be a way for him to make up to the college for his extended absence.

The letter, especially the new idea for the screenwriting workshop, eased his conscience. It also helped take his mind off Jane. He finished the bottle of champagne and collapsed into bed.

"Trust me," Ravenna said.

Perry made a harsh kind of cackle.

"Is that some kind of show business term, like 'the bottom line'?"

"What are you talking about?"

" 'Trust me.' That's what Archer Mellis always used to tell me."

"Don't get paranoid, now."

"How can I not get paranoid when my old friend gives up on my movie after only one place turns it down?"

"Vaughan has *not* given up on 'The Springtime Women,' he's simply put it on the shelf for a while. And don't say anything to him you'll regret. He's a good producer; he's *bankable*."

"That fucking Mellis screwed this up. He bad-mouthed me to that snippy asshole from Unified, I know it."

"If you start trying to figure out who's doing what to you and who else and why you'll go nuts in this town," Ravenna said. "Now settle down and eat your squab salad."

Perry sighed and took a sip of wine.

"I'm sorry," he said. "Listen, I really appreciate this — everything."

They were sitting at a table with a candle beside a lovely, lighted pool, in the back of a beautiful house in Beverly Hills. It was not Ravenna's own house but one of her successful new actress clients had loaned it to her while she was shooting a film on location in Ecuador. Ravenna had canceled other plans and had Perry over to calm down and plan some solid strategy. He had called that morning and sounded like he was going to pieces after hearing the news that Vaughan had struck out at Unified with "The Springtime Women" before it had even got to the stage of a meeting with Perry. They simply said they already had two films in development set in Greenwich Village and could not at this time consider another.

"I still don't understand why Vaughan can't get it going somewhere else with Harrison Ford as part of the deal."

"Darling, he's not part of the *deal*."

"You mean Vaughan was lying to me?"

"No, he told me Harrison in fact did read the story and liked it very much."

"So, doesn't that mean anything?"

"Someone of Harrison's stature can't commit to a project until he sees a *script*, darling. We're not even close to that."

"So what am I supposed to do, twiddle my thumbs till Vaughan decides to get off his ass and try to do something with it again?"

"Of course not. You're going to try to get another of your stories into development."

"I haven't even thought of one."

"That's why you have a super agent, mister. This afternoon I looked through that book of stories you gave me and I know just what you should do. It would make a very nice little film, and it could be done for under eight."

That meant eight million, Perry knew now, and was a real bargain.

"In fact," Ravenna said, "I don't know why you haven't thought of this one yourself."

"Which one?"

" 'Rich and Ripe' of course."

It was a short story, almost a vignette, that was originally in *Playboy*, about a Boston matron who has a Harvard boy to tea, hoping to seduce him, but he has no idea what she has in mind and is shocked when it finally becomes apparent to him. He flees.

"But nothing happens," Perry said.

"Darling, nothing happens in *any* of your stories."

"Thanks a lot."

"Don't get sensitive, please. This is the seed of a delicious idea — in the film, of course, the matron succeeds in seducing the boy, and they have an absolutely splendid, hilarious affair. You'll simply have to pitch it that way for producers."

"I'm not very good at that."

"Remember a marvelous little novel back in the sixties called *One Hundred Dollar Misunderstanding?*"

"Sure. Robert Gover. A preppy guy doesn't understand this black girl he's fallen for is a hooker, because he doesn't know her language."

"See? In your story, the preppy doesn't know the *matron's* language. And you carry it through a whole affair, shooting on location in Boston."

"That's not bad at all."

"Not bad? It's beautiful."

"So what do we do now?"

"I'll send you on the rounds. The best producers in town. It won't be easy, but I'll pull it off."

"Why won't it be easy? Is the word out against me? Because of my quitting the series?"

"That's nothing. People quit all the time. The problem is, you're an unknown quantity."

"For God sake, I wrote a TV pilot that became a series, and I've written all those stories. My books."

"But none of that counts, you see. You haven't done a *feature.*"

"That's crazy."

"It's the business. But getting you in is my problem. Once you get in, though, you have to sell yourself."

"I have to tap dance."

"We all do."

Ravenna got up and shucked off the lounging robe she was wearing. She took off the bra of her bikini and made a perfect dive in the water.

Perry had a bite of squab and some more wine. Ravenna was fabulous. She was not only solving his professional problems, but was evidently about to take care of his sexual needs as well. The flimsy bra lay on the tile edge of the pool, like a signal, a gauntlet thrown. Perry had lusted for Ravenna from the moment he first saw her, but he feared that he would really fall for her, that she was the kind who might really make him stray from his marriage. Well, now that Jane had taken off without so much as a good-bye on Christmas, wasn't he free to do as he pleased?

When Ravenna got out of the pool, dripping, Perry stood up. His penis was standing too. He went over and picked up a towel and started drying her off. She didn't protest. He rubbed her down and then turned her to him, pressing his mouth against hers, digging his tongue in. She pressed against him for one throbbing moment, then pulled away and put on her robe.

"Finish your salad," she said. "It's time to go home."

"Hey, what the hell! What's going on?"

"Nothing whatsoever," she said.

"I thought —"

"Let's get this straight, darling. It's my job to get you work, not to get you laid."

She tied the cord of her bathrobe, slipped into her high-heeled clogs, and undulated into the house.

Perry felt old.

He even looked old. He didn't look old when he stared full face in the mirror, it was when he caught himself in the glass of a window, unsuspecting, sideways. His California diet that had enabled him to lose six pounds hadn't done much for his middle, which was still flabby, but it made the skin of his neck sag. It looked like the neck of a turkey.

That's what he felt like, preparing to make the rounds of the powerful producers.

A tap-dancing turkey.

Worse, an *old* tap-dancing turkey.

Perry took another hard look in the mirror and made himself smile.

His teeth were brown. The tobacco smoke from his pipe had started to stain them years ago, but he never had worried about it. He chalked it up as a kind of occupational hazard of being a writer. Didn't most good writers smoke pipes? Hell, they posed that way on book jackets!

But now the stain seemed gross, a sign of the general decomposition of his body, a telltale mark of advancing age and Eastern-style decadence.

He asked Ravenna to supply him with a dentist.

"I didn't want to mention it," she said, "but I'm glad you asked."

She gave him the name of a dentist in Beverly Hills who worked on her actor and actress clients, people whose teeth had to sparkle if they wanted to get any jobs.

Arnie Lawler looked more like an actor himself than a dentist. Perry had the feeling it was actually the tanned, suave George Hamilton peering into his mouth.

"I'm afraid we can't do anything for you," Arnie said, offering a Perrier in his office following the examination.

"I just want to have my teeth cleaned!" Perry said.

"I'm afraid you've let them go too long. Also the gums. I'd want you to have gum surgery before we even considered taking you on."

"You mean you're turning me down? You won't clean my teeth because they're too dirty?"

"If you have the gum work, we'll be happy to reevaluate your situation," Arnie said. "But I can't make any promises."

Perry went home and gargled some Chardonnay. Holy God, even his *teeth* had been rejected. He couldn't stand the thought of making the rounds of dentists, hoping to have one take him on. He decided he would simply try to keep his lips over his teeth in the event he was called upon to smile while taking any meetings.

He prayed these producers he was going to see would at least be polite.

Most of them were quiet men, a bit aloof and studious, proud and self-possessed. There was nothing ostentatious about them, either in their personal dress or office decor. They wore no flashy clothes or gold chains, but sported the casual elegance of highly polished loafers, fine slacks, and long-sleeved shirts of muted colors, buttoned at the neck, without a tie.

Their offices were located on the sun-parched lots of once-mighty studios that were now simply part of the intricate web of the Industry's interwoven system of production, engaged in their own trimmed-down enterprises and renting out space to independents. Producers who were individual entrepreneurs did not belong to any company's hierarchy but simply had an office at Fox or MGM, or Paramount, or the gigantic Burbank lot that once was all Warner Brothers and now was home for not only that major but also a host of lesser, newer companies, any one of which might come up with tomorrow's biggest smash hit. The independent producer was not a mere employee of the studio where he kept his office but simply had a deal with that company, a two- or three- or four-picture deal that gave him a base rather than a home. Perhaps at least partly because of that temporary situation the offices tended to be starkly if tastefully furnished. A fine rug on the floor, a few new prints on the wall, indicating an educated appreciation of the arts. Nothing that hinted of flash or glitter.

The personal manner of the powerful producers not surprisingly matched the style of their dress and office decor. They looked their guest directly in the eye, and after their secretary or assistant had brought a hospitable cup of coffee or tea or glass of Perrier, they spoke of the type of material they wished to involve themselves in to bring to eventual fruition on the screen. Then, perhaps lightly placing hands together at the fingertips, the host gave a brief, sometimes almost imperceptible nod to the guest to indicate granting him the opportunity of presenting his own proposal.

In their studied detachment, their polite but cool attention, the sense they conveyed of a calm and almost gracious condescension that stemmed from their superior understanding and mastery of life, these men rather reminded Perry of Freudian analysts. In these meetings, he had the odd sense he was in a psychiatrist's office, about to have his words and thoughts scrutinized by some scientific process beyond his own ken. After he then poured out his words in what seemed a rush and tumble of childish enthusiasm, his attentive listener would nod, perhaps pose a few pertinent questions, and then conclude the session with a phrase as standard to his own procedure as the "Yes, go on" of the therapist or the "Bless you, my child, go and sin no more" of the priest. Standing, the producer would extend a well-manicured hand, and, bestowing a thin smile like a benediction, utter the ritual words that finalized this discreet little ceremony: *"We'll get back to you."*

A far cry it was from the bad old days of Hollywood when certain uncouth moguls of legend flung shoes and epithets at actors and treated those writers that circumstance forced to their presence with the gross disdain of an immigration officer confronting a criminal alien. No, if these contemporary men of success in the esteemed field of film production bore any relation to their predecessors it was to the fictional image of Scott Fitzgerald's Monroe Stahr, that most perceptive and elegant of all tycoons. But unlike Stahr, these new moguls were not doomed by an outmoded system that chained them to a certain corporate fate, but rather, like independent princes, moved about the glittering kingdom as they chose, negotiating their own fate, deal by deal.

Of course, sad to say, there were still throwbacks to the former men of crass behavior and foul language, those who had not learned to modulate their voice or their scorn, especially for writers. Perry took a meeting with one such Neanderthal, a belching young mastodon who munched on a meatball sub while he laid on Perry the disgusting old line about writer's rights in a deal being known as "the schmuck rights." A real producer had in fact once used that term to a real writer (maybe more than once, maybe by more than one obnoxious mogul) who of course had recounted the story into legend, so the character Perry had to endure was not even being original, or even *au courant*, just offensive.

"For God sake, Ravenna," Perry complained when he got

home later and called his culprit agent, "why did you send me to that poor man's Attila the Hun?"

"Because, darling," she said with patient, instructive emphasis, "*he gets pictures made.*"

That was a phrase Perry was to hear often in the coming weeks, a judgment that separated the men from the boys, as it were, the final, most basic criterion in the whole entertainment community of Los Angeles; or, as articulated in the local argot, this basic, unadorned, do-or-die determinant was — for sure — *the bottom line.* The only relevant question to be asked of or about a man engaged in the enterprise of producing feature films was not whether he was good or bad, an angel or an ax murderer, benevolent entrepreneur or bestial burner of innocent babes in cradles, but only "Does he get pictures made?" The question is not why or how he gets them made, or how good they are when he gets them made, but only *does* he get them made.

Take Ned Gurney, for instance. It was sad as hell that Ned couldn't make it in the movies. It was really unfair, but it seemed with each passing week, hell, every day, every hour, his chances grew fewer, his hope was diluted; no matter what the reasons for his project getting hung up, the bottom line was he hadn't made it. Maybe he never would. And all his charm and ingenuity and savvy and past accomplishments on Broadway didn't mean zilch.

Perry was truly sorry. He was not only sorry for Ned's sake, he also was sorry for his own. He wished they could go on working together, enjoying their easy working relationship, the give and take of ideas and creative insights, the fun of imagining a new scene or story line. If only Ned had made it in the movies Perry could be working with him right now, getting on with his own script instead of just hanging around and waiting for the phone to ring.

All that nice cozy dreaming about making movies with Ned was based on *if*, and Perry realized now that *if* was really an East Coast word, an intellectual word, a word that had no place in the lexicon of Los Angeles, a word that fell somewhere below *the bottom line.*

Besides, the distinguished, *successful* producers with whom Ravenna had so astutely arranged for him to take meetings were every damn bit as civilized as Ned Gurney! The only problem was none of the admirable gentlemen had called him back.

Perry checked with his answering service several times a day — whenever, in fact, he left the condo for any length of time at all, reasoning that during the twenty minutes he had taken to run some things over to the dry cleaner was probably the very time that the crucial call had come. Usually, however, his only messages were from the few other people he saw for a drink or a dinner, or some kind of telephone salesperson of encyclopedias or hot tubs (he always called them back now, knowing the odds were they were unemployed actors and actresses in need of hearing at least a sympathetic voice and a polite refusal), but with disturbing frequency there were no messages at all. Of course the answering services in Los Angeles — they were surely one of the major industries of the region — were not so downbeat or insensitive as to report that you had no messages, that no one in the whole world had found any reason to call you, so instead of saying anything negative, like "Nothing" or "Nobody called," the person at the service handling your line said simply, "All clear."

Perry had begun to wince on hearing those two plain syllables, felt a rush of embarrassment that the person on the other end (probably an unemployed actor — or maybe, even worse to contemplate, an unemployed *writer*) knew he was of such small significance that he had no messages at all.

"All clear."

Perry would mumble a thanks and hang the phone up quickly, trying to put the message — or nonmessage — out of his mind.

After several weeks of hearing nothing at all, Perry took the bull by the horns and called Ravenna to ask what the hell had happened to Phil Clausen. Now there was a guy he had really enjoyed meeting with, a successful producer who had expressed an interest and respect for Perry's work — he hadn't actually read any of the stories, nor had he chanced to catch "First Year," but he had heard excellent comments on both, and was pleased that writers of quality material were now coming out here and trying their hand at film. He seemed genuinely absorbed in Perry's explanation of the plot he wanted to do in film terms, and said he looked forward to reading the copy of the original short story Perry left with him. Like the others, he promised to get back to him.

Ravenna was in a meeting when Perry called to ask about Clausen, but her secretary promised she'd get back to him as soon as possible. Perry hung around the condo all day, looking out the window and doing the L.A. *Times* crossword puzzle and watching the soaps on TV, but Ravenna never called back. Sure enough, when the next morning he went out to pick up the dry cleaning, he came back to get a message that she had called while he was out. Even though he was disappointed and frustrated that he'd missed her, he was secretly pleased that he had a message, so the service knew he had some action in his life.

"Listen," Perry said, speaking with speed and urgency when he finally connected with Ravenna, "what the hell ever happened to Phil Clausen? Shouldn't I have heard something from him by now? And if not, couldn't you call him? I mean, the point is, of all the people I've met, he's the one I'd really like to do business with. I honestly felt a rapport with the guy, and I think he would really appreciate the kind of thing I want to do, you know?"

"Darling, I'm afraid Phil passed," Ravenna said sorrowfully.

"He *what?*"

For a moment Perry panicked, wondering if Ravenna was using some L.A. show biz shorthand for passed away. Surely not.

"You mean he gave it to someone else?"

Perhaps he had shown it to some leading director to enlist as a further element in putting together a powerful presentation to offer to a studio.

"Darling, I'm trying to tell you Phil Clausen decided against the project."

Perry was stunned.

"Why?" he asked.

"Sweetheart, I'm an agent, not a psychic. There's a number

of good ones in town, but I haven't heard of any who can read the minds of producers."

"But didn't Phil say anything? About the story?"

"He said he was passing on it."

A crucial distinction in just the order of words in a sentence: not passing *it on* but passing *on it*.

"Damn," Perry said. "Do you think he really read the story?"

"Did you leave it with him?"

"Of course!"

"Well, then either he did or he didn't," Ravenna said, with a rising edge of irritation in her voice. "All I know is he *passed on it*."

The phrase this time sounded to Perry almost like "pissed on it," which was probably closer to the truth.

"Goddam it, Ravenna, I told you in the first place I wanted to send the story *first* before I had meetings about it with any producers, so I'd know if they'd read the thing."

"And *I* told *you* it's not done that way. You pitch the idea and then you leave a copy of the treatment — or story, or book. Whatever."

"But it doesn't make sense. It's backwards. Look, it's simply logical that if you're going in to talk to a guy about a story, he ought to read it first. Then he knows what you're talking about."

"That's not how it's done out here."

"Why not, if it makes perfect sense?"

"Darling — don't blame me. I didn't make the rules."

"Well who did?" Perry shouted. "And where are they written down? Can I go out and buy a rule book, so I can play this ridiculous game?"

"Why don't you go out and take a walk on the beach," Ravenna said, more soothingly now, as if trying to comfort a distraught child. "You know, that stretch you like out at Venice? It'll do you good. Clear your head. Sweetheart, I've got to scoot —"

She made a kissing sound into the telephone and then hung up.

Perry stood for a moment still clutching the receiver, the kiss ringing in his ear.

Thank God for the Vardemans. Maybe they hadn't been able to get Perry's movie off the ground exactly when he wanted (he knew they would in time, of course, they were eminently "bankable," as Ravenna put it in the argot of the business), but simply having them as friends out here was a crucial source of comfort.

"I've been to almost a dozen producers now," Perry told them, pouring out his heart between gulps of Japanese beer, "and the plain fact is, I've struck out."

Pru Vardeman pulled her silk shawl up tighter around her neck and shivered slightly, as if a chill wind had just blown past. She was wearing a pair of dark glasses with enormous round lenses, and looked like some kind of wealthy celebrity on the lam. The spot the Vardemans had chosen to meet Perry — a newly opened sushi bar on a side street in Playa del Rey — was a perfect place for assuring anonymity from the press or a prying public. Perry was in fact disappointed in their choice of a rendezvous, thinking it might boost his sagging morale to be seen with his prestigious friends in one of the popular luncheon spots of the entertainment elite (He had suggested the Polo Lounge of the Beverly Hills Hotel), but their overextended schedule only allowed them a quick late lunch on the way to pick someone up at the airport, so Pru had suggested this tiny, almost hidden spot as both convenient and amusing.

Vaughan tilted back his head, dropped a giant prawn in his mouth and washed it down with a slug of Kirin.

"Moss-back," he said, "I bet you're a lousy meeting."

Pru winced as she picked at her squid.

"Gawd," she said, "it sounds like you're calling him a lousy lay."

"That I wouldn't know about," Vaughan said, emitting a belch and rubbing his stomach. "All I know is there are writers who give good meeting and writers who don't, and it's got nothing to do with how good they are at writing."

"What the hell am I supposed to do?" Perry demanded. "Suck off these guys in their office?"

"Please," said Pru, putting her fork down and readjusting her shawl.

"Excuse me," Perry said, "but for God sake, I'm not a nightclub act, I'm a writer."

"Didn't your agent tell you," asked Vaughan, "you've got to learn to tap dance?"

Perry finished off his beer and ordered another.

"Listen," said Pru, leaning forward across the small Formica table, "why don't you go to your friend Ned Gurney with this and be done with it?"

"Are you kidding? You guys are the ones who told me he didn't have a snowball's chance in hell of getting a feature off the ground."

Pru sighed.

"That was months ago."

"Don't you read the trades?" Vaughan asked. "Ned Gurney's hot now."

Perry could feel his own face getting hot.

"What do you mean?" he asked. "How?"

Vaughan popped another prawn.

"He finally got Nirvana to do his picture. They signed Meryl and Warren for the leads."

"Sonofabitch," said Perry.

He heard himself laughing, a hoarse, croaking kind of cackle. The friend — or former friend — he'd betrayed because he had no clout had magically, overnight, become hot.

"We've got to run," said Pru, sipping the last of her tea and rising. "Sophia's flight is due in at four."

"You're picking up Sophia Loren?" Perry asked.

"Sophia Kolski," said Vaughan, "the new Polish sexpot. Just came off a big French flick."

Vaughan molded an outline of a voluptuous body in the air with his hands.

"She's hot right now," he said with a wink.

"At *the box office,*" Pru added, taking Vaughan firmly by the arm. "We hope to make a deal with her — a *business* deal."

Vaughan winked again, pulled out his wallet, and peeled off a couple of twenties he tossed on the table as Perry rose feeling dizzy.

"Please, finish your lunch," said Pru, giving him a quick peck on the cheek and starting out.

"Wait!" Perry called. "I want you guys to read something."

He bent down and grabbed the briefcase he had stuck beneath the table, rummaging through it with trembling hands and pulling out a folder encased in a handsome green binding. He shoved it at Vaughan, who instinctively backed away, as if Perry were trying to hand him a snake.

"It's a treatment," Perry explained. "Instead of just giving the short story to producers, I thought it might help if I left them a real screen treatment, but I've never done one before, so I wanted you guys to look it over, tell me if it's OK. OK?"

Vaughan tucked it under his arm and nodded, moving now toward the door.

"Tell me what you think of it — honestly!" Perry called after the departing couple.

Vaughan waved the folder at Perry as he hurried out, looking back over his shoulder and saying just as he disappeared, "We'll get back to you on it!"

Perry sat down again at the little table, staring at the white raw pieces of fish. They didn't look very appetizing, but they seemed quite fitting fare for him now.

They of course were cold.

XIII

I'M HOT!" Ronnie Banks exclaimed, raising aloft a bottle of beer from his perch on a stool at the bar of La Traviata.

Perry recoiled, as if Ronnie had announced he had just become a vampire.

Damn. The whole point of getting together with Ronnie was to try to find someone who was *not* hot, someone who would be sympathetic to the devastating news Perry got hit with out of the blue that morning.

He had to tell someone, and yet he didn't want to reveal this shameful secret to anyone who wouldn't understand what it was like, or who might even think less of him for knowing it. He wanted to lay it on someone who was out of work, had little or no money, no hot prospects, was generous of spirit and liked to drink.

Actors. Actors were the best bet. First Perry had thought of Lon Ridings, who had played the scholarly father of Laurie, but his last sight of the poor guy, pressing his near-nude body (except for those damn jockey shorts, for God sake) into the dirt at the side of Ned Gurney's patio, was too depressing. He didn't want someone *that* far down. Then he thought of Ronnie Banks, the young guy they'd all originally wanted for the role of Jack but who was turned down by the network. He seemed like a nice, hard-luck kind of guy who liked to booze it up a little. He had talked to Perry about getting together sometime, and in fact had sent him an invitation to a play he was in, but it was way out in the depths of the Valley in some kind of makeshift little theater in a converted auto-body shop behind a shopping mall. It did not seem likely that Ronnie Banks had just signed a contract for millions for some kind of multipicture deal, and Perry decided he was the ideal guy to meet for dinner.

And now he was hot.

"Hey-ho, no need to sweat it, my man," Ronnie said when he saw Perry's obvious dismay, "I'll only be hot for the next couple days."

"Hey, listen, I couldn't be happier for you!" Perry said heartily, trying to cover his embarrassment as well as his guilt. "What's your good news?"

"Got a bit in a new feature — but don't worry, it's only ten lines!" Ronnie assured him as he guided him up to a barstool.

"Congratulations, really. That's swell."

"What's happening?" Ronnie asked. "You look like someone's got a contract out on you."

"That's what I feel like," Perry admitted.

"Should we make sure to sit with our backs to the wall at dinner?"

"Good idea. Listen, I really can't talk about it yet — what's happening. I'll tell you after I get a few drinks in me, OK?"

Ronnie looked concerned, serious.

"You don't have to tell me at all, Perry. Whatever it is."

"But I want to. I've got to tell someone."

Ronnie nodded, and finished off his beer.

"Let's get a booth and be comfortable," he said.

"Great."

Perry was glad they'd come to La Traviata. It was a dim, cozy, inexpensive restaurant on Melrose Avenue in Hollywood where a number of entertainment people, including some stars, hung out when they didn't feel like being seen. They of course did not become invisible when they drank or dined at La Traviata, but according to some unwritten edict the place was not classified as fashionable, so columnists and their stringers never sniffed around it, no tourists ever heard of it, and local civilians who went there never bothered the stars by hounding them for an autograph while the vulnerable celebrity was in the midst of trying to swallow a long string of linguine. It was rather like a neighborhood restaurant for people who lived in a place so spread out and transient that they really had no traditional-type neighborhood.

Perry didn't feel like eating at all, but he made himself order. Since nothing sounded appealing to him, he simply ordered things he used to like to eat, in hopes he would like them again — baked clams, veal parmigiana with spaghetti, beefsteak tomato and onion salad, and the house special, creamy cheesecake with fresh strawberries for dessert.

Everything tasted like cardboard. Perry picked at his food and rearranged it on the plate and even made himself swallow a lot of it, but only because he wanted to maintain some pretense of being all right. The only thing he really wanted was the wine, which he poured down not in any appreciation of its taste but rather like a man pouring water on the burning engine of his car in a desperate effort to quench the fire. Before they got to dessert Perry ordered a second bottle of Verdicchio. Ronnie was drinking it too, of course, but tonight he was way behind his thirsty friend.

Perry felt if he just got enough wine inside him he'd be able to confess his shameful new secret, and when at the end of the meal it still seemed too difficult, he was sure that the brandy would enable him to speak freely. The brandy was great — not the taste, which was flat and colorless, like everything else, but the sting to his gums, the burning sensation in his throat.

"Elena — *dahling!*" Ronnie exclaimed, and jumped up to greet a svelte, glamorous woman who suddenly loomed above the table, appearing to Perry almost like a vision or dream, a beautiful, slightly wavering image reflected in a clear pond. He knew her, yet did not know her — certainly not as Elena.

"Ronnie, *dahling,*" the gorgeous woman cooed in a sexy, familiar voice. Holy God! Of course!

"Ramona Selden!" Perry blurted out, identifying the former call girl of the Washington elite.

But of course that was only on "Checkmate," the prime-time

soap opera that rose to overnight popularity four or five seasons ago, momentarily challenging the numbers of "Dallas" and "Dynasty," until it for some reason peaked, waned, and was canceled last year.

"Elena Allbright, this is my friend Perry Moss," Ronnie said in introduction, then added, giggling, " 'Checkmate,' " meet 'The First Year's the Hardest.' "

Perry caught his breath as "Ramona Selden" slid into the booth beside him, extending her hand and saying, "Of course, you're the writer. I loved the pilot — then didn't they turn it into some kind of cop show?"

"Pretty much," Perry croaked.

"The first year *was* the hardest," Ronnie said.

"Aren't they *all*," said Elena-Ramona, giving Perry's wrist a quick, sympathetic squeeze with her long, elegant fingers.

"I loved you!" he declared with feeling, then quickly, to the background accompaniment of Ronnie's wild giggle, added, "I mean as Ramona Selden of course."

"Thank you. Wasn't she a wonderful bitch?"

"You had 'em fooled, Elena," Ronnie said. "No one could guess Ramona was played by a real cream puff!"

"Come on now, don't ruin Perry's image of me, I worked hard at it!" Ramona said, giving Perry a lovely, intimate wink.

"Can you join us for a brandy?" he asked, shocked by his own daring.

"Ooh, I'd love to," she said, "but I'm meeting my new heart-throb in the bar. I just saw Ronnie and wanted to say hello — *and* enlist his sympathy in my latest plight."

"Men?" Ronnie asked.

"Worse," said the lovely Elena. "Money."

"Already?" Ronnie asked.

"Broke again," she nodded.

Perry's jaw dropped, and he looked quickly at Ronnie and Elena to see if this was some kind of put-on, a comic routine for a newcomer, but they both seemed depressingly serious, even pained.

"I've been there," said Ronnie with a funereal look and a quick hit of brandy, then let go the giggle and said, "Hell, I'm almost there again!"

"Hang tough, pal," Elena said rising, giving Perry one last thrilling squeeze of the wrist. "Lovely to meet you, Perry. Don't let this place get to you."

"Thanks, really, it was really great —" he burbled as she winked and went off, and as he watched her long, shapely legs move in rhythm to her picturesque ass, he called after her, "It was an *honor!*"

"Elena's OK, huh?" Ronnie asked.

"She's fabulous — but hey, she's not really broke, is she? What was all that about?"

"Sure she's broke."

"Elena Allbright? Ramona Selden? How could she be broke? She's a star!"

"You don't think stars go broke?"

Ronnie let out a whistle.

"In this town everyone's broke — or was once, or will be. It's built into the system. No matter how much money you make."

"I feel like you staged this whole thing for my benefit," Perry said.

"What are you talking about?"

"That's what's wrong — I mean, what I was trying to tell you — that I just found out today."

Perry leaned forward across the table, glanced furtively around the room to see if anyone was bending an ear toward him, then cupped a hand to his mouth and said in an urgent whisper:

"*I'm broke too!*"

Ronnie leaned back and guffawed.

"Welcome to Hollywood," he said.

Perry insisted on paying the tab with his American Express card — what the hell, by the time the bill came in he might have struck it rich again — so Ronnie insisted on taking him out to Pablo's in Santa Monica for a drink after dinner. Perry felt a little dizzy when they walked out of the restaurant, so he didn't mind leaving his car in La Traviata's parking lot and going in Ronnie's rattling old Renault.

259

"I thought Stu Sherman — that's my accountant — was pulling some kind of joke on me," Perry said over his brandy at Pablo's. "I mean, I never even heard of anybody paying forty-seven thousand dollars in taxes. Hell, that's more than I used to make in almost *two years!*"

"They got it all figured out, so you can't get ahead."

"I thought rich people didn't have to pay taxes."

"That's *really* rich — you're probably just middle."

"I used to think one hundred and sixty-seven thousand in a year made you rich."

"That just puts you in the fifty-percent bracket. Without any good tax shelters, probably. You got to have millions to come out ahead."

"I just got enough to get through the next month or so."

"Well, you own your own condo, don't you?"

"Do I? I won't be able to pay the mortgage after next month. Fuckin' mortgage is three grand. If I can't pay it, I guess they'll take it away from me — so how can I own it?"

"Sometimes I'm glad I'm mainly poor."

"Shit. When I only made twenty-six-five a year I was never broke."

"Nah. That's not enough to be broke on."

"What the fuck am I going to do?"

"What about that deal you had with the Vees?"

"Fuck the Vees."

Perry put his head down. He could feel himself shaking.

"Hey man, we got to get you *up!*"

Perry lifted his head.

"I'm sorry," he said.

"Forget it. We're going to get you glad. I could use a little glad myself."

Ronnie lived in a one-bedroom apartment in the Valley. Posters of sixties rock groups, names from psychedelic days, hovered and pulsed on the walls, fading in and out of Perry's brandy-filtered vision: Jefferson Airplane, the Grateful Dead, Led Zeppelin. Perry thought of a Sunday afternoon in a farmhouse around Haviland when he first went up there to teach. There was sweet

wine and homemade bread and Joni Mitchell on the stereo. "I've
looked at life from both sides now . . ." It was another lifetime,
a time of innocence. He saw the way the sun lay across the rug
on that distant Sunday, like a visual echo. Ronnie only had beer,
no brandy or wine. Out of a little bureau drawer, a tobacco can,
a substance, he took something white, in a cellophane Baggie.
He made tiny lines on a hand mirror. Ronnie rolled up a dollar
bill. Perry laughed. "Don't laugh near this, for God sake. You
blow anything away, I'll sue!" This was it, at last — the hip new
Hollywood, just like in the newspapers. Coke!

Broke was all right after all. Money was funny. Perry was glad.
Nothing was bad.

"Hey, I'm high!" he declared.

"Hi ho, hi ho," Ronnie sang, " 'tis off to glad we go . . ."

Down again. What goes up comes down. Law of nature. Law
of supply and demand. Whatever happened to Ayn Rand? There
is no brandy handy. Have no fear, there's always beer. No good,
but better with grass. Ronnie rolls a joint, passes to Perry. He
tries, but only coughs. Damn. Dim. The outlook is dim, grim.
Grimy. Dustballs growing in the corners. Ought to get out of
here. Relax. Nothing to fear. Nothing to fear but fact. Fact is
you're broke. No joke. Walls of the world closing in. Head in a
spin. Tailspin. Failspin. Fact: fucked.

Perry woke to the smell of old socks and stale beer. A pain was
in his neck, a pounding in his head. He'd spent the night on
Ronnie's couch. Now it was day, you could tell by the glare
behind the dusty drawn slats of venetian blinds. Perry rose, stag-
gering, walking on nails to the kitchenette, and opened the refrigerator. Beer. Mustard. A glass jar of dill pickles. Moldy piece
of cheese. He sniffed a half-empty carton of milk and put it back,
then leaned against the wall, seeing black. He blinked and went
to the sink, ran some water in his cupped hands and splashed it
at his mouth. He stumbled back to the couch.

He woke again later to sizzling sounds. Was he being electro-
cuted? Was the house about to explode? Like his head? None of
the above. Ronnie was frying bacon. Making coffee, feeding it

to Perry black. Trying to bring him back. Perry remembered he was broke, his car was miles away over mountains in the parking lot of La Traviata, his wife was on the other side of the country in a house that used to be his, too, in Haviland, Vermont. He pulled a pillow over his head and tried to blank out his mind, but the sizzling sound persisted. Hell.

The rain came. It was unrelenting, unceasing, day after day, for nearly three weeks. It was nothing to be concerned about, Ronnie assured Perry, it happened like this every year around January. It did not fall in scattered showers and storms that occurred throughout the year, like rain in the East, rain that lasted a day and night or at most a couple of days before the sun returned and the world was given a chance to dry out. This rain came in one dramatic, overpowering rush that overwhelmed the senses, leaving the mind as well as the body feeling drenched.

The rain filled up the streets and overflowed the swimming pools. The rain came down the hills and into the canyons, blocking roads with torrents and mudslides. The rain got under the hoods of cars and into the crevices of houses, dampening everything. The rain got into your soul. It never let up. It kept beating down.

Perry stepped in a puddle and suddenly realized that in Vermont at this time of year, the rain of course would have turned to snow. What a miracle! What a fabulous, brilliant conception it was to have the hard drops of water transformed into soft, lovely, intricately beautiful flakes of snow, snow that caressed and silently covered the earth with a clean blanket. Perry could suddenly see it, that winter world he had always known and taken for granted, covered with snow like a blessing. The vision of it was so intense it made him close his eyes, and when he blinked them open again he could feel tears. Hell. He was homesick, like a little kid.

He went back to his condo and got into bed and hid under the covers, trying not to think of where he was, and where he might have been. He got up after dark and had a big tumbler of a hearty Napa Valley Zinfandel. He needed to get a little buzz on to take his mind off the rain. And thoughts of Jane.

"Urgent."

That was the last message left by Ravenna with his service. The two before had just said to call her, the last one said *urgent*. It was almost three in the afternoon when Perry got back to his condo from another night of carousing with Ronnie that ended up with his passing out on his buddy's couch again. It was getting to be a habit. He had hoped to just sink into his own bed and "General Hospital" while sipping some Pepto Bismol and munching on a bag of nachos. When he really wanted to hear an "All clear" from his answering service he got an "Urgent." Of course he had to return the call, even though his head was splitting.

"Darling, you've only got two hours!" Ravenna practically shrieked.

To live?

"Two hours to what?" Perry asked, using all his powers of concentration to frame the question.

"To get to Larman Kling's office."

"Who's he?"

"*Sweetheart.* Larman Kling did *Planet Zero,* and his latest is *Schtick,* which happens to be outgrossing everything this week at the box office. He's hot right now."

No wonder the urgency. No wonder Perry had to get to this guy's office by five o'clock. He was hot *right now.* By nightfall he might be cold again. The only question was why anyone who was hot was interested in seeing *him.*

"What's it about?" Perry asked suspiciously.

"A project he thinks is ideal for *you!* He was gaga about 'First Year.' Went bananas when I told him I represented you."

"What's the project?"

"Darling, go find out! And hurry, I don't want you turning up a minute late to this meeting and you've got to get to Century City. *Ciao.*"

Perry hung up the phone and started taking off his clothes, dropping them on the floor, leaving a trail as he headed for the shower. He switched on the cold water and made the mistake then of going to take a look at himself in the mirror.

He was old.

Maybe the shower would make him new. That and a handful of aspirins were his principal hope.

Larman Kling was not like the cool, sophisticated brand of independent producer whom Perry had so much admired in his initial round of meetings. Nor was he one of the meatball-chomping Neanderthal types. In fact he was not like anyone or anything Perry had encountered before, in Hollywood or elsewhere.

"Sha-*boom*, sha-*boom*, sha-*boom*, sha-*boom*," Kling chanted as he clapped his hands in rhythm to his words while he stalked (frenetically) back and forth through his office.

"It's the *pace*, the *pace*, the *pace*; that's the key to this story," Kling explained, rubbing his scalp with his knuckles so hard it made him squint. Perhaps that was the source of some interior electric body current that caused his reddish hair to frizz out as that of a cartoon character who has just stuck his finger in a live socket. He was wearing basketball shorts, sandals, and a T-shirt with a large red bug stenciled on it that served as the symbol of one of his hit horror movies. He suddenly wheeled and pointed a finger at Perry.

"Can you get it? Can you hear it? Can you *do* it?"

"The story, you mean?" Perry asked.

"The pace!"

"Well, I think so, sure."

"Let's *hear* it, then!"

He beckoned to Perry, motioning his head as if trying to coax the right answer out of a thickheaded student.

"Sha-boom?" Perry said, hesitantly.

"Let's hear it!"

Perry cleared his throat.

"Sha-*boom*, sha-*boom*, sha-*boom*, sha-*boom*," he chanted, as Larman cocked an ear and listened, tapping his foot and nodding. Soon he began to smile and join in, pacing and clapping and chanting his "sha-booms" along with Perry's, stepping over and around the water beds and mattresses that composed the only furniture of his spacious office. The place looked like a wholesale bedding showroom, but instead of being located in an old warehouse, it was here in this long glass-walled penthouse at the top of one of the towering futuristic office buildings of Century City, on, appropriately enough, the Avenue of the Stars.

Perry's head was still pounding from his excesses of the night before; fighting the effects of booze and cocaine with aspirins was like trying to defend against ICBMs with blasts from a BB gun. Each "sha-boom" he uttered was like a nail driven into his brain; still, he pressed on, wanting to please the eccentric producer, wanting to have a shot at the job. He didn't even know what the story was yet, only what the "pace" was supposed to be, yet that was not the most important factor.

The most important factor was that Perry was broke. This assignment, if he got it, could save the day. The going rate for a feature was a hundred grand. That would bail him out and give him enough to get through the next six months, after taxes — at least he hoped so, he wasn't sure any more. At any rate it was the best hope he had of saving his dire financial situation. Of course, he still had his integrity, and he wasn't going to take on the job if it was something about giant bugs terrorizing a small town in Oklahoma. He knew it was no such thing, of course, or Kling would never have sought him out for the work. Perry was known as a "people writer," that is, a writer who only did stories about ordinary, law-abiding citizens, plagued by the familiar problems of daily life in the 1980s, rather than by invasions from outer space, or the Brontosaurus That Ate the Bronx.

Thankfully, Kling stopped chanting, nodded his approval, began scratching his head again, and, locking his hands behind his back, began to pace the room while he recounted the plot of the movie he wanted to make. He reminded Perry of Harpo Marx with a voice.

"The power is the power is the power," he said, launching into his story. Kling seemed to suffer from some sort of compulsion to repeat almost everything he said at least three times, a practice that, instead of making things more clear, made them incredibly more difficult to follow. As best Perry could tell, the story was about an ordinary American family who discovers its seemingly ordinary pet possesses psychic powers, and, when the six-year-old son learns to interpret the dog's insights, discovers that the next-door neighbors are part of an international narcotics ring. The story was an original idea of Kling himself, and he had already commissioned a script by a veteran Hollywood screenwriter, but was disappointed. In other words, this potential job was a rewrite.

"I don't even know if I can rewrite someone else's material," Perry said.

"The point, the point, the point," said Kling, wagging his head with enthusiasm, "is I don't want a literal rewrite, I want you to read this script and then put it out of your mind, throw it away, stow it, shove it, and create your own powerful interpretation of the story."

"I've never done anything on that — uh, well, on psychic subjects," Perry said. "Why would you ask me to try? I mean, I appreciate it, but I would think you'd prefer someone who knows the genre."

"You're fresh, fresh, fresh, so fresh!" said Kling. "That's what I want, the fresh I saw in your TV show, and out of that will come the power."

"Well, I'll certainly think it over," Perry said.

Kling pressed a copy of the script on him, and then, evidently exhausted, went to lie down on a mattress in a corner of the room. Perry took that as his cue and left, hurrying out to the first bar he spotted in the big Century City complex.

After he had a Mexican beer he called Ravenna.

"Not only is the story crazy," Perry complained, "this Larman Kling is some kind of madman. I mean, I'm talking *goofball*."

"Darling," Ravenna said, "he gets pictures made. Now read the script and think it over. If you do this, it will not only solve your cash flow problem, it will mean you've broken into features."

It was true. It didn't matter if you wrote a script of the worst movie ever made, it only counted that you'd written a feature that got produced, released, and distributed. Perry had found out that this was the secret of Cyril Heathrow's success. He had once had one script produced, and since then was consistently paid sums in the $250,000 range for turning out other scripts, even though no others had been filmed.

With all these practical matters in mind, Perry read the script that night, as he gulped down some wine. Given the basic idea, it did not seem all that bad. He called Kling the next morning and asked him what he thought was missing from it.

"The magic, the magic, the magic!" the intense producer exclaimed.

Perry promised to think about it further.

What was to think about?

A man who had $4,000 in cash and a $3,000-plus a month mortgage that was part of a monthly nut of $10,000 (which meant you had to make twice that to have it after taxes) was being offered an opportunity to make $100,000 without breaking the law, and in the process, advance his career.

So what was the problem?

Perry stoked up his pipe and settled back on the couch to face his decision honestly. He admitted to himself what was bothering him about this seemingly golden opportunity. Oh, of course he had known it all along but it was too worrisome, too confusing — and at the same time too childishly simple — to deal with head-on, and so he had kept pushing it back.

The truth was that a year ago — hell, even a week ago, before he knew he was broke — he would have laughed scornfully at any suggestion that he might even remotely consider doing a rewrite of a script about a family whose dog possessed psychic powers.

Are you *serious*?

Yet here was the virtuous writer himself, thinking over the offer, for no other reason than desperately needing the money.

There was a term for that.

It was called "selling out."

It was against all the values and dreams that Perry had grown up with, a mockery of the lofty ideals of his literary heroes.

Hey — can you picture Henry James being in the same room with Larman Kling, much less considering doing a rewrite for him? Surely not even Scott Fitzgerald, in the depths of his own dark night of the soul in Hollywood, took on assignments whose plots revolved around psychic pets!

On the other hand times had not just changed, time itself had seemingly been put on fast forward, like the speeded-up tapes on a video cassette recorder. Henry James was not just a tintype now, he was more like some ancient God, as remote as Zeus. Fitzgerald was a figure of legend, and the games and wars that meant so much to him now seemed closer to the life of Troy than of today's Los Angeles.

Maybe that's the sort of thing the Vees had in mind when they said the term "selling out" (which they hadn't even *heard* for ages) seemed "quaint" to them, a relic of the nineteen-fifties, like hula hoops and Ike buttons, a problem for that now primordial creature of the post-war American world, the Man in the Gray Flannel Suit.

Perhaps they were right, perhaps Perry was needlessly flailing his conscience and letting outmoded cultural guilt get him down simply because he was trying to apply the standards of the past to the realities of the present. When he thought of it that way, he saw that there were damn good reasons for his taking on this assignment *besides* the money involved!

By doing this rewrite he could learn more about the craft of filmmaking, a craft he wanted to master. He'd be working with a successful producer — OK, so he wasn't the most intellectual or sophisticated of the new breed of movie moguls, but the bottom line was (remember?) *he got pictures made.* Besides, the reason Kling wanted *him* to take on this assignment was to bring some class to the project. Perry was getting the opportunity for the very reason that he was regarded as a *quality* writer. He could write quality dialogue — hell, that's what he was being hired to do! If Kling had wanted Harry the Hack he could easily have found hundreds of such eager robots, but no, he had purposely sought out a writer of quality. And he wanted the very best that Perry could deliver.

Despite this impressive accumulation of evidence, Perry felt a sudden yearning to talk it over with Jane. Maybe just because he was so used to doing that during the past five years. She seemed to have a knack for pointing out angles he hadn't observed, for alerting him to possible pitfalls he hadn't been aware of, and even for showing him positive aspects his own deliberations had overlooked. He even went and sat in front of the phone for a minute or so. Then he sighed, trying to imagine explaining to Jane the advantages of doing a rewrite job and the need for quality dialogue in a script about a psychic dog.

No.

She was too far away from the realities of the business, too far out of the picture. Maybe if she had stuck it out, had stayed here until he got it all together, she could have advised him as intelligently and sensitively about this as she had about so many other things. Of course, if he had been a little more intelligent and sensitive about her own feelings out here, had thought just a little about her own welfare instead of devoting total attention to his own, maybe she would be here now, beside him.

Damn. It was too late for that kind of thinking. Besides, it was just a cop-out. The fact was, Jane was simply too far away to be of help now. From clear across the country, in a farmhouse in Vermont, this whole thing would sound crazy. He was the one who was here, it was his own ass that was on the line, and he damn well better deal with it. Perry told himself it was time to stand on his own two feet and think for himself, anyway. He stood up and went to the refrigerator, throwing his shoulders back as he walked. He got out another beer and opened it, beginning to feel cheerful and confident.

The outdoor terrace of the Polo Lounge was the perfect place to celebrate. The colors of the clothes of the beautiful people (not just socially, they really looked physically beautiful, too, tan and sleek and perfectly proportioned) blended with the tropical blooms of the flowers, the stately green palms and the pink hotel, everything softly illumined by the warm sun.

Perry was back on his Perrier, the drink of success. The drink of people who were so together and confident they didn't need a drink. At least not at lunch. It made him feel crisp, clearheaded, concise.

"You look a lot better than last time," Pru Vardeman said, no longer scrunched beneath her silk shawl but expansively throwing back her shoulders and tilting up her chin as she smiled on Perry and, at the same time, nodded acknowledgments and blew occasional kisses to actors, producers, directors and agents of note who were also having the pleasure of lunching here this lovely day. Vaughan, sticking to his personal style in Ivy League jacket and tie, raised his own Perrier to toast his pal.

"We've all come a long way from Harvard Square, Moss-back," he said with a satisfied grin.

Perry laughed.

"From Mr. Bartley's Burger Cottage to the Polo Lounge!" he said.

Pru laughed too.

It was like old times.

At last.

The Vees were delighted at Perry's landing the job with Larman Kling, who they assured him had moved beyond his earlier horror flick and sci-fi stuff and gained high regard as an artist with the success of *Schtick*; but more important, was hot right now. This was not only good news for Perry but for the Vees too; if Perry had a feature credit under his belt it would make it much easier for Vaughan to eventually make "The Springtime Women." Instead of being a handicap to a project Perry would be an important element once he had the feature credit in his cap.

"Oh, and I almost forgot," Vaughan said. "I read that treatment you gave me. Not for me, but I think it might be just what Phil Clausen's been looking for. I hope you don't mind I sent it to him."

"Huh? Hey, no, thanks, but he already passed on it."

"Well, he mentioned that, but he thought he'd like to take a fresh look at it. Anyway, it can't hurt."

"Hell no," said Perry, shrugging loosely, relaxed, warm not only with the sun, but success.

He could feel a pleasant sensation, a sort of glow in the area between his stomach and his groin.

He was hot.

When Perry got back from lunch and called his service, instead of the familiar "All clear," he had seven messages. It was as if the word of his being hot, a desirable person to call, had gone out through the atmosphere. There was a message to call his public relations person, who no doubt wanted to get his new deal in the trades as well as the atmosphere. Perry smiled, feeling glad he hadn't fired the guy out of fear of being broke. It was small-time to try to cut corners and save a few bucks. "Don't think poor" was one of the vital rules of survival in this high-stakes game he was playing now — not just playing, but winning.

When he called Ravenna, her secretary got her right away. No delays, nothing about being in a meeting, when she was simply filing her nails, oh no. Not for a hot client. He hoped she had closed the deal so he could get right to work; he was anxious, eager, to get that sparkling dialogue onto the page, to establish the sha-boomlike pace of the story of the psychic dog. He had already begun to wonder if perhaps Ravenna, with her wily negotiating power, had even got him a little more than a hundred grand for the job; maybe a little sweetening of the pot, up to — say — one-twenty-five?

"*Darling*," she cooed, "I think we have our deal."

"Great," Perry said, "how much?"

"Well, Ralph Stilleta — he's business affairs for Ursa Major — is a real hardass. He started at thirty, told me he was absolutely holding the line at thirty-five, but I got him to thirty-seven-fifty! *With* a guarantee on the back end of another five if it goes to film!

Perry was speechless for a moment. Had Ravenna confused him with some other client?

"I don't understand," he said.

"What's that?"

"I don't understand. What's this shit about thirty-something? You said I ought to get a hundred."

"Perry, I beg your pardon. I said no such thing. That's out of the question."

"You, Ravenna Sharlow, did not tell me I ought to get a hundred grand for doing a feature? And isn't one of the whole points of my doing this to get a credit for a feature?

"Darling, this is a *rewrite*."

"But it's a rewrite of a *feature* — and besides, it's not really a rewrite. Kling told me he wanted me to read the first script and then throw it away. Do what I want."

"Darling?"

It was Ravenna's patient, instructive tone.

"Yes."

"A rewrite is a rewrite is a rewrite."

"You sound just like Larman Kling."

There was some other successful person who said things in threes also, wasn't there? Oh — sure. Gertrude Stein. Perry had almost forgotten about her.

"I guess I have no choice," Perry said.

"This is going to turn things around for you, sweets."

"All right. I'll do it."

Ravenna blew him a kiss through the phone.

Earlier, when Perry thought he was going to make at least a hundred grand on this, he had called Liz Caddigan and asked her to dinner. Now he called back and canceled. He figured under the circumstances he would only be thirty-seven-and-a-half-percent effective. Liz would probably be able to ascertain the exact figures of his new deal.

He called Ronnie Banks. Maybe a little hit of coke would bring him up again.

XIV

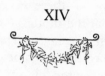

H E DIDN'T TELL anyone but his agent he was moving to the Valley.

Before he came to Los Angeles that name always conjured up in his mind bucolic scenes from the lovely old movie *How Green Was My Valley,* and the lilting folk song "Down in the Valley" — gentle meadows and babbling brooks, heather and fern and sparkling pond. But here it meant the San Fernando Valley, a flat, featureless, anonymous expanse of sun-baked tracts, a grid of endless, seemingly identical streets of Dairy Queens and dry cleaners, used-car lots and Laundromats, storefronts with secondhand furniture sitting out front on the sidewalk, cement-block bars with slits for windows.

Of course there were nice places in the Valley, expensive places.

"The Valley is really coming up these days," Ravenna said encouragingly. "Have you seen the new boutiques on Ventura Boulevard?"

Perry couldn't help thinking of the Vardemans' snide references to the Valley, locating it on their own social map.

Pru said the Valley was where one went to get inexpensive maids and baby-sitters. It was silly to seek such help in Beverly Hills when the rates were so much better in the Valley.

Vaughan had dismissed a novel once that was being promoted as "an inside peek at Hollywood" by protesting, "that's not about

273

Hollywood, for God sake, it's about failed television writers who live in the Valley."

Perry wasn't really living there, of course, he was simply staying with Ronnie Banks while he put his condo on the market. He was renting it out at a loss — there was no way he could get the three grand a month that the mortgage cost — but he couldn't concentrate on writing while realtors and prospective buyers roamed in and out. Ronnie invited him to come out and split the modest rent of $400 a month, using the fold-out bed in the living room, and it worked out fine.

It was good for Perry, not being alone right now. He and Ronnie had become real pals. They went out for pizza or Chinese food at night, drank, smoked some grass, occasionally did a line or so of coke, talked about the theater, women, art, you name it.

The only problem was the goddam script.

"So how is it going, are you into the flow, can you feel the flow, do you know?"

"Larman, great to talk to you!" Perry said, pressing his hand on his temples as if that might help force out a positive, upbeat response. He glanced at his typewriter and the card table set up beside it with his paper and what there was of the script so far. Then he turned away, as if not actually looking at the script while he spoke would make it easier to tell the necessary lies.

The fact was he only had three pages.

He had worked every day for two weeks and he only had three pages. Oh, he had written many more but he had torn them all up. After a fabulous start, it seemed as if the whole thing had shut down on him, like an iron gate.

"It's going great!" he shouted into the phone. "Yeah, the flow is flowing, I mean it's growing, growing every day, I just can't stop it flowing!"

"I can't wait to see, when can I see, can you bring some pages up to me?"

"Oh, well yes, hell yes, just give me about a week, another week, to put what I got together and get some more!"

What the hell else could he say?

Larman Kling's secretary came on the line and made an appointment for Perry to come up the following Wednesday at ten in the morning. Larman wanted to read the pages while Perry was right there with him.

Holy God.

He had to do something. He had to get words on paper by a week from tomorrow. Whatever he had to do to make that happen, he would do it.

FADE IN

EXT — JOHNSON HOUSE — DAY

A small yellow frame house on an ordinary block in an ordinary American midwestern town. There is an elm tree in the front yard. A toy red wagon is sitting beside it. DANNY, a boy about ten years old, freckle-faced and natural in muddy jeans and a St. Louis Cardinals T-shirt and Little League baseball cap worn backwards, comes out of the house, looks around, puts two fingers in his mouth and whistles. There is no response, and DANNY now cups his hands to his mouth, closes his eyes, and tilts his head back, calling as loud as he can.

DANNY
Here Spot, here Spot, here Spot!

Perry read the page over, smiling. He stood up, clapped his hands, and stuck a clenched fist in the air, triumphant.

He felt like a Rocky of writing!

The chips were down, but he was going to come through to glorious victory, he was going to win in the end, against all the odds. On the verge of being broke, abandoned by his wife (she had become increasingly villainous in his self-explanation of their separation, a deserter who left the ship at the first signs of a leak), the great but unappreciated literary man was relegated by the crass commercial creeps of Hollywood to a low-paying rewrite of a turkey script about a psychic dog, conceived by a hysterical producer who seemed to be a mad combination of the Marx Brothers and Gertrude Stein.

Did the great writer despair and throw in the towel, slinking back East in defeat with his tail between his legs and his pride dragging behind him like a leash?

No way, José!

The coke had worked.

It acted like a jolt on his imagination, enabling him to break through and write the story of the ordinary family and their psychic dog! Well, not all of it yet, but twenty-five pages of it — enough to show Larman Kling.

When he was high, it seemed fabulous.

Well, he was no fool, he realized part of that response was due to the drug, and when he'd read the stuff he'd written when he'd come down and was straight, it didn't seem nearly as wonderful. In fact it didn't seem wonderful at all.

"Run, Spot, run."

Holy Mother of God.

A grown man had written that line. A professional writer, one whose short stories had been published in distinguished magazines and won prestigious prizes.

"Run, Spot, run."

Hey, wait a minute. Who the hell said a rewrite of a script about a psychic dog was supposed to be a great work of art, anyway?

Perry had a glass of wine and read over the pages again.

Maybe it wasn't so bad after all.

It was better than nothing.

It was worth the $100 a day it cost in coke to keep the pages coming out.

Perry figured that was a business expense.

Larman Kling was pacing the room as he read, dropping the pages as he finished them, casting them away like leaves that wafted down through the air to settle on the floor or on one of the many mattresses or water beds. Perry had no idea if this shedding process meant that the eccentric producer didn't like what he saw or was so engrossed in the script, so totally transported by the story, that he didn't even want to be bothered by putting

276

back the pages, perhaps wasn't even aware that he was spilling them all across the room.

Perry could feel his heart pounding. Just before coming up he had slipped into a men's room of one of the restaurants on the ground floor of the building, and had a hit of coke. It was already wearing off, and as Larman Kling kept pacing and tossing off pages and mumbling without really uttering any words, Perry's panic began to rise. He also had a stabbing headache that wasn't helped by the sunlight blasting through the glass walls of the enormous room, striking Perry's eyes like a fist.

Larman Kling tossed away the last page and continued to pace, fiercely rubbing his head now with his knuckles, then suddenly turned to Perry and started to bark. Like a dog. The sound came out in sharp, staccato sounds — "Erf! Erf! Erf!" Perry didn't know if he was supposed to bark back, so he simply nodded, wanting to make some response, some acknowledgment.

The worst part was that Perry had no idea if Kling's outburst of barking meant that the script was so wonderfully real he felt exactly like Spot, the heroic dog, or whether he thought the script itself was a dog. Was he barking in praise or complaint?

As Perry was trying to decipher the riddle of Kling's behavior, the producer suddenly went down on his hands and knees, barking louder, starting to growl, and walking toward Perry on all fours. Perry sat frozen, not speaking or moving, feeling he was locked in a nightmare.

As Kling came closer, panting now and wagging his tongue, Perry prayed that the imaginative producer would not for any reason lift one of his legs and spray.

"You haven't got the dog, that psychic dog, or any kind of dog, or anyone or anything else," said Kling, staring up into Perry's eyes.

Perry's heart accelerated, feeling both fear and anger. What was he doing, sitting on a mattress in a high-rise penthouse in Los Angeles, while a man on all fours criticized his work?

"You didn't like anything?" he asked.

Kling stood up, brushing himself off.

"That's all in the past, the distant past, over and done and past now," he said. "But I don't give up on a good man, no. We start now. The dog is the start, the key, the open sesame, we get you knowing the dog, the rest will come, oh yes, you'll see — come with me!"

They went in Larman Kling's private limo.

"The Arvendale Kennels!" he told his driver.

"Where's that?" Perry asked.

"Inglewood. Near the Forum. You like basketball? The Lakers? Speed, finesse, speed."

"Yes," Perry said. "Absolutely."

Kling pulled down a panel that brought forward a miniature bar. For a moment Perry's heart leaped, hoping they could have some champagne, or at least a little wine. He could use something.

"Take your pick, select, everything chilled," Kling said.

Perry leaned forward and saw to his dismay that the bar contained only an array of vegetable juices. He selected a can of V-8, figuring he could at least pretend it was a Bloody Mary.

Kling took a papaya juice, shut the bar, and slipped a tape in the stereo deck. Perry braced himself, praying it was nothing jarring, no heavy metal rock or angry punk. He couldn't even have stood a Beethoven symphony.

Thankfully, the tape wasn't even music.

It was surf sounds.

Kling took two black masks from a kind of pocket below the bar and handed one to Perry. What the hell, were they going to commit a crime? Perhaps steal a psychic dog from the Arvendale Kennels? Evidently not, for the mask had no eyeholes. Kling slipped his down over his head so it covered his eyes, then leaned back in the seat, motioning Perry to do the same.

"Relax," he said. "Clears the head, empties the mind, prepares for new absorbing."

Perry did as he was told. Except that he couldn't empty his mind. Everything indeed was black now and there was only the sound of surf, which was supposed to be soothing, but Perry kept picturing scenes of past mistakes, embarrassments. If only he had stuck with Ned Gurney he might be sharing the benefits of his being hot now, might be working on a class picture, writing a quality script, and conferring daily with a civilized man. Instead he was in the back seat of Larman Kling's limo, masked, sipping V-8 juice, listening to surf sounds, and speeding toward a dog kennel in Inglewood for what incredible purpose he didn't even want to guess.

"Come down, down here, with us!" Larman Kling called.

He was on all fours, nose to nose with an Airedale. He was sniffing the dogs, rubbing up against them, barking at them.

"Got to learn their language, how they speak, think!" he explained.

Perry did what he was told. He got down on his hands and knees and tried to talk to the dogs. A menacing-looking Great Dane growled at him.

Perry flinched and moved on to a friendly terrier who licked his face.

"Speak!" Kling ordered.

Perry barked.

The terrier barked back.

Kling, smiling, urged him on, barking himself.

Is this what I was born to do? Perry wondered. Is this where I'm supposed to be, in my life? This was not even a story he would want to recount at faculty cocktail parties. For a moment he wanted to crawl over and bite Larman Kling, severing an artery and rendering the mad producer blessedly unconscious. He looked over at Kling, who was barking now even more enthusiastically, gathering a whole pack of dogs around him, waving to Perry to come and join in the canine conference. Perry understood of course that Kling was doing all this to try to help him get into the script, to be able to write the part of the dog. He realized, with a powerful, disorienting mixture of appreciation and revulsion, *this man is trying to help me.*

Kling went even further in his effort to do all he could to aid Perry's blighted attempts at writing the psychic dog script. He got him an office to work in. Kling had another picture in preproduction on the Unified lot, and he secured a room in one of the barrackslike buildings for Perry to work in. He even arranged for Perry to pick out his own furniture from the constantly shifting pieces in the studio warehouse.

Perry lay on the soiled red couch, trying to think through a scene. The couch, a straight-backed wooden chair, and one of those mammoth old-fashioned desks were the only objects in Perry's new office. He did not try to spruce it up or personalize it with any pictures or posters on the wall. That stuff was for hicks who didn't understand the fleeting nature of the business. He was a veteran now. Or becoming one fast.

He did not use the coke any more, simply because it hadn't worked. It only gave the illusion it worked, and that was finally worse than the blank piece of paper. Perry was so pissed off at having fallen for the coke he even stopped using it at night, for fun. He simply drank wine and smoked grass, but he didn't do those at work, not while he was trying to write.

He was doing the script cold turkey.

Or trying.

Larman was trying to help. He was dropping in every day and trying to inject his own ideas into Perry's blank brain.

Perry sat at the typewriter and made himself write. After a while, exhausted, he would have to lie down on the soiled red couch. He tried to think about what he was doing, tried to understand why the hell it was so damn hard.

He was being paid to spread his mind, to force it to open against its own instinct, to accept the entry of an alien idea.

This hurt.

Well, what the hell did he expect, hadn't he read about it all his life, wasn't it one of the oldest cliches in the book, the hoariest and the whoriest? Ha. But it wasn't so funny now, not so glib and easy as it was in jokes and objective journalism, for now it was happening to *him*. This ache was not academic, it was — *ugh* — ugly, radiating real pain that spread and burned to the core, the private center, the self.

The pulsating pain was all the worse because Perry knew he himself had caused it. He had sought this violation, had invited, for pay, the intrusion of a foreign mental object (the dog of a script) into the very inner sanctum of the psyche, the delicate creative part of it. Of course it would hurt, he knew all along it would hurt. He expected the pain, was ready for it. He planned to do simply what people have done in such situations for centuries — close his eyes and brace himself, grit his teeth and think of the reward, the blessed benison, the life-sustaining *money*.

But you don't get paid just for closing your eyes and letting them shove their merchandise up your mind.

Once they stick it in you, you have to nurture and feed their seed, shape it and make it grow as if it were your very own — but you have to make sure it comes out according to *their* image, the specifications of what they want, what they are paying you to deliver.

Perry understood this, he knew the rules of the game and had every intention of obeying, yet now in the very act, he was struck by the fear that he might not be capable of carrying it out, of completing his part of the bargain.

Dizzy with fear, he got up from the couch and forced himself back to the typewriter.

Failed television writers who live in the Valley.

He tried not to think.

He made himself write. After two more weeks of this he handed in twenty new pages. He waited. Waited for the phone to ring. Waited for Larman Kling to knock at the door. On the fourth day of waiting he went in to the studio, started up the stairs to his second-floor cubicle, and was pushed out of the way, pressed against the wall by two moving men.

They were carrying out the soiled red couch.

"Hey, that's mine!" Perry protested.

"You in room two-twenty-seven?" one of the movers asked.

"Yes! I'm working for Mr. Larman Kling — you better call his office and get this straightened out."

"His office is who called us," the other mover said. "Told us they wouldn't be needing that space any more."

That's how Perry found out he was fired.

They took away the furniture.

Of course Kling's business affairs people settled up with Ravenna, paying almost the full price of the aborted script.

"What the hell do I do now?" Perry asked.

" 'et back on the 'orse," Ravenna said.

"What? I can't understand you."

"Sorry, I was flossing. I said you ought to get back on the horse that threw you."

Of course. What else could he do? Turn tail and run?

The word went forth that Perry Moss was "available."

That was the official designation of his situation within the Industry.

It sounded more dignified than "unemployed" or "looking for a job" yet it still made Perry cringe. He felt like a woman who was being described as "easy," or "looking for some action."

Anything.

Well, that wasn't the case, dammit.

He was going to be particular. He should never have taken the job with Larman Kling in the first place. At least he had salvaged thirty grand from the psychic dog fiasco, and even though after he paid all his percentages and taxes that would come to around seventeen-five, that would carry him a few more months in his new, reduced Valley style of living.

He made the rounds.

Of course he was back to the world of television. There was no use trying the powerful producers of features again, not after having been fired off his first feature, but even though the word was out all over town, he was graciously welcomed to meetings by the people who produced television shows.

He took his notebook and briefcase and he listened to their ideas. There were ideas based on popular songs, on magazine and even newspaper articles. There were ideas based on what a producer's ten-year-old son had said at breakfast, or what happened to a network executive's maiden aunt on her Jamaican holiday, or the childhood fears of a director's TV repairman's cousin's plumber. There were ideas out there everywhere, like dust motes, as plentiful and also as ineffable as phantom butter-flies or ghosts.

He made a list of tag words of some of the ideas he'd been pitched: Gay, Geese, Gangs, Roller Derby, Rape, Circus, Camp, Cult.

None of them grabbed him.

He was going to keep looking.

"What are you waiting for?" Ravenna asked, "the perfect wave?" Not even her gibes made him panic.

He was going to wait, and in the meantime, he was not going to waste his time.

He was going to try writing his own stuff again. You didn't have to have an assignment from a studio or a network to write a short story. You didn't even have to make a deal with a magazine. All you had to do was sit down and write the damn thing.

So, between meetings, Perry tried to sit down and write some short stories.

The trouble was, they kept coming out like scripts.

Instead of being able to write a simple, descriptive sentence to begin a short story, like "The freckle-faced kid named Sammy walked out his front door and picked up the morning newspaper," it came out like this:

FADE IN

EXT — SAMMY'S HOUSE — DAY

A freckle-faced boy, SAMMY, walks out the front door of his family's house, looks around, sees the morning paper, stoops down and picks it up.

SAMMY
(to himself)
I wonder how the game came out?

MOTHER
(voice-over)
Sammy! Come to breakfast, dear!

And on and on.
Except it didn't go on and on.

It stopped.

At first Perry panicked because he couldn't write stories any more. Then he realized he was simply in the wrong place. You wrote stories back East, where the sentences went all across the page. Perry was relieved. There was no sense in his trying to write prose on the Coast, where he'd come to write scripts. It was like trying to make himself ski on the desert or hike in the ocean. He stopped trying to do the impossible.

The problem was what to do with his time. The time in between the meetings. The meetings were the peaks of the day, and the rest of the time was like an empty bowl that had to be filled.

He tried to read books, but that was hard too. The look of a page of print seemed thick and crowded, like New York City, where everything was jammed together, buildings and people and cars. A printed page was like the East, the past. Out here in Los Angeles, in the future, everything was open, flowing, like the traffic on the freeways.

This was not a place of words but of pictures. Pictures had space in them, they were not filled with black lines and dots. They had color and motion. Yes, out here, the pictures moved. It was a place of moving pictures. Perry put aside books — they seemed heavy and opaque, like bricks — and filled his mind with pictures, moving pictures.

He went to movies and watched television. He watched everything — news and soaps and sitcoms and game shows. The only thing he didn't like to watch was the morning talk shows. There were too many people on telling about their latest triumph — the hit movie or best-selling novel they had written or directed or starred in, the Meditation Cookbook that had just been sold to paperback for a million-five, the one-act play produced in a little theater in a small town in the Appalachians that was going to be produced as a feature film starring Jeremy Irons and Dolly Parton. He didn't want to hear that stuff. Not now. Not till he had something going of his own, some slim thread that might lead to magnificence. Right now, he would even settle for sustenance.

The other thing he couldn't stand to see on the morning talk shows was the national weather map. It reminded him where he was, down there at the left-hand corner, and seeing that, envisioning his position on the map, now gave him a sense of dizziness, of being off balance. He sensed some deep interior pull, almost like magnetism, that made him feel he ought to be in the upper right-hand corner of the national map, the little part like an ear sticking up that was actually New England. That was nonsense of course, it was some kind of childish response like he had about wanting the rain to turn to snow, just because that's the way he had always known it, but he simply solved this daily disturbance by not turning on the TV until nine o'clock, when the game shows began. If he woke early and wanted to watch something, he either found old reruns on UHF, or played a tape of an old movie.

But after nine A.M. all television was good as far as Perry was concerned. It was moving pictures and gabble and applause and laugh tracks, and all that filled up his mind and stopped it from hurting. The problem was when the commercials came. Even though the commercials too had moving pictures, somehow they allowed other thoughts to creep in, let his mind slip off to regrets and mistakes and fears. He was trying hard not to do dope or drink during the day, so he had to find some way to plug up the leaks the commercials left in his mind.

The answer was games. The little electronic jobs you plugged in and held in your hands and played by pushing a button. Football and basketball and hockey. The games made little bleep-bleep sounds that helped fill his mind during the commercial breaks. He held the games while he watched the tube and was safely plugged in and tuned out.

Despite these ingenious efforts to relax, Perry couldn't help noticing that his heart kept beating too fast. It wasn't the coke, because he'd stopped doing it. He was only drinking wine and occasional brandies and smoking grass. The grass was supposed to calm him down. Still, he kept being aware of his heart pounding, as if it were trying to get his attention. He didn't want to think about it, he figured it was part of his mental set, his anxiety, and if he just kept calm and cool it would slow down, just as he was trying to slow down.

But it didn't.

He woke in the night with his heart pounding like a steam engine, as if he were a guy running the Boston Marathon and trying to make it up Heartbreak Hill. He was drenched in sweat.

He figured he'd better see a doctor. He didn't want to ask Ronnie, because he would recommend a doctor in the Valley who catered to starving actors. If something was really wrong with him he wanted to see the best. He didn't want to ask Ravenna, either. After being turned down by her dentist, he didn't want to suffer the humiliating possibility of being rejected by her doctor as well. More important, he didn't want her to suspect anything was wrong with his health.

Who wanted to represent an aging writer with bad teeth who had been fired off a feature *and* had some kind of problem with his heart?

He called the Vardemans. In a sense they were the last people in this town he wanted to see — for he didn't want these powerful, successful friends to know of his overall plight — yet he knew they would be able to recommend a first-rate doctor. Even more importantly, perhaps, Perry had a deep longing, a crying need, to remind himself of his past, that he *had* a past, that he once was a bright, carefree, enthusiastic young grad student hanging out in Harvard Square. The Vees were at least a link to that time. Maybe he could get them to reminisce about the old days, not even talk about Hollywood at all except to recommend a good doctor.

Vaughan finally returned his call after three days, and sounded jovial enough till Perry said he wanted to get together for lunch and mentioned he was "staying" out in the Valley for a while. As much as he hated to admit it, Perry felt it was too degrading to actually lie and pretend he was living someplace where he wasn't. Vaughan put him on hold while he discussed it with Pru. He said Pru couldn't make it right now, she was really tied up, but Vaughan could meet Perry the next afternoon at three o'clock at the Bob's Big Boy in Studio City.

Meeting at one of the chain of Bob's Big Boy fast-food stops was even a cut below the hidden sushi bar in Playa del Rey, and three in the afternoon did not even come under the category of a late lunch, but Perry really had little choice. In fact he was grateful that Vaughan was making time to see him at all.

Vaughan had come from lunch with the new head of Unified, having struck a two-picture distribution deal with that studio for "multi buckos," and evidently the new success had stoked his hunger, for he ordered a double cheeseburger with french fries and onion rings and a double thick chocolate malt. He explained the lunch he had just come from was primarily ritual, consisting of "sparrow food at some fancy fern joint," and so he was glad to be able to chow down. Perry, watching his diet, had coffee and fruit cup, and started reminiscing about Mr. Bartley's Burger Cottage back in Harvard Square.

Unfortunately, Vaughan didn't seem in the mood for reminiscing about the good old days. Nor in fact did he ask Perry about what was going on with him now or what had brought him to be "staying" in the Valley. Once Vaughan finished his feast, he seemed nervous. Glancing at his watch, he said he had to be back at the fucking Polo Lounge for some shmoozing with a new young actress, a "hot little twat" from Argentina. On the way out, anyway, Perry got the name of his doctor, a "top internist" in Beverly Hills.

"Good man," said Vaughan, "especially if you picked up any rash or running sore in the general area of the gonads. No embarrassment. *Mucho* discreet."

Perry thanked him, and watched as his old pal got into his low-slung Trans Am and peeled away in a blaze of expensive rubber.

That night Perry was shocked and a little suspicious when Ronnie told him Elena Allbright had invited them both to a dinner at her place the following evening.

"Thanks," Perry said, "but you really don't have to drag me along."

"What does that mean?" Ronnie asked.

"It means I can hang out here and do some burgundy and watch the tube."

"But Elena wants you to come. She got a part in a pilot, and she's celebrating not being broke."

"Then I doubt she wants to have people around who remind her what it's like being down on your luck."

Perry simply did not believe that the glamorous actress, once the embodiment of sex and power in the role of Ramona Selden, would invite an out-of-work writer who had just been fired off a picture. Especially now that she was working again herself.

"Hey, are you being coy or something?" Ronnie asked.

"Listen, I know you're a good friend and a kind, sensitive man. I'm sure you probably asked Elena if she minded my tagging along, but to tell you the truth, I don't want to feel like a social charity case."

"Old buddy, you're letting this town get to you. Elena specifically asked me if I would bring you. She likes you. She likes your work. She wants you to come to her party."

Perry finally believed the hostess really wanted him. It was a concept he had forgotten — the feeling of being wanted, of being desired as company for others. It reminded him of the time, not all that long ago (though it now seemed another existence), when he took for granted that his presence at any function of literate people was a welcome addition. Why, back in Vermont — hell, even in some of the finest homes of Boston and New York — he was not just a plus for a hostess, he was a goddam *plum*.

He was glad he went. There were buckets of fried chicken, bowls of potato salad, and lots of wine and beer. There was a crowd, forty or so, a nice crowd. Perry recognized a few of them as actors or actresses who had either played some part or come to read for some part on "The First Year," and seeing them made him feel stronger, as if he had more substance, for they knew him from a time when he was somebody. He felt lighter, more buoyant, when he talked to the ones he had known through the show.

Elena not only came over to give him her warmest smile and a comradely hug, she said there was someone there who had been a fan of "First Year" and wanted to meet its creator. Perry was pleased, of course, and when that someone turned out to be none other than Lynn Redgrave, one of his own favorite actresses, he was overwhelmed. There weren't any other stars at the party, it wasn't that kind of party, but it turned out Elena had once done a guest spot on the old "House Call" series that Lynn had starred in, and they became buddies. Evidently Lynn was one of the stars who would go to places just because she liked the person who had asked her. She seemed quite at home in this otherwise rather motley crew, and even with her splendid English accent she seemed what Perry thought of as a down-home kind of person. When she came over to express her enthusiasm about "The First Year's the Hardest," he was practically immobilized with awe and gratitude.

"It was *mar*velous," she said, giving him a firm, friendly hand-shake and making him feel energized and warmed by the aura of her natural vibrancy. "Please do more, won't you?"

"Well, sure, I mean, I hope I will —" he stammered.

"You will," she said. "You must, of course!"

He almost believed he would for a moment; he felt if he could get a fix of that confidence and vigor of hers every day he really *could*, no matter what the odds.

Back at Ronnie's, he felt so grateful for having been invited, for having been paid attention to, he got almost maudlin.

"I really want to thank you," he said.

"Fuck off," Ronnie said. "I didn't even invite you. I got points with Elena for bringing you."

"Well, I'm glad you got *something* for all you've done for me. I only wish I could really do something for you, too — I mean, to pay you back."

"You're coming up with the rent, aren't you? That's the deal."

"Hell, I don't mean that. I mean, everything's trade-offs in this town, right? You scratch my back and I scratch yours?"

"That's how it works sometimes, sure."

"Well, I mean, the least I could do for you is make sure you got a part in something I got produced. I mean, I'd love to do that, it would really make me feel good to be able to do that."

"Great. You write a TV remake of Moby Dick, I want Ahab. None of this Ishmael shit. I've had it with doing Ishmael."

"I'm serious."

"OK. If something happens like that, it happens."

Perry took another slug of his brandy and then suddenly, unexpectedly, he burst out crying.

"What's wrong?" Ronnie asked.

"I feel like a fraud," Perry sobbed.

"Why?"

"I don't really know if I'll ever do it again. Have something on the air. I'm no damn good to you. I don't even have any power. Nothing."

Ronnie got up and walked over so he was standing above Perry.

"You got to get off this," he said. "I'm your friend."

He sat down beside Perry and put an arm on his shoulder.

"I'm sorry," Perry said, choking on the sobs.

"Go ahead. Spill it out."

Perry put his head in his hands and just bawled.

Ronnie sat beside him, patting him on the shoulder.

Perry believed that Ronnie in fact was his friend, and that made him think of Al Cohen, and it made him bawl even more. He'd forgotten about friends. Forgotten about everything that mattered. Or used to matter.

On his way to see Dr. Harlow Sampson a week later, Perry's heart started pounding faster than ever as he began to worry not about his condition, whatever it was, but whether this top internist — no doubt an Internist of the Stars — would take on his case. What if, like the Beverly Hills dentist, the Beverly Hills doctor found that Perry's heart was pounding *too* fast, that it was really an embarrassment, a sign of slovenly health care over the years, and he would have to go elsewhere and try to get into acceptable shape for being taken on by a really class doctor?

Perry was relieved that at least Dr. Sampson was an older man, a courtly-looking, gentle man, with a tapered gray beard, the kind of man who might out of benevolence take on his case even if he weren't in the best of health.

"Your resting pulse is one-thirty," Dr. Sampson told him over the consultation glass of Perrier in his office. "The top range of normal is eighty to a hundred. So you're right. Your heart is beating too fast. But your EKG is fine. I take it you're in the entertainment business?"

"Yes. I'm a writer."

"Writer, actor, whatever. The business itself causes stress. That's your only problem."

"Are you saying I should quit?"

"People have to make a living. Many of my clients are in the business. I can prescribe something for you."

"What?"

Dr. Sampson was making out a prescription.

"It's a beta blocker. It will keep your pulse down."

"Hey, thanks. Thanks a lot."

"Try to take it easy," the kindly doctor said. "Next thing you know you'll have a hit. That's the best medicine."

He smiled, and shook hands.

The prescription was like magic. He took the pill and his heart didn't pound.

Perry felt calm now. He felt even more calm when he met with Mona Halsted. Why hadn't he thought of her before? Well, the time just hadn't been right. When he met her that glittery night at the Vees' his head was all into "First Year" and his newly hatched feature fantasy with Vaughan. When Jane brought her up again on that last walk on the beach at Venice, Perry still was clinging to the feature dream as an immediate possibility, the jackpot that was just around the corner. Now he was more realistic. More in the mood for Mona. She was, after all, not only a sensitive and sympathetic person, she actually knew and admired his work. Oh, was he in the mood for Mona.

He felt ashamed that he had put her down for seeming so

motherly. Right now, he would take all the motherly warmth and comfort he could get. And she exuded it. She made him feel secure, almost at peace, simply by being in her presence. She looked, if anything, more motherly now than she had at the party — or at least more traditionally motherly, in the old-fashioned sense. She did not look so much like Sada Thompson playing the mother in "Family" now; without Ms. Thompson's bright lipstick, she reminded Perry more of one of those Norman Rockwell mothers. Her makeup was so faint and artful as to seem like a natural blush. Her smile was serene, reassuring. Perry would not have been at all surprised if she had reached out onto the air-conditioner outside her office window and pulled in a fresh apple pie.

The story she wanted to do as a TV movie was a story about death.

Perry perked up. At least that was serious. It was something in fact he felt very in tune with these days.

It was not about a man, but that didn't lessen Perry's interest. It was the story of a young woman who learns her father is dying of cancer. She has never been close to him, yet she sacrifices not only her career by leaving her important job with no advance notice, she breaks off an engagement with a man she loves, all in order to be with her father during his last days.

Before she continued, Mona said, "I have waited for the right person to do this story. It's very important to me. The fact that you might be the one to write it would be like a dream come true."

"Thank you," Perry said.

He felt all right about himself for the first time in a long time. He felt almost as worthwhile as he had before he came to Hollywood.

Mona stood and came around her desk and pulled a chair up next to him.

"I want to confess to you," she said, "the real reason I want to do this story."

"I'd like to know," Perry said.

Mona nodded, and took a deep breath.

"I was born and grew up in a small town in Nebraska," she said. "I was an only child. The daughter of a judge. He was a stern man, remote and godlike. I was afraid of him. I clung to my mother. When I went off to college, my father developed a terminal cancer. He asked me to come home, to be with him in his last months of life. I would have had to take a semester off college. Leave my boyfriend. My sorority sisters. My plans. I was frightened. I refused. I turned away from my own father when he was dying."

Mona took out a handkerchief. She wiped at her eyes, then blew her nose.

"What I want to do now," she said, "is tell the story of a daughter who made the decision I wish that I had made myself. A daughter who sacrifices her own wishes and desires for the sake of comforting her father, even though she's never been close to him. Of course, she will become close to him — in our story. It would be like a kind of atonement, I suppose. It would be like showing others a better way to behave than I did. And it would, most of all, I hope, be a tribute to my father."

When she finished, Perry had to wipe his own eyes.

"It would be an honor," he said, "to try to do justice to that story."

To make the situation even better, the story had been presold to Judd Wizener, known as one of the most perceptive and kindly men in television, the head of TV and movies for his network. Mona was sure he'd be delighted to have Perry as the writer.

Perry called Ravenna and told her he had found "the perfect wave."

The deal was struck quickly. He would only get $35,000, in three payments, but that was not the point. The point was at last he had a subject worthy of a real writer. It fit something he had forgotten, some words of Yeats about doing only those things you could be proud of, and count all else "extravagance of breath."

Yes.

Now all he had to do was write a treatment for approval by the network before he began the actual script.

Perry got right down to work.

It was hard. It was hard to capsulize a real story like this, hard to put it in TV terms. He found himself struggling. Damn. If he couldn't do this one with all the circumstances right he might as well give up.

He smoked a little grass, but that didn't help.

He knew that Mona was anxiously waiting to hear, to have him get going on her dream project.

Finally, one night in frustration, he remembered Archer Mellis's original words of advice.

"Don't even think about television."

Yes! That was it, that was the key. He was worrying too much about pleasing the preconceived pap notions of network people. That was crazy. This was going to be read by the sympathetic eyes of Mona and then of the kindly Judd Wizener.

Perry had a beer and went to his typewriter. He poured out his deepest feelings about this story, not just the plot but the heart of it, his vision of it. He wrote all night, stopping only to have more beers, but not getting drunk, just keeping going, just like the old days. It was like staying up with a great story that ran its own course, that wrote itself!

At dawn he had twenty-two pages that were like a letter to Mona. He showered, shaved, and took it in person to her office. He heard back from her two hours later.

She loved it.

She was sending it over to the network right away.

When Perry hung up the phone he smiled and took a deep breath, then another. He felt he could really breathe again. He went to the kitchen and made a cup of instant coffee, feeling clean and sharp. He should have been bushed, but he felt more alive than he had for months. He didn't want to go to bed. He wanted to do something, wanted to take some kind of action, now that he felt capable of such a thing.

He called Ned Gurney. He had missed him enormously, but feared if he called after the news that Ned finally got his feature going, it would sound like the worst kind of sucking up. Now that Perry had something hot of his own in the works he felt it was all right to call Ned. He invited him to lunch at the place where Ned had first taken him when they met, the restaurant in Westwood that reminded Perry of the Copley Plaza in Boston.

Ned was gracious, as always. Perry apologized to him about breaking his word on the option of "The Springtime Women," and Ned admitted that it had hurt, but he had put it behind him. Perry said he didn't think anything was going to come of it anyway. Poetic justice, maybe, for his being so underhanded in the greedy effort to get it made. Ned merely shrugged.

"You know what that piece should really be?" Ned asked.

"Maybe it should just be what it is," Perry said. "A short story."

"Maybe. But in dramatic terms, it really should be a play."

"You think it could be?"

"Of course. You could do a beautiful job with it. And on the stage, you as the writer would really have control."

"I've heard that," Perry said. "What an amazing thing it sounds like. It's almost worth writing a play just to have that experience."

"Especially after your recent experience, I bet."

"Yes. But now I've really got my teeth into something good."

He told Ned about Mona and the story of the daughter whose father is dying, and Ned was very pleased that Perry had something of substance to work on, and a good producer to work with.

"I hope someday," Perry said, "I might even get to work with you again."

"I'd like that," Ned said. "Who knows, we might even do something back East, on Broadway."

"You think you might go back?"

"I miss it," Ned said. " 'Spoons' is going well, and of course I have high hopes for it, but I think I'll be able to use a change of pace when it's finally finished."

Perry nodded. He didn't want to ask anything more specific or try to make any real plans that might seem impossible, for he didn't want to break the spell. It was as if, in that room with its Boston aura, they were temporarily back East, up in the right-hand corner of the national weather map, where snow fell softly in winter and leaves turned red in the fall.

"Thanks," Ned said when they parted, "this was civilized."

*

Perry paced the apartment and drank pots of black coffee, waiting to hear from Mona about the reaction from the network. A week passed. He was tempted to put a little brandy in his coffee, but he kept himself dry during the day, in shape, ready for the word to come down, ready to be told to "go for it."

When Mona finally called, it was not to give him the go sign, but to tell him the network wanted to have a meeting about the project.

Perry immediately stiffened.

"Didn't Judd Wizener like it?"

"Perry, he *adored* it."

"So why do we have to meet with him? Does he want to talk casting already?"

"Dear, we aren't meeting with Judd."

"Why not? I thought he adored the project."

"He's not with the network any longer, dear. Evidently, this treatment of yours is the last thing he read."

"My God! What happened to him?"

"He's gone into independent production."

Perry sat down.

"I thought he was strong. I thought he was entrenched."

"Things happen," said Mona.

"So who are we seeing? Who's in charge?"

"JoyAnn Wales."

"Who's *she*?"

"A brilliant young woman, I understand. Came to the network three years ago from Boeing."

"From Boeing Aircraft? What is she, a test pilot?"

"An engineer. Absolutely brilliant, I'm told."

"What the hell do engineers know about stories?"

"Now Perry. We mustn't be defensive before we've even taken our meeting."

"Well what did she say about it? Did she like the treatment? Did she get the point?"

"I'm sure she adored it. All I really know is that she has some notes."

"Holy God."

Some notes.

Some suggestions, no doubt, on how to improve his fragile story from a hotshot young woman aerospace engineer.

When he hung up, Perry poured a tumbler of wine.

JoyAnn Wales was a small, physically delicate young woman with a voice like sandpaper. Her blond hair was worn in a feathery bob, and her dress, a gossamer sort of thing that added to the impression that she might be blown away by the first breeze through the palm trees, was a wash of soft pastels. But her voice anchored her. Her voice was in a constant state of irritation, as if inflamed.

"When is this thing supposed to take place?" she asked harshly.

"Right now," said Perry.

"We see it as universal," cooed Mona, "but in a contemporary scene and setting."

JoyAnn picked up the script and started flipping through it, slapping back the pages as if they were bad children.

"They sound like they're wearing hoopskirts," she said.

Perry could feel his pulse picking up.

"What gives you that idea?" he asked.

"This daughter — for Christ's sake, she leaves her job, forgets her career, dumps her man, to go play nursemaid to this grungy old fart?"

"That's her father," Mona pointed out.

"Is that supposed to explain why she's such a wimp?" JoyAnn demanded.

"She's supposed to be a decent person," Perry said. "Evidently you find that hard to identify with."

"What Perry means," Mona said, "is that we're trying to portray a young woman whose loyalty to her father makes her sacrifice some of her own desires of the moment."

"If she wants to make it with him, we might have a story here. The last incest piece we did got a forty-three share."

"Perhaps Perry and I can think this through again, with your notes in mind," Mona said.

JoyAnn stood up.

"The bottom line is," she said, "I just don't know where these people are coming from."

She tossed the treatment back to Perry. It fell to the floor in front of him. He did not pick it up. He got to his feet, feeling at the same time a fierce anger and a wild sense of freedom.

His heart was beating wildly, even though he had not only taken his beta blocker before the meeting, he had also popped a Valium he'd borrowed from Ronnie just for good measure. He felt that his pounding heart was a good sign, a sign he was still alive, still human. He considered his pounding heart to be a triumph of nature over chemistry, even over Hollywood.

"I can tell you where *I* am coming from," he said to JoyAnn Wales. "I am coming from Vermont. And I am finally going back. Now. In the nick of time."

JoyAnn looked puzzled, and turned to Mona.

"I'm afraid he doesn't get the picture," the sharp young executive said.

"Oh, I'm afraid he does," said Mona, standing up herself now.

Perry placed his hands on JoyAnn's desk, leaned toward her, and said, with pleasure and fervor, a single word:

"*Ciao.*"

Outside the building, he hugged Mona.

"You can have what I wrote," he said. "Free of charge. Maybe you can make something of it, somewhere else. Or here. Wherever. Let me know if I can do anything."

Mona smiled.

"Don't worry," she said. "Give my love to Vermont. And to Jane."

He turned and started for his car and Mona called after him.

"Perry?"

"Yes?"

"God speed."

He had never heard anyone say that before.

"Thank you," he said.

Perry called American Airlines and booked a tourist-class seat on the next available flight to Boston.

"Do you wish to make a return reservation?" the ticket person asked.

"No. This is one-way," he said. "No return."

When he spoke the words he suddenly felt as if lead weights were lifted off him. He felt he could fly to Boston without even getting on the plane, just by walking out the door and taking the first step East.

Despite this new feeling of freedom, Perry did not yet have the courage to call Jane. It took all the chutzpah he could muster to call Al Cohen and ask if he could stay with him and Rachel for at least a night; on the floor, anywhere.

Perry felt guilty that Al wasn't even angry. In fact, Al wasn't even surprised, but he seemed very pleased.

The Cohens' living room looked to Perry like a longed-for safe harbor.

First he cried.

Then he launched into breast-beating tirades against his own phony behavior, his betrayal of their friendship. This eloquent self-flagellation was stifled only by Rachel's sticking a beer and a sandwich into his hands. Once Perry's mouth was full, Al shut him up with what he said was the final word on the subject, courtesy of Robert Frost:

"Home is the place where, when you have to go there,
They have to take you in."

"Home is also the place," said Rachel, "where you have to listen to all the Robert Frost that is quoted without complaining to the management."

Perry winced, remembering that night an eon or so ago before he went West, when after a wonderful dinner and too much brandy he yelled at Al for quoting something of Frost, bitching that the poet and his observations were out of fashion, or some such arrogant nonsense. It sounded to him now like something the Vees would have said.

"Will you forgive me?" he asked. "You have every reason to turn me out in the cold."

"But to quote Mr. Frost yet again," said Rachel, reaching out and giving Perry a tweak on the nose, "home is 'something you somehow haven't to deserve.' "

"I love it," Perry laughed. "The quote, and being here."

He spent the first night on the Cohens' couch. The next morning he had coffee and juice and bacon and eggs and toast and then he walked alone to the woods that bordered the house where he once had lived.

In the woods he inhaled the smells of spring. He sank to his knees. There was a crocus just beginning to bud and he leaned to it, touched it, and knew, in a surge of comprehension that was almost like a blow: *this is the gold*.

He bowed his head. The day was fresh and warm, and sunlight lay across the hard ground. Perry had an urge to get closer to the earth. He remembered Lon Ridings, the actor, and how he had disrobed down to his jockey shorts and pressed his flesh to the dry dirt alongside Ned Gurney's patio. He knew how the man must have felt, how he must have wanted to burrow on down into his own grave. That was not what Perry felt now. He did not want to take off his clothes, he simply wanted to lie flat out on the earth and dig his fingers into the soil.

He could feel his heart beat. It was not pounding any more. It did not feel as if it might explode and burst right through his chest. It was making a lovely rhythm against the earth. He lay there a long time, and then raised up on his elbows. Slowly, he crawled to the edge of the woods and peered at his old house.

A woman walked out the door and looked toward him, but she didn't see him yet. He wanted to go to her. He wondered if that were possible. First he stood up. Then he put one foot in front of the other. He felt wobbly, like a colt. He took another step. Simple things. He was learning them all over. He was doing something miraculous. He was moving toward the woman he loved.

He was walking.